Episcopal Scotland
in the Nineteenth Century

# Episcopal Scotland
# in the Nineteenth Century

MARION LOCHHEAD

JOHN MURRAY

To Henry,
for help and friendship

Printed in Great Britain for
John Murray, Albemarle Street, London
by Cox & Wyman Ltd, London,
Fakenham and Reading

# Foreword

The nineteenth century is now past history and we are becoming sufficiently detached from it to see it in perspective. It was an age of strong and of great personalities in every walk of life, and the Episcopal Church in Scotland was not without her share. It is around some of them that this vivid account of Episcopal Scotland in that day and age has been written. It is a medium in which Miss Lochhead is particularly happy and for which she has a special facility. Those who are familiar with her writings will know what to expect and they will not be disappointed.

It is a pleasure to me to write a Foreword to this, Miss Lochhead's latest book which, while primarily of interest to Episcopalians, will, I am sure, appeal to all those who are interested in the religious life and history of nineteenth century Scotland.

✠Francis Glasgow and Galloway, Primus.

# Contents

# Illustrations

\*　　　　　　　　　　ix

## Illustrations

# Acknowledgements

I am grateful to the Bishops of the Church in Scotland for their encouragement of this book; especially to the Most Reverend Francis Moncrieff, Bishop of Glasgow and Galloway, Primus, for so kindly writing a Foreword, and to the Right Reverend Kenneth Carey, Bishop of Edinburgh, for reading part of my typescript and making most helpful suggestions. For similar help I am indebted to the Very Reverend George Martineau, Dean of Edinburgh; the Reverend Canon Henry Reid; the Reverend Canon Roland Walls; the Reverend Canon Kenneth Woollcombe, Principal of the Theological College who also arranged to have the portraits of Bishop Jolly and Bishop Forbes in the College photographed for reproduction.

For other illustrations I am grateful to: Mrs. and Mr Bowlby of Greenlaw (for those of Bishops Gleig and Walker); the Right Reverend Edward Easson, Bishop of Aberdeen; the Right Reverend Duncan MacInnes, Bishop of Moray; Lady Christison; Mrs. Ann Dallas (for her drawing of Greyfriars, Kirkcudbright) and the Reverend C. A. Simister; the Very Reverend Provost Douglas of the Cathedral of the Isles, Cumbrae; the Very Reverend Provost Douglas of the Cathedral of the Isles, Cumbrae; the Very Reverend Provost Currie of St. Ninian's, Perth; the Very Reverend Provost Haggart of St. Paul's, Dundee; the Very Reverend Provost Foskett and the Cathedral Board of St. Mary's, Edinburgh, Hubert Fenwick, Esq. A.R.I.B.A.; and Messrs. Valentine of Dundee, Cowper of Perth and Andrew Paterson of Inverness.

My thanks go to the following for kind permission to use copyright material: to Lady Christison for the books by her father, Bishop Anthony Mitchell, and to Messrs Mowbray for his *Biographical Studies in Scottish Church History;* to Miss Helena Perry for those of her father, Dean William Perry; also to Messrs. Mowbray for his *Scottish Liturgy*, Messrs. Hodder & Stoughton for his *Life of Anthony Mitchell*, The Cambridge Press for his *Oxford Movement in Scotland;* and S.P.C.K. for his Lives of *Alexander Penrose Forbes* and of *George Hay Forbes;* to Peter Anson, Esq. K.S.G. for his *Call of the Cloister* and also to S.P.C.K.; to the Misses Hale for the privately printed account of Lansdowne House School by their aunt, Miss E. M. Hale; to the Garden and Governors of Trinity College, Glenalmond for *The History of Glenalmond* by G. St. Quintin; to John Murray for Lady Monkswell's *Victorian Diarist*.

I have been unable to trace the owners of copyright of A. J. Mason's *Memoir of George Howard Wilkinson*.

The Reverend Canon William Cooper, Forbes Librarian at the Theological College has lent me rare books, and been most helpful and encouraging. The National Library of Scotland has, as usual, proved a treasury of material, especially in The Dowden Collection of Pamphlets. The London Library has also provided useful source-material.

Sir John Murray, K.C.V.O. has published some of these chapters as articles in *The Quarterly Review*. To him, and to Mrs. Osyth Leeston I am, as always, deeply grateful for constant encouragement and stimulus. The Editor of *Scan* has also published three articles.

# Preface

## The Scottish Episcopal Church Today
## The Working Church: Her Position
## and Administration

The Scottish Episcopal Church is a province of the Anglican Communion along with the Church of England, the Church of Ireland and of Wales, and the Episcopal Churches in Canada, America, Australia, South Africa, Australia; everywhere, in fact, throughout the world whether or not English-speaking. With all of them she is in full communion, sharing the same creeds, upholding the same Apostolic Succession and threefold ministry of Bishop, Priest and Deacon; one with them in sacramental worship, with her own Prayer Book similar to that of the Church of England, although different in some details, chiefly in the service of Holy Communion. From this Scottish Liturgy is derived the Prayer Book of the Church in America.

Her major difference from the Church of England, like that of the other provinces, is in her disestablishment from the State. The Church of England is, in fact, unique among the Anglican Churches in being established, bound by legal ties to Crown and Parliament. Neither has any authority in the government of the Scottish Church. Most of the other Anglican provinces might be called *unestablished*: the Scottish is *disestablished* for political reasons, by an event which may or may not be regretted. Her disestablishment is the source, cause and explanation of many things in Scottish Episcopacy today: her comparative poverty offset by ample freedom, her lack of historic parish churches and cathedrals. This lack is shared by the Presbyterian Established Church of Scotland and is due, in part, to circumstances affecting them both: the poverty from which Scotland has never long escaped, the violence of the Reformation in a country which took religion violently, and, on the Borders, to English invasion. The glory of Gothic, the nobility of Norman in great cathedrals and in parish churches, the beauty and sanctity of buildings which for centuries have been the centre of prayer and worship, can only here and there be found in Scotland. Only in a few places was a church of medieval foundation taken over undamaged, and used for worship, and most of these belong to the Established Church. Our cathedrals have all been built in the nineteenth century; a few of our churches go back to a much earlier date. Of these, Rosslyn Chapel – the Collegiate Church of St. Matthew, to give it its full title – is the private chapel of the Earl of Rosslyn and also a Mission Chapel of Edinburgh Cathedral with the Bishop as patron. It is the choir of what was planned as a great church by Sir William St. Clair in the fifteenth century, and is a gem of stone work, famous for its prentice pillar and its carvings of The Dance of Death, the Seven Virtues and Vices, and The Angelic Orchestra.

The Priory Church of St. Mary, South Queensferry, is also of the fifteenth century, built by the Carmelites; restored by the Episcopal Church in 1890 it is owned by trustees, of whom some are diocesan officials and some members of the Dundas family on whose land it was built. At Kirkcudbright there is the Franciscan Church of the Grey Friars, of the same period, which was secured for the Church in 1919. Under the care of the church in Lanark is the Chapel of Sancta Sophia at Douglas, once, in Queen Mary's day, the dower-house of Douglas Castle: she is said to have stayed there. In the eighteenth century it became a school or place of learning (hence its new name and dedication). Since 1960 it has been a Mission Chapel, restored and furnished with the utmost seemliness.

At Kilmaveonaig, Blair Atholl, the tiny church of St. Adamnan, on a site where that saint preached, has been a place of worship since the thirteenth century or earlier; rebuilt in the fifteenth century it was held and used by an Episcopal congregation before the disestablishment of 1688–9 and ever since. Among private chapels the most notable is that of St. Michael and All Angels at Glamis, which goes back to the seventeenth century and which serves local Episcopalians.

These are cherished exceptions to the rule or pattern of nineteenth-century building. For this poverty in beauty of architecture it is hard to find any solace; difficult to find much comfort in the number and solidity of our Victorian churches built in our days of prosperity, for then we followed the convention of Victorian Gothic and failed to create any expression of our own austere yet lovely tradition.

The poverty caused by disestablishment, lack of tithes, inherited wealth, endowments and the like, and by the absence of any official status, is balanced and, in the opinion of some, outweighed by our freedom. The Scottish Church can revise, as she has done twice in this century, her Prayer Book with no other authority than that of her own Provincial Synod. She would not make any drastic change without consulting her sister churches in the Anglican Communion; but Parliament has no voice in this or any other discussion. She is free to regulate her worship, her teaching, her discipline, her administration.

The Scottish Episcopal Church has seven dioceses: Aberdeen and Orkney; Argyll and the Isles; Brechin; Edinburgh; Glasgow and Galloway; St. Andrews, Dunkeld and Dunblane. Of these, Edinburgh alone is post-Reformation, founded by Charles I. The others trace their decent from medieval and earlier dioceses, Brechin in one direct line, the other five, of united names, in a history of permutations, a kaleidoscopic pattern. Aberdeen and Orkney were separate until 1857, Argyll and the Isles until 1819, Argyll having been previously held with Ross, and the Isles with Orkney and Caithness. Moray was for a time held with Edinburgh, then with Aberdeen, finally with Ross; and Ross went with Caithness, with Moray, and for a while by itself: since 1851 the three, Moray, Ross and Caithness have been one united diocese. Glasgow continued an Archbishopric after the Reformation until 1704, when the office of Archbishop was given up by the Scottish Episcopal Church; the see was then vacant for twenty years, held for a brief time by Bishop Duncan, again vacant as a separate bishopric, and from 1773 till 1837 held with Edinburgh, as was Galloway. In that year the united Diocese of Glasgow and Galloway was formed. St. Andrews, also once an Archbishopric claiming the primacy in medieval Scotland, became a bishopric in 1704. Here too a vacancy occurred; then four successive Bishops were styled Bishops of Fife. Dunblane, separate until 1776, then joined Dunkeld, and these two were united with St. Andrews in

3

1837. St. Andrews and Dunkeld both go back to the ninth century, which can be surpassed only by Glasgow's descent from St. Kentigern and Galloway's from St. Ninian.

The present map or pattern is of the nineteenth century. Each diocese has its cathedral, but only three – Aberdeen, Edinburgh and Glasgow – have their cathedrals in their name-city. Argyll and the Isles have two cathedrals: St. John's, Oban, and the Cathedral of the Isles, or Collegiate Church of The Holy Spirit on the Isle of Cumbrae in the Firth of Clyde. Brechin's cathedral is St. Paul's, Dundee; Moray, Ross and Cromarty have St. Andrew's, Inverness. St. Ninian's, Perth, the cathedral of St. Andrews, Dunkeld and Dunblane, was the first to be built in Scotland since the Reformation. Those in Edinburgh and Inverness were also built as cathedrals: the other four, in Oban, Aberdeen, Dundee and Glasgow were churches which grew in size and importance, were the Bishop's churches, and were in time made cathedrals. The Cathedral of the Isles is unique in its foundation and purpose as will be told later. St. Mary's, Glasgow, was consecrated as recently as 1907.

They are all very new, as church history counts time, but the dioceses are old, and many of the congregations making up each diocese have an unbroken history from the seventeenth, some even from the sixteenth, century. That they did not always meet in a church did not make them any less a congregation; the reason for that will appear.

There is the cathedral but no cathedral close, no Bishop's Palace, no Deanery within the precincts. The Bishop has his official residence, generally called Bishop's House, and usually, though not in every case, in the cathedral city. The incumbent of the cathedral is styled Provost (as in some of the new English cathedrals), not Dean. The latter is, in the Scottish Church, a diocesan dignitary, although also, *ex officio*, a member of the Cathedral Chapter. He is the Bishop's second-in-command, his delegate upon occasion, appointed and authorized by him to act in his absence; to act, that is, wherever a priest can function, not in the Bishop's own sacramental and episcopal rites. He can, for example, institute the incumbent of a charge, preside (in the Bishop's absence) at diocesan meetings, and, when a see falls vacant, he is authorized by the Primus or senior Bishop to summon the diocesan electors: but he cannot confirm or ordain. The Dean visits each charge in the diocese, inspects registers and buildings; fills, in short, very much the place of the Archdeacon in the Church of England.

The Scottish Episcopal Church has no Archdeacons, although she has more than once had them by courtesy or by accident. Two Victorian Bishops appointed a cleric to that office, undeterred by its non-existence. Bishop Wordsworth of St. Andrews appointed the incumbent of St. Ninian's, Alyth, who promptly ordered his hat and gaiters, and refused to give up either costume or office. The same honour was bestowed by Bishop Ewing of Argyll upon Mr. Ikin of Ballachulish, with the title of Archdeacon of Appin, and in the present century a Rector of Kirkwall was known as the Archdeacon of Orkney.

Each Cathedral Chapter consists of the Bishop, the Dean, the Provost, the Canons, the Lay Chancellor and other lay officials. The Canons, each holding an incumbency within the diocese, are chosen alternately by the Bishop and the Diocesan Synod.

Incumbents are called Rector, not Vicar. The difference is one of legal-ecclesiastical origin. Fowler defines *Rector* as the incumbent of a parish where the tithes were not appropriated to a monastery or other religious community, or impropriated to a lay person or a corporation, *Vicar* as one whose tithes were thus appropriated or impropriated. Tithes do not, however, occur in the disestablished Scottish Church. (The Episcopal Church in America also uses the style *Rector*; and the *Oxford Dictionary* states that in Brittany the parish priest is known as *Recteur*, not *Curé* as in the rest of France, and that the curate is *Curé* not *Vicaire*.)

When a see falls vacant the Dean summons the clergy and lay electors to nominate and vote for a new Bishop; a lay elector is chosen by each congregation. The election must be approved and confirmed by the other Bishops who form the College; if the electors fail, through disagreement or other cause, to elect a Bishop, the right of election falls to the College.

The seven Bishops elect one of their number, usually the senior in consecration, as Primus or Presiding Bishop. He presides over meetings of the College, the Provincial Synod, the Representative Church Council; he is styled Most Reverend, whereas the others are Right Reverend; but he is not a Primate; he is *Primus inter pares* with no unique authority, no rule over his fellow Bishops, and no rights within their sees. Only during an episcopal vacancy does he, or another Bishop appointed by him, perform the episcopal acts and functions in that see, and he authorizes the Dean to call the electors. At the consecration of a new Bishop the Primus is first among those consecrating him; the Bishop-elect is presented to the Primus by two others and they, with all the other Bishops present, join in the act of consecration. The custom is to have the Scottish Bishops joined by two or three from other provinces of the Anglican Communion – from England, Ireland, Wales or overseas, as may be arranged. This is a token of the unity of the whole Anglican Communion and of the fact that nationality is of no account in the Apostolic Succession. On some occasions an Orthodox or an Old Catholic Bishop has taken part in the consecration, thus showing a wider unity in the Catholic Church.

Patronage continues but only in a democratic and representative form, not as an inherited right of a layman, the local landowner or another, to present a clergyman to the living. In some charges the Bishop is patron, but in most it is the Bishop and Vestry together, and the latter, being composed of elected members of the congregation, men and women, is entirely representative. The approval of both Bishop and Vestry is desirable, that of the Bishop necessary; he could refuse to institute. There are many factors about an election but one of the most effective is the tradition of the congregation in the matter of churchmanship, ritualistic observance and so on. The priest, once elected, is instituted by the Bishop (or in his absence by his delegate, the Dean) who says:

'Receive this charge which is both mine and thine,' stressing his share of the pastoral work, his relation as Father-in-God to his clergy and laity.

The Scottish Church has her own Theological College in Edinburgh. The Principal, if (as is nearly always the case) he is also Pantonian Professor of Theology, is *ex officio* a Canon of the Cathedral. There is also, in Edinburgh, a Choir School attached to the cathedral; and there are fourteen church day schools in the province. The Church has an orphanage at Aberlour in the diocese of Moray. Lansdowne House School in Edinburgh, founded as a private boarding-school, is now a day school for girls of all denominations, but continues the plan of its founders that 'the religious teaching given shall be in accordance with the standards of the Episcopal Church in Scotland'. Trinity College, Glenalmond, is an Episcopal foundation with more than a century of Episcopal tradition but the boys need not be Episcopalians. It is a boarding-school, the first in Scotland to follow the pattern of the English public school. The Bishops are on the Council; the Primus and the Bishop of Edinburgh are on the Council of Lansdowne House.

As for the governing bodies of the Church, the Episcopal Synod or College of Bishops, which is both a governing and a judicial body, hearing and deciding appeals, meets once a year, oftener if desired by the Primus or by any four Bishops. The Provincial (formerly called the General) Synod has two chambers: the first of the Bishops, the second of the Deans, the Principal and Vice-Principal of the Theological College, other representative priests (one in ten of each Diocesan Synod) and laity (half the number of the clergy), with other five lay members elected by the College of Bishops, and two lay members *ex officio*: the Registrar of the Episcopal Synod, and the Convenor of the Executive Committee of the Representative Church Council. Lay members may be men or women; only one office, that of the lay elector of a Bishop, is still reserved for men, who must be communicants and not less than twenty-four years of age.

The Diocesan Synod consists only of the clergy, but this is likely to be changed to admit laity, for it is seen to be an anomaly that they should be absent from this smaller body when they have their place, along with the clergy, in the higher legislative court – the Provincial Synod. The laity, both men and women, sit on the Diocesan Councils which deal with finance and other practical matters and are the focus of all the Diocesan Boards and Committees. To these each congregation elects its Lay Representative.

The Representative Church Council has been called 'The Board of Management' of the Church. Meeting once a year it convenes all the Boards, it administers trusts and funds, manages all the finances, the business, the mechanics of the Church. It consists of the Bishops, the Deans, the active clergy and those of the retired who have been in Holy Orders for twenty years before retirement, and clergy who serve the Scottish Church overseas; of lay representatives, one from each congregation, and various lay officials. The Annual Report of the R.C.C. provides the statistics of the Church and is known as The Blue Book. The Year Book and Directory, known as The Red Book, gives the picture of each diocese and each charge, with an outline of history. Between them the external life of the Church is made known.

The stipends of the Bishops range from £1,264 to £2,000; that of priests is based on the cost of living, the minimum being about £930. Those stipends are paid partly from the central funds of the Church, partly by the congregations. The Stewardship Campaign of recent years has instituted in most places a system of planned giving.

It is still a small Church. The returns of 1964 show a membership of 96,500, of whom just over 55,000 are communicants. Of the seven dioceses, Glasgow and Galloway is the largest with over 32,000 members, Edinburgh coming next with 20,000: Argyll and the Isles is the smallest, with 2,292 members, though widely scattered in area. The proportion of communicants to total membership is rather more than half.

Three of the Anglican Communities work in Scotland; one of them is of Scottish foundation. The Community of St. Mary and St. John in Aberdeen is the descendant of the Scottish Society of Reparation, founded in 1870 with the primary object of reparative devotion to Our Lord in the Sacrament of the Altar, the secondary one of teaching and caring for children. This Society has a Third Order of Associates living in the world. Also in Aberdeen is the Community of St. Margaret of Scotland, a daughter of the Community at East Grinstead. The Sisters of St. Peter the Apostle, whose mother-house is at Laleham, have a Retreat and Guest House at Walkerburn, near Peebles, where most of the Retreats and many conferences and summer schools are held. A group of these Sisters has recently been called to work in Dundee. Bishop's House, Iona, also receives guests, and the chapel is served by guest-priests.

Retreats are regularly and frequently conducted at Walkerburn by the Society of St. John or Cowley Fathers, the Community of the Resurrection, the Benedictines of Nashdom, the Friars of the Society of St. Francis. These have their Scottish Tertiaries or Oblates or Companions.

The Home Mission work of the Church is increasing. Its very wide range includes Church extension, moral welfare, education, the care of old people and of orphans, youth work, hospital visiting and prison chaplaincies. Overseas there are two Scottish Missions that will soon have filled a hundred years of service. The work in Chanda, in the diocese of Nagpur, India, was begun in 1871; that in the diocese of St. John, Transkei, South Africa, in 1872. Their story is too great to be fitted into this domestic history of the Church in Scotland, but is one of her most triumphant acts of out-going and of service.

Behind this factual record of the Church lies a vivid history, which is the explanation of her modern conditions and of her difference from the sister Church of England in certain circumstances and externals. This book has tried to tell the story, concentrating upon the nineteenth century. The limitation of time has been decided partly by space; a full account would demand two large volumes, partly because this period, in which the Church, set free, began to grow and come towards her modern way of life, is the one least known even to her members.

Greyfriars Church, Kirkcudbright

# The Background of History
# 1688 And All That

For many reasonably well instructed Scots Episcopalians the nineteenth century remains dim. They know something about their Church today, a little, perhaps, about the first decades of this century; of the century of penalties and persecution, from 1688 until 1792 they have some vivid pictures. In fact, the average idea of Scottish Episcopacy might be summed up as: *1688 And All That*. In that year William of Orange gave an audience to William Rose, Bishop of Edinburgh, and asked him about the allegiance of his Church:

'I hope you will be kind to me, and follow the example of England.' To this the Bishop replied with more candour than diplomacy:

'Sir, I will serve you as far as law, reason or conscience will allow me.'

William took his meaning, turned on his heel and left the audience. The Church of luckless loyalty to the Stuarts went into the wilderness of disestablishment, disendowment and disfavour. An Act of Parliament in 1689 established Presbyterianism as The Church of Scotland.

This is the first picture. Others belong to the eighteenth century, to the penal days after the Forty-Five. One is of priests imprisoned in Stonehaven gaol for having illegally continued to officiate, and of the good Episcopalian fishwives clambering over the rocks to hold their babies up to the windows of the cells for baptism by true priestly hands. Another is of a priest holding the services in the hall or passage of a house with the permitted four around him, and as many others present, within sight and hearing, as could be crammed into the rooms on either side, or stand at the open door and windows. Then there is the Seabury picture. As a young man this American stayed, for a time, in Edinburgh. One Sunday he asked his host to direct him to an Episcopal chapel. His host took up his hat, saying:

'Follow me, but at a distance; do not speak'; and led him to a wool-store in Carubbers' Close, off the High Street, where a congregation of The Faithful Remnant had met since being turned out of St. Giles. When the penal days were coming near an end, and the American War of Independence had been won, Samuel Seabury, now an Episcopal priest in America, was elected Bishop of Connecticut, the first to be elected to the American Episcopate since the war. The English Bishops refused him consecration because he could not swear allegiance to King George. In the disestablished Church in Scotland there was no such impediment. Seabury was 'a godly and well-learned man', worthy of the office of Bishop. He came to Scotland, and in 1784 was consecrated by Bishops Kilgour, Petrie and Skinner in the upper room in Bishop Skinner's house in Aberdeen which served as chapel for the faithful Episcopalians. The impoverished little Scottish Church, not yet free from her disabilities, could transmit the living, apostolic succession.

These are vivid pictures, brave episodes, part of our heritage. There are many others, and to know our Church it is necessary to know about 1688 and all that. The trouble lies in our national tendency to see history in episodes and ignore those which we cannot fit into a pleasing picture of the whole.

For many Scots, ecclesiastical history begins with the coming of the missionary saints to Scotland: Ninian, first, and then Kentigern, Columba, their comrades and their successors; holy men teaching pure doctrine. After a time appear the Roman Catholic priests and Bishops, not so holy, although many of them good men, if misguided; they can be tolerated, even mildly admired, being safely held in the past. Later the priests and Bishops become bad, the doctrine becomes corrupt, laden with errors and accretions. Then comes the Reformation when the Reformers restore purity, even if, as is being more and more admitted, they were harsh in the process; the times demanded harshness. The extremists, including the later Covenanters, are somewhat embarrassing to the tolerant, well-mannered Presbyterian of today, but were undoubtedly brave men; and so the story moves on through the eighteenth and nineteenth centuries, with growing tolerance only marred by occasional outbreaks of acerbity. Somewhere in this ordered process lurks Episcopacy: an intruder, rather a nuisance. Everyone knows about Catholicism, but not many are quite sure what to make of this Episcopacy. There is nothing wrong with it in England, where it is established and very respectable and well-bred, but in Scotland it appears out of place.

This is all very neat if also angular and flat. It is the picture in the mind of the average non-Episcopal, not intolerant Scot. The Scots Episcopalian finds it all out of line and proportion; he maintains that the Episcopal Church is neither new nor intrusive, but the direct descendant in faith and order of the Church of St. Ninian, St. Kentigern and St. Columba which, in turn, is in descent at the remove of only a few centuries from the Church of the Apostles themselves. This Scottish Church continues the Apostolic Succession with her threefold order of Bishops, Priests and Deacons, with her Sacraments, with the Scriptures, the Creeds and Tradition. In her teaching and apologetics she refers to both Scripture and Tradition, to the Fathers of the early Church, to the Liturgy with its central Act of the Eucharist. In worship, discipline and doctrine she claims to hold the faith once delivered to the saints.

Establishment is not of the *esse*, perhaps not even the *bene esse* of the Church; it is an historic accident. The Church of England is now the only part of the world-wide Anglican Communion to be established as the Church of the State with resultant privileges and honours, hindrances and difficulties. An accident of history, a lapse, some might say, of diplomacy disestablished the Episcopal Church in Scotland, whether for her good or ill and that of Scotland being matter for argument. Nationalism is distinct from establishment, and much more intimate. There is a distinctly Scottish tradition, and a proud one; there are qualities and distinctions which come from our history, from our racial temperament, and it is of the *bene* and the *plene esse* of our Church that, being Scottish, she should be a little different from the Church in England, Ireland, America, Africa or elsewhere. But the very essence of our life is our catholicity, our heritage expressed in our motto: 'Evangelical Truth and Apostolic Order.' The chain of episcopacy has, in times of confusion been dropped, not broken; it has never been lost.

At the break with Rome, in 1560, the extreme Reformers triumphed. Something of the diocesan system lingered in the Presbyteries, and superintendents were appointed, though not consecrated, to something resembling the authority of Bishops. In 1560 the Convention of Leith ordered the restoration of the Episcopate. The validity of the restored order is doubtful because the consecration of the Bishop of Caithness who laid hands on the new bishops was itself dubious. This 'titular or pseudo-Episcopacy' as Andrew Melville called it, lasted for twenty years; his criticism of these prelates as mere 'cyphers and creatures of the King' was not unjust. This union between crown and mitre brought little good. In 1592 the Scots Parliament repealed Episcopacy and restored Presbyterianism which was far from being subservient, even from being decently respectful to the Crown. One minister declared that all kings were devil's bairns; Andrew Melville, more mildly, told James VI he was only 'God's silly vassal' ('silly' meaning weak, not witless). James retorted that the monarchy and Presbyterianism agreed as well as God and the devil. The debate continued with zest and acrimony on both sides, but the King's power increased. In 1600 three titular Bishops, of Ross, Caithness and Aberdeen, were appointed; Bishops in Presbytery returned in 1606, and in 1610 a true and valid Episcopate was restored, not by the Act of Parliament which legalized it, but by the valid consecration of three Scottish Bishops, Spottiswoode of Glasgow, Lamb of Brechin, Hamilton of Galloway, by the Bishops of London, Ely, Rochester and Worcester. The fact that these consecrating Bishops were English has been made a reproach, and an argument that Episcopacy is merely English. This is irrelevant. The nationality of a Bishop has no more to do with his office and authority as Father-in-God, successor of the Apostles, maker of priests, transmitter of Order, than has his family, his private character, his scholarship or his politics. These four English Bishops were in the Apostolic line, and so could transmit the succession to the three Scots, who in turn transmitted it to others, and who ordained priests and deacons. It is worth noting, however, that the Archbishops of Canterbury and York deliberately withheld themselves from this consecration, thus making it clear that they had no authority over the Church in Scotland.

'Thus the line of true Episcopal succession, broken in 1560, was restored to Scotland,' wrote Anthony Mitchell, Bishop of Aberdeen, in his *Story of the Episcopal Church in Scotland*; or the line, dropped rather than broken, might be said to have been picked up again.

The seventeenth century was, in spiritual endowment, a golden age for the Church of England, however much she suffered materially during the Commonwealth; it was the century of Herbert and Vaughan, of Hooker and Jeremy Taylor, of Bishop Andrews and Bishop Ken. In Scotland, too, there was this wealth. The Church had priests like William Forbes and John Forbes of Carse, Bishops like Wedderburn and Leighton. They might have brought peace and unity to Scotland, but the Church was caught in the net of politics, bound in luckless loyalty to the throne; in the second quarter of the century to a king as luckless and blundering as he was good and devout, who loved the Church to the point of martyrdom – Charles I.

Before his tragic reign began, Episcopacy lived in a peace made uneasy by her royal defender, James VI and I. The Five Articles of Perth in 1618 ordered:
1. Kneeling at the reception of Holy Communion.
2. Private Communion of the sick.
3. Private baptism in case of need.
4. Observance of holy days: Christmas, Good Friday, Easter, Ascension, Pentecost.
5. The Confirmation of children.

These, although expressing a very moderate devotion, were anathema to the Presbyterians. Their sacramental implications were understood and detested.

One does not kneel to a mere symbol; the act implies worship. Communion of the sick stresses the fact that what is given is no mere token or reminder of a Feast held long ago, but very Food for the soul, medicine of immortality. Private baptism of a child like to die declares belief in baptismal regeneration, and Confirmation belief in the grace bestowed by that sacramental act.

In 1633 Charles I founded the see of Edinburgh, and the High Kirk of St. Giles became a cathedral. In quick succession appeared three books of order or discipline: The Book of Canons, The Ordinal, and The Scottish Prayer Book of 1637 still popularly known as Laud's Liturgy, although Archbishop Laud had done no more than make suggestions and help in the revision. It was chiefly the work of two Scottish Bishops, Wedderburn of Dunblane and Maxwell of Ross, yet it was not their Liturgy either. It was a Catholic Liturgy derived from the Liturgies of the Primitive Church, with the essential Rite or Canon of the Eucharist as its centre. It was Catholic but not Roman, owing less to the Western Rite than does the English Office in The Book of Common Prayer, deriving more from the Eastern Orthodox Church. Like all the Orthodox Liturgies it contained the Epiklesis or Invocation of the Holy Spirit upon the Elements.

This Book has created a legend. Its introduction into St. Giles by the Dean caused a riot, the story of which is still cherished by pious Presbyterian opinion even if not held *de fide*. According to this legend, one Jenny Geddes hurled her stool at the Dean's head, yelling: 'Daur ye say Mass at my lug?' To suggest that Jenny Geddes is a spiritual forebear of Mrs. Harris is still, in some quarters, to risk a charge of heresy, and for proof of the incident a stool is exhibited in St. Giles. That there was a riot, chiefly of local toughs, is true.

In the same year The National Covenant was drawn up and signed; it bound signatories to the defence of the Protestant religion 'against all innovations and corruptions' (in Bishop Mitchell's phrase); and in the south of Scotland it was signed by a multitude of people. The north was more reluctant. Aberdeen, led by her learned Episcopalian 'Aberdeen doctors' refused the Covenant. The south, however, made a large majority, and there was a violent reaction against Episcopacy. The Assembly of Glasgow deposed the Bishops, excommunicating some of them, and rejected the Five Articles, the Liturgy, the Canons and Ordinal: in fact, Episcopacy in general and particular. Clergy who would not subscribe the Covenant were deposed. What was later to be called 'the rabbling of the curates' proved a popular sport. The victorious Presbyterians were literally up in arms against the Episcopalians, sending Montrose with an army against Aberdeen. The Doctors – Forbes, Baron, Scroggie, Leslie, Sibbald and Ross – fled; and with them departed 'more learning than was left behind in all Scotland beside'. Penalties were imposed on all who did not sign the Covenant, Private meetings or conventions for worship were forbidden (a fact overlooked by the later Covenanters and their defenders) and religious frenzy became sadistic and perverted. It spread beyond sectarian violence into the cruel witch hunts.

The Civil War broke out and raged disastrously. The Scots of the south fought against their King and gave him over to his bitter enemies; then, by reaction, remorse, or some complexity of emotion they were enraged by his execution. For most Scots this was the murder of a King of Scots by the English; for Scots Episcopalians it was the death of a martyr. Charles II was proclaimed King. That adroit cynic had no hesitation about signing the Covenant; he only asked for a pen. No one can blame him; it was an extorted signature after a course of domineering pressure. Something in him had changed and hardened after the shock of his father's death. He would outwit his adversaries by any means; he would not be a martyr, he would not if he could avoid it go upon his travels again. He was King; he signed; his private intention and reservations were his own business. These Scots did not deserve honourable treatment.

After the Restoration, Charles established Episcopacy in both Scotland and England. In Scotland, only one Bishop, Sydserf of Galloway, had survived the war. He was translated to Orkney. Four new Bishops were consecrated in 1661 by the Bishops of London, Carlisle, Worcester and Llandaff: the four being James Sharp, Robert Leighton, Andrew Fairfoul and James Hamilton. The latter two already in priestly orders; Sharp and Leighton had first to be episcopally ordained deacon and priest. Sharp became Archbishop of St. Andrews; he was hated by the extreme Presbyterians with a hatred that led to his dreadful end, murdered in the sight of his daughter. Hamilton, Bishop of Galloway, who had been a Presbyterian minister, also suffered an evil fate. It is narrated with sappy unction by that pungent historian, Robert Wodrow, in his *Analecta*:

'It's remarked by several that few or none of the Bishops after the Restoration that had taken the Covenant died a natural death. Mr. Sharp, his exit is known.' (A superb example of meiosis!) Bishop Hamilton had spoken ill of a zealous Covenanter, one Gilbert Hall, stricken by palsy:

'Now, God has stopped that man's mouth which we could not

all get stopped': admittedly a statement devoid of decency let alone charity. Retribution was swift.

'Within a very little time, riding home from some place, on the road his [Hamilton's] tongue fell a-swelling, and before he got home it was swelled to that degree that it hang out of his mouth, and he died in great anguish.'

If there were more Christian charity in the world there would be fewer good stories.

The Scots Bishops were, however, most of them devout men, true Fathers-in-God, and one of them, Robert Leighton, Bishop of Dunblane and, later, Archbishop of Glasgow, came within measurable distance of sanctity. He was a scholar and theologian; he loved books, but he loved souls more. Living humbly and frugally, he served his flock and taught the faith. Seeing more clearly than most what was the essence of that faith, common to all Christians, he tried with great patience and gentleness to reconcile Presbyterians with Episcopalians; but this was a hopeless venture in an age which sought strife. The *perfervidum ingenium, odium theologicum* or sheer thrawnness of the Scot defeated him. Yet his gentle spirit lives and works today.

Parliament had no more notion of tolerance than the Scotsman in the street. Episcopacy must now be imposed, and ministers who would not accept Episcopal authority were now, in turn, ejected. The wheel had turned and would turn again. Neither side can be absolved from blame; but in the mind of the average Scot only the Episcopal, never the Presbyterian tyranny is remembered. Again the bitterest struggle took place in the south, and especially in the south-west. In the north-east, Episcopacy continued, through calm days and stormy, as, in some parts of the Highlands, Roman Catholicism still lived and would continue to live. The ejected ministers were stubborn and bitter, the bitterness intensified by Parliament's attempt at conciliation by offering Indulgences (in this world, not the next) to those who would conform. The Indulged or restored ministers were hated, if anything, more bitterly than the original Episcopalians. Some of the ejected ministers and their adherents became Covenanters, extreme, irreconcilable, disowning allegiance to both King and Bishop, rejecting both legal and ecclesiastical decrees. They were proscribed, hunted, persecuted; some of them suffered a terrible death, and the shadow of this black period lies across our history, although the lawlessness of those Covenanters, like the sufferings of the later Episcopalians, is forgotten. Under James II the persecution was increased. That unhappy monarch surpassed his father in political blunders; he had great courage, he was devout, he served his country well in helping to make the Navy, but all except the most fervent Jacobites may be tempted to agree with Austin Farrer that 'James the Second should never have occurred'.

And so we come to 1688, to his flight, to the coming of his daughter and son-in-law, Mary and William of Orange, to that fateful interview with Bishop Rose, to the disestablishment, the tale of luckless loyalty and the years in the wilderness. That loyalty must have been in will and honour rather than in emotion. Fealty to Charles I is easy to understand; he loved the Church with all his soul, he was of pure life, he had the sad and haunting Stuart charm. James had transferred his allegiance to the Church of Rome, his morals were not immaculate, he had neither the melancholy dignity of his father nor the humour, intelligence and fascination of his brother, the second Charles, but he was the anointed King to whom the oath of allegiance had been taken, for whom his subjects were bound to pray. Vows are not to be broken for expediency or for the unworthiness of the person to whom loyalty is vowed.

The wilderness was not, at first, perilous, though it was bleak. The Church endured, especially in that home and cradle of Episcopacy, the north-east. For a time it was tolerated or at least ignored. Queen Anne, when she came to the throne, showed the Church favour and the Church responded with loyalty. Had she been succeeded by a son, Scotland would have been spared much bloodshed; Episcopacy would have grown in strength, some measure of peace might have been gained between the Established and the disestablished Kirk. The degree of toleration varied from district to district. In some places the non-juring Episcopalians were ejected; in others the matter of deposition was overlooked; in some, indeed, the Episcopal incumbent was so popular that he was protected. In one parish the Presbyterian incomer was conducted to the boundary and made to swear he would not return. This was in the north; in the south-west the rabbling of the curates was performed with fervour. But for the twelve years of Queen Anne's reign there was at least an uneasy peace. In 1712 the Act of Toleration restored liberty of worship with the use of the English Prayer Book; but with the death of the Queen and the coming of German George the brief truce ended. Their Jacobite sympathy in the Rising of 1715 brought upon Episcopalians the open and active hostility of Crown and Parliament. A Penal Act of 1719 forbade the non-juring clergy to officiate in the presence of more than nine persons beyond their own household; ordered them to pray for King George by name under pain of six months' imprisonment. Some clergy and congregations 'qualified' by taking the oath of allegiance, and thus began a schism within a Church already harassed from without:

'The Episcopal clergy, though thus deprived, by the calamities of the Church, of their temporal livings and of the civil authority which belonged to them when members of an Establishment, still retained their spiritual character which no civil power gave them and which no civil power could take away. They continued, in poverty and humiliation, to minister to such as adhered to their suffering Communion; and their Bishops . . . from time to time consecrated other Bishops to keep up the succession.' So a later Bishop of Edinburgh, Daniel Sandford, recorded. That Episcopal Act was essential. From these consecrations 'the present Bishops of the Episcopal Church in Scotland derive their spiritual character and authority'.

Episcopacy continued, the Apostolic Succession was maintained, but what we know of the worship and practice of the Church in the late seventeenth and early eighteenth centuries is not greatly to our comfort, and not at all to our complacency. A picture of the Faithful Remnant gathering Sunday by Sunday for a plain but worshipful Celebration of the Eucharist is dream, not reality. The difference in outward form between Episcopalian and Presbyterian was slight. Episcopalians retained the Lord's Prayer, the Doxology and the Blessing: their services, with extemporary prayers and metrical psalms were otherwise very like those of their separated brethren. The resemblance appeared even in the Celebration of Holy Communion. It is an almost shattering disillusionment to find a description, by a contemporary, of the Church's worship; and that contemporary no hostile witness but a great and learned Bishop, Thomas Rattray of Dunkeld. He wrote in 1720:

'Let us now look back to the state of this Church with regard to public worship which indeed, at the Revolution and for a long time after, was very lamentable and has scarcely deserved the name; for we had no such thing as any offices or liturgies used among us'. The service began with a metrical psalm followed by extemporary prayer 'during which most of the congregation sat irreverently upon their breech'. At the end, they stood for the Doxology but did not all wait for the Blessing. 'All the time it was a-pronouncing, they were running out of the church like so many sheep breaking out of a fold.' Until the reign of Queen Anne there were few Prayer Books; the clergy relied on their memory or their powers of extemporization even in the Communion Office. This was celebrated no more often in the Episcopal than in the Presbyterian Church, in many places only once a year, preceded by a sermon of preparation on the eve. There was no seemly ritual of priest at the altar and people going up reverently to kneel and receive the Sacrament. Tables were set out 'as it had been at a common meal', the Consecrated Elements handed from one to another, 'while the attending elders shoved the plates with the Consecrated Bread along the table for their greater convenience', a sermon being preached the while. And the Elements had been consecrated, sometimes, by an extemporary prayer: 'How defective it must frequently have been may easily be judged, considering that many of them had no notion of its being the Sacrifice of the Christian Church, only they repeated the words of the History of the Institution.'

Enough bread was consecrated but only a little wine. 'When it was exhausted they had a little barrel or some other vessel at hand from which they filled more, and straightway used it without any consecration at all.'

More than a century after Bishop Rattray, Bishop Forbes of Brechin described the early Roman custom of adding new wine to the residuum of that already consecrated. This Scottish act was thus not peculiar; but the unseemliness, even the irreverence is still shocking, even if the essentials of the Rite were retained, and even if we allow for the circumstances, for the people being imperfectly taught, the clergy, many of them unlearned, for the antagonism surrounding them, the anxiety and insecurity. Episcopalians dared not call attention to themselves; the more closely their services resembled those of the Presbyterians the better for them. Safety lay that way. Their doctrine was their own affair, but its outward expression might bring attack. An earlier account by Sir George Mackenzie confirms that of Bishop Rattray:

'We had no ceremonies, surplice, altars, cross in baptism, nor the meanest of these things that would be allowed in England by the dissenters.' So it continued until the peace of Queen Anne.

Then copies of the English Book of Common Prayer began to be introduced. The Scottish Book of 1637 was still rare. Some of the clergy, remembering that Liturgy, 'did yet interject a prayer of Invocation for the descent of the Holy Ghost to bless and sanctify the Elements, to make them the Sacramental Body and Blood of Christ'. Some used the first post-Communion prayer as Oblation. These two features, the Oblation and the Invocation, distinctive of the Scottish Liturgy, were never entirely forgotten. The Prayer Book of 1637 was not generally reprinted or distributed, but its central and distinctive part, the Prayer of Consecration and the Prayer for the Church were printed in a series of 'wee bookies' which were in common use for the rest of that century. For every Office but the Eucharist the clergy and people used the English Book; for that Rite they returned to their own.

There came a slow return of ritual. In the other kirk, Robert Wodrow noted, with disapproval, that Episcopalians used the Prayer Book at burials, the clergy wearing their 'habits'. Complaint was made to the Court of Session about those prelatical customs but 'no redress is likely to be got'. Other customs gravely displeasing to Dr. Wodrow were the Communion of the Sick and signing with the cross in baptism.

Bishop Dowden has pointed out that Presbyterian mob-intolerance in the early days (as distinct from Government hostility) was aroused not by Jacobite loyalty but by Episcopal ways of worship. One priest, James Greenshields, who had taken the oath of allegiance to the new monarch, was haled before the Presbytery of Edinburgh and imprisoned for having used the Prayer Book. His appeal to the Court of Session was dismissed: he took it to the House of Lords who granted it, and overturned the judgement of the Scottish Court to the rage and scandal of zealous Presbyterians and the benefit of Episcopalians, for from this came the Act of Toleration of 1712 already mentioned, passed 'to prevent the disturbance of those of the Episcopal Communion in that part of Great Britain called Scotland in the exercise of their religious worship, and in the use of the Liturgy of the Church of England'.

The Church had, for a time, peace to make her soul. She turned to a new reverence in worship, to a deeper knowledge of divine truths. Eucharistic doctrine regarding the Sacrifice and the Presence on the altar, never wholly lost, was gradually recovered and made clear. The Apostolic Succession had always been upheld. Episcopalians might differ little, for a time, in outward forms from the Presbyterians but they had their Bishops. There was, as it were, always that thin purple line. There came also a new stimulus in teaching about the Eucharist. In Bishop Dowden's words:

'The main impulse towards the adoption of the views of the Eucharist which afterwards became general, reached Scotland from the south'; from the English non-jurors who held fast by the teaching of the early Church and that of the great Caroline divines. These non-jurors numbered nine Bishops and some four hundred priests of whom many were Fellows of Oxford and Cambridge Colleges. They had their own Liturgy, finding that of the English Prayer Book imperfect in its Eucharistic expression.

Bishop Rattray was of this school, steeped in patristic and liturgic learning and devotion. His teaching (given in his *Works*, published in the nineteenth century by The Pitsligo Press) is typical of the sacramental tradition of the Scottish Church:

'That we may have a right understanding of this tremendous and mystical service, we must observe:

'That our Lord Jesus Christ, as our High Priest after the order of Melchisedek, did, in the same night in which He was betrayed . . . offer up Himself a free and voluntary Sacrifice to His Father, to make satisfaction for the sins of the world, under the symbols of bread and wine . . . That having eucharistized or blessed them, that is, not only given thanks to God over them . . . but likewise offered them up to God as the symbols of His Body and Blood, and invoked a blessing, even the divine power of the Holy Spirit to descend upon them. . . . He gave them to His disciples as His Body broken and His Blood shed. . . .

'That this sacrifice of Himself thus offered up by Him as a High Priest was immediately after slain on the cross, and after He had, by the power of the Spirit, raised Himself from the dead, He entered into Heaven, the true Holy of Holies, there to present His Sacrifice to God the Father, and in virtue of it to make continual intercession for His Church whereby He continueth a priest for ever.

'That He commanded His apostles and their successors, as the priests of the Christian Church to do (i.e. to offer) this bread and cup in commemoration of Him, or as the memorial of His one Sacrifice of Himself once offered . . . and thereby to plead the merits of it before His Father, here on earth as He doth continually in Heaven.'

Rattray further taught that the priest rehearsed the history of the Institution to show the authority by which he acted, by the words: 'Do This', and also to consecrate by the words: 'This is My Body. This is My Blood.' The bread and wine became 'the symbols or antitypes of the Body and Blood of Christ'. The Epiklesis was effectual 'for procuring the descent of the Holy Ghost upon them, whereby they become the spiritual and life-giving Body and Blood. . . . As Christ offered up His Body and Blood under the symbols of bread and wine as a Sacrifice . . . so here the priest offereth up this bread and cup as the symbols of this Sacrifice, and commemorateth it before God with thanksgiving; after which he prayeth that God would favourably accept this commemorative Sacrifice by sending down upon it His Holy Spirit, that by His descent upon them He may make this bread and this cup (already so far consecrated as to be the symbols or antitypes of the Body and Blood of Christ) to be verily and indeed His Body and Blood; the same Divine Spirit by which the Body of Christ was formed in the womb of the Blessed Virgin, and which is still united to It in Heaven, descending on and being united to these elements and invigorating them with the virtue and power and efficacy thereof and making them one with It'. [*Symbol*: 'An object representing something sacred.' *Antitype*: 'That which is shadowed forth or represented by the type or symbol.' – *Oxford Dictionary*.]

This last paragraph is vital in the history of Eucharistic doctrine. Eucharistic worship was thus supremely Trinitarian:

Oblation made to God the Father, the pleading and commemoration of the Sacrifice of the Son, the Invocation of the Holy Spirit. The same pattern is found in the Orthodox Liturgies of the East.

The Epiklesis or Invocation in the 1637 book was this:

'Hear us, O Merciful Father, we most humbly beseech Thee, and of Thy Almighty goodness vouchsafe so to bless with Thy Word and Holy Spirit these Thy gifts and creatures of bread and wine that they may be unto us the Body and Blood of Thy most dearly beloved Son.' Then followed the Words of Institution.

The Epiklesis of the non-jurors was this:

'We beseech Thee to look favourably on these Thy gifts which are here set before Thee, O Thou Self-sufficient God; and do Thou accept them for the honour of Thy Christ, and send down Thy Holy Spirit, the witness of the Passion of our Lord Jesus, upon this sacrifice, that He may make this bread the Body of Thy Christ, and this cup the Blood of Thy Christ; that they who are partakers thereof may be confirmed in godliness, may obtain remission of their sins, may be delivered from the devil and all his snares, may be replenished with the Holy Ghost, may be made worthy of Thy Christ, and may obtain everlasting life.'

The Epiklesis was one of the Usages of the Scottish Church; others were the Oblation of the Elements upon the altar, the commemoration of the faithful departed in the Prayer for the Church, the use of the mixed chalice (of water and wine) after the example, it was held, of Our Lord at the Last Supper, baptism by immersion, the use of chrism, the holy ointment, in Confirmation, the Sign of the Cross, the anointing of the sick and reservation of the Sacrament for the sick and dying. Three at least of the Scottish Bishops in the early eighteenth century, Falconar, Gadderar and Campbell, defended the Usages, Campbell declaring them essential. Others did not hold to them. But in general the tradition of worship was so followed that in 1743 a priest in Perthshire could report:

'The majority of those who use the Scottish Liturgy is so great that there are but very few who do otherwise, and those few mostly in the south, or in parts mostly overaw'd by the laity. I am persuaded that most of the clergy of my acquaintance, and with great sincerity I can say it for myself, would much sooner resign our several charges than give up the Scottish to use the English

Communion Office; yes, the greater number even of our laity would desert us did we attempt it.'

The Church had emerged from the spiritual shadows before she entered the darkness of danger and persecution after 1745. But the light of holiness and holy teaching had never been quenched. Among those who had shone it forth was a young priest in Aberdeenshire, Henry Scougal, son of Patrick Scougal who was Professor of Divinity in King's College, Aberdeen, before the disestablishment. Henry Scougal died, still in his twenties, in 1678. Among his Works is a Sermon of Preparation for the Holy Sacrament. It is difficult to believe that his people could have been slovenly in their approach to the altar after such instruction:

'What are those wonders we expect to see? A little bread broken among us, a little wine poured forth and drunk? The outside of this ordinance is very poor and mean, hath nothing in it that may dazzle or delight the vulgar eye, that may please or affect a carnal mind; but those whose eyes are open to the right apprehension of spiritual and divine things, can easily see through the coarse and contemptible veil, and discern astonishing wonders in this ordinance, wonders of power and wisdom and love.'

He showed the Eucharist as something very far from a mere sign or a subjective recollection of the one perfect Sacrifice of perfect Love. He was in the tradition later to be followed by Bishop Rattray and many others. Extreme Protestant doctrine never had any place in Episcopalian teaching.

'If we consider what is represented to us in this sacrament, we have therein occasion to behold the most wonderful and astonishing spectacle that ever was seen in this lower world: the only begotten Son of God suffering for the sins of the world; the Lord of Glory hanging between two thieves. For in this ordinance Jesus Christ is evidently set forth and crucified before our eyes.'

There could not be a stronger or clearer assertion of the doctrine of the Real Presence and of the Eucharistic Sacrifice.

'Our faith comes not only by ear. Our other senses contribute unto it that we may say in some sense with the beloved disciple that we have not only heard but have seen with our eyes, we have looked upon it, and our hands have handled the Word of Life.'

Scougal must have taught his people reverence, but neither he nor they knew any splendour of ritual and ceremonial. The simplicity of the Sacrament was itself a glory.

'There might have been contrived a more sensible resemblance and tragical representation of the death of Christ . . . but it is a mean and low devotion which outward objects do excite by their natural strength. We see so much as to awaken our souls, but not so much as to keep them awake without themselves. The outward object serves to excite our faith but then leaves it to its proper exercise and employment. Faith takes the hint which sense doth give it' – an admirable complement to St. Thomas Aquinas's '*Praestet fides supplementum sensuum defectui*'.

The church where this doctrine was preached would be bare of ornament, lacking in any sensory aid to devotion. Faith must make do with very slight hints from sense; but the faithful knew they were at the foot of the Cross, in the Presence of the Crucified, pleading His Sacrifice:

'This Sacrament doth not only represent a wonder that is past, but exhibits a new. The bread and wine that are received are not bare and empty signs to put us in mind of the death and sufferings of Christ. Our Saviour calls them His Body and Blood, and such, without question they are, to all spiritual purposes and advantages.'

That is the very core and essence of the teaching of the Scottish Church then and for many years to come: the doctrine of the Presence of Grace and Power, or of Power and Efficacy. It is emphasized in another passage in which, also, Scougal repudiates, though mildly, the doctrine of transubstantiation:

'We are not obliged to believe that, after consecration, the bread and wine do vanish and the Body and Blood of Christ succeed in their turn. Our sense and reason assure us of the contrary, the Scriptures nowhere affirm it, nor did ever the ancient Church believe it. . . . These words of Our Saviour are spirit and life, are to be understood in a spiritual and vital sense; but though these elements be not changed in their nature and substance, yet they undergo a mighty change as to their efficacy and use.'

In the Eucharist Christ enters the hearts of His worshippers, becomes the food of their souls, so quickening them 'with His Life and spirit that they may have no wills and affections of their

27

own, no desires or inclinations different from Him . . . in a word, that it may not be any more they, but Christ that liveth in them'.

These worshippers were at the foot not only of the Cross but of the Throne of Christ in glory; they were in the presence of Christ the King, the eternal priest pleading in heaven His own Sacrifice. This conception was recurrently lost by both the medieval and the reformed Church. It continues like a thread of pure gold through the Scottish doctrine of the Eucharist.

Scougal is a mystic and in his conclusion becomes almost a poet:

'Doubtless when these sacred and venerable mysteries are performing, the holy angels do stand by, and the place is full of blessed and glorious spirits who delight to look and pry into them; and all the orders of the heavenly hosts shout and raise their voices together.'

He wrote a mystical treatise *The Life of God in the Soul of Man* which had a great influence. He was one of the *Mystics of the North East* of whom the Rev. G. D. Henderson has published a learned and sympathetic account. Another of those mystics was John Forbes of Carse, who wrote *The Spiritual Exercises*, and yet another was James Garden, who wrote *Comparative Theology*. All three were at one time or other Professors of Divinity at Aberdeen. James Garden had a brother George who translated *The Spiritual Exercises* into Latin.

The Gardens were both influenced by certain French mystics whose doctrine came near Quietism: Madame Guyon, Madame Bourignon and Pierre Poirot, all of them flourishing in the late seventeenth century. Madame Guyon was a disciple of Fénelon and shared the disfavour into which he fell during his dispute with Bossuet. Poirot published her works, including *A Short Method of Prayer*, and those of Madame Bourignon. He himself was a Protestant.

Their Scots followers did not fall into the error of Quietism or into the extreme introspection of these French teachers; but the doctrine and practice of contemplation, of waiting upon God, came like balm and nourishment to those whose outward way of worship was hampered.

It was a small group, interesting in its limits and its intensity: all of them Episcopalians, all of the north-east, all gentry and men of learning: the Gardens, Lord Pitsligo, Lord Deskford, the son of the Earl of Seafield, William 14th Lord Forbes, Sir Patrick Murray of Auchertyre, Dr. George Cheyne, and Dr. James Keith. Dr. George Garden held the charge of St. Nicholas, Aberdeen, continuing to preach after the disestablishment, refusing to pray for William and Mary or to read any royal proclamation. Summoned to Edinburgh he disregarded the decrees of the Privy Council, was demitted from office but continued to preach and to function as a priest. His politics did him no harm with the Faithful Remnant but his devotion to Madame Bourignon made him suspect of a tinge of heresy, and kept him, it is said, from a bishopric.

His brother James was deprived of his Chair of Divinity for political reasons. James Keith and George Cheyne were medical doctors, practising in London. They kept in touch with Madame Guyon by letters, theirs translated by an exiled Scot, the Chevalier Michael Ramsay. Dr. Cheyne was a notable figure, in size Falstaffian and:

'Not only a good portly man and a corpulent, but almost as witty as the knight himself, and his humour being heightened by his northern tongue, he was exceedingly mirthful.' He was a friend of Alexander Pope.

Dr. Keith wrote many letters to Lord Deskford which give us an idea of the spiritual life they shared. They used a little language of their own; Our Lord was referred to as Little Master or L.M. They practised the Presence of God:

'Weekly attend to L.M. and render His Presence familiar to you, and He will be your joy, your centre, your counsel, your guide and your all. *Laissez tomber* and *passer outre* are most useful advice, and never to be forgotten, especially in the troublesome occasions of life.'

Again: 'My spirit is often present with you before our blessed Little Master. Let us never stop at the many rubs that are thrown in our way . . . but taking as little notion of 'em as possible, sink down into the Nothing where only our security lies, and there we shall be where He would have us.'

Only a positive sense of the Presence of God kept him from an almost nihilist passivity:

'A total resignation to the Divine Will in all states and circumstances, outward and inward, will certainly bring and preserve that solid joy and peace which the world neither knows nor can deprive us of . . . The children of L.M., whose kingdom is not of this world, must continually attend to His still voice and faithfully abide in His Presence. . . . Here they are sometimes taken into the enlargements of God and into the liberty of His chosen.'

They had need of inward calm, being now assailed by disputes within the Church, and the centre of strife was the Episcopate. Loyalty to the exiled monarch, now James VIII and III, was carried to such a quixotic degree that he was allowed to nominate Bishops and approve or disapprove of those elected by the Church. Throughout the troubles, the diocesan Bishops had, from time to time, consecrated others without diocesan jurisdiction, to fulfil episcopal functions and maintain the Apostolic Succession; rather in the way Rome consecrated Bishops *in partibus infidelium*. In 1720 these non-diocesan Bishops formed themselves into a College, and King James could, when he chose, nominate men to be consecrated. There was a certain confusion, and from confusion strife between the diocesan and the collegiate Bishops, chiefly over the Usages, the collegiate Bishops opposing, the diocesan defending and practising them. This undercurrent of trouble ran beneath the torrent of political persecution which raged for nearly eighty years, from the Hanoverian accession in 1714 until 1792.

The persecution which broke out after the Fifteen blazed into fiercer flames after the Forty-Five. Episcopalians were implicated more deeply than before. Although not all of them were Jacobite, all of them were made to suffer.

After Culloden the Church dwelt in the shadow of death. The virulence of persecution of the vanquished foreshadowed the methods of the Nazis. The Duke of Cumberland would have been happy in Hitler's Germany. The Church was attacked with devilish skill in what was vital and essential.

Robert Chambers, not himself an Episcopalian, wrote in his *History of the Rebellion of 1745*:

'The persecution to which the Church was subjected was of a nature even more severe than those with which the Presbyterians were visited in the reign of Charles II.'

The Penal Laws of 1746 and 1748 went further than those of 1719. The clergy were now forbidden to officiate unless they took the oath of allegiance to the Hanoverian dynasty and abjured the Stuart; and this oath must be taken before September 1746. If they failed to do so, and continued to officiate they could be arrested and punished: for the first offence by six months' imprisonment, for a second by transportation to the American colonies. It was white martyrdom for them, and an effective drainage of life from the Church.

No non-juring priest might celebrate for more than four persons; and after September 1746 no priest, even if he took the oath, might officiate unless he had been ordained by a Bishop of the English or the Irish Church. As most of the clergy had been ordained by their own Scottish Bishops they were caught, effectively – or would have been caught had they lacked courage and resourcefulness. The next Act, of 1748, not only declared that all letters of order must be granted by an English or an Irish Bishop, but that all previous registrations by clergy ordained by Scottish Bishops were null and void: a singularly malignant piece of backward legislation and one entirely beyond the just powers of the State.

'Thus was Scottish Episcopacy proscribed and annihilated as far as Act of Parliament could do it,' Bishop Mitchell has written. 'The Scottish clergy were now prohibited from conducting worship even with the statutory numbers in any house but their own.'

The faithful laity were penalized by being debarred from voting, from Parliament, from the universities, and as far as the law could work, from worship. Fortunately the law was not omnipotent, although it came very near crushing the life out of clergy and laity alike. Robert Chambers has paid tribute to the faithful and heroic priests who continued to serve their people:

'They submitted with meekness to a fate which they could not controvert. Instead of flying to the fields, and publishing their grievances at conventicles, they sought to administer those ordinances to private friends which they were prohibited from dispensing to a congregation. Individual clergymen have been known to perform worship no less than sixteen times in one day.'

The law was evaded, very adroitly, often successfully, always with the risk of martyrdom. Every Episcopalian ranked as a private friend of the priest, and a considerable congregation could gather in and around his house, always leaving only the permitted four in his immediate presence. One house, that of the famous poet-priest, John Skinner of Linshart, was conveniently built in L shape; people crowded into the angle, and the priest read the service from the window. One day when he was about to read his sermon a silly hen, fluttering in and out, scattered the leaves of manuscript.

'A fowl shall never shut my mouth,' declared Skinner, and from that day he preached extempore.

Indeed neither a fowl nor human authority could stop his mouth or his pen. His poetic talent, admired by Burns, expressed itself in satire, and it is said that a lampoon against an influential local lady, a stern Presbyterian, brought him to prison. His captivity was shared by his small son who insisted on going with him: the son grew up to be a Bishop, and was one of those who consecrated the American Samuel Seabury to the Episcopate.

These were the years of suffering and heroism, of that courage, endurance and loyalty which make the splendour of the Scottish Church. It is a tradition rightly cherished by Episcopalians, little known by other Scots, and is indeed so valiant that there is a danger of our living in a dream of the past.

In time, the persecution grew less bitter. Again the Faithful Remnant – so small a Remnant now – were, at best tolerated, at worst ignored. Malignant neighbours and informers could still cause trouble, but more and more the Piskies were left in peace. The clergy continued to serve their people, even to serve them openly. There were few churches or chapels, for it was safer to meet in a house or a store, as, long ago, the tiny community of Christians had met in some Roman villa.

John Skinner returned to his flock, and was visited by that genial gossip, Ramsay of Ochtertyre. He found a bare little church, the altar set beneath the pulpit, little to offend Presbyterian eyes. It might almost have been a Presbyterian service 'until the reading of the Liturgy dispelled the illusion'. By this time the Liturgy was in general use. It included the Litany read by the curate, Skinner himself celebrating the Communion. Ramsay liked the singing of a hymn at the Offertory: 'It made almsgiving go hand in hand with praise and prayer.' He was impressed by the devotion of the people, by their fine, serious faces. The ways described by Bishop Rattray were now happily forsaken.

Skinner used to sit late at night reading and writing – poems as well as sermons; he refused to have his window curtained or shuttered, for his light made a beacon for wayfarers between Linshart and Longside. It might be too large a claim to make him patron saint of poets and priests alike – as we can name George Herbert – but he was a true man of God, a faithful priest, valiant for truth, and a rich and vivid personality.

He is matched in vigour by Robert Forbes, who had received him into the Church, for young Skinner had been a Presbyterian. Forbes was incumbent of the church in Leith, and became Bishop, first of Ross and Caithness, then of Ross and Argyll. The pattern of the dioceses continued, for a long time, to vary. And in those impoverished days, when clergy were few, a newly elected Bishop did not give up his charge, even if it were within the see of another Bishop. To this charge he gave most of his time, visiting his diocese at intervals to preach and to confirm. The strictly episcopal functions were maintained, the work of administration and organization was slight.

Forbes was a whole-hearted Jacobite, imprisoned after the Forty-Five, and from the stories of his fellow captives and other first-hand material he compiled his *Lyon in Mourning*, that great and poignant record of the sufferings of the vanquished, and the misfortunes of Prince Charles Edward. He treasured some relics, including a bit of the gown and apron worn by the fugitive prince when disguised as Betty Burke the maid-servant.

'Oh, he is an honest man,' Prince Charlie said of him, 'and I hope soon to give him proof how much I love and esteem him.'

Forbes has left a rich legacy. Part of it is in his *Journals* of his Episcopal tours, one in 1762, the second in 1770 in days of comparative peace. They are among the most delightful of diaries, vivid word-pictures of the man himself, his journeys, his encounters, and of the Faithful Remnant in their sober piety and faithfulness.

The *Journals* show him as Father-in-God. In another aspect, as teacher, scholar and liturgiologist, he is seen in his *Catechism: Dealing Chiefly with the Holy Eucharist*, and in the edition of the Scottish Prayer Book which he, along with Bishop Falconar, produced in 1764.

His teaching continues that of Henry Scougal, declaring but not defining the Real Presence. To the question:

'Are not Christians to believe the Consecrated Bread in the Holy Eucharist to be the Body of Christ and the Consecrated Wine to be the Blood of Christ?' comes the answer:

'Yes, certainly they are, because Our Saviour Himself in the Institution of this most Holy Sacrament has expressly declared the Bread to be His Body, and the Wine to be His Blood.'

This is developed:

'Though we cannot believe that the Bread and Wine are the very natural and substantial Body and Blood of Christ that were on the cross, yet we are to believe them to be so in a spiritual manner, that is to say that the Consecrated Bread and Wine are the Body and Blood of Christ in power, virtue and effect.'

Here again, as in Rattray, is the characteristic doctrine of the Scottish Church, and the Power effecting the change is no other than the Holy Spirit, Christ's 'Divine Substitute upon earth, by which He is present with His Church unto the end of the world'.

The Presence is there, not by transubstantiation but by the power and blessing and sanctifying effect of the Holy Spirit working in and with the Elements.

Forbes quotes both the Epiklesis of the Prayer Book of 1637 and that of the Liturgy of St. James, made known by Bishop Rattray:

'We beseech Thee, O all-sufficient God that Thou wilt graciously look upon these gifts set forth in Thy Presence, and favourably visit them for the honour of Thy Christ, and send down the Holy Spirit, the witness of the sufferings of Our Lord Jesus Christ, upon this sacrifice that He may make this Bread the Body of Thy Christ and this Cup the Blood of Thy Christ.'

Almostly exactly in these words did the non-jurors pray. Forbes lays great emphasis upon the Epiklesis, the 'invisible power and operation of the Holy Ghost by which the Sacramental Bread and Wine, in the act of consecration, are made as powerful and effectual for the ends of religion as the natural Body and Blood themselves would be if they were present before our eyes'.

A later Bishop Forbes, he of Brechin, was to find this definition inadequate.

Liturgy followed doctrinal teaching. In 1764 Robert Forbes

and Bishop Falconar issued their revision of the 1637 Book which continued in use until the present century. It was to be deprecated, as we shall see, by another scholar-Bishop, Dowden of Edinburgh, because of its omitting 'that which refers to the purport of the thing prayed for'. The 1637 Rite prayed that the consecrated Bread and Wine 'may be unto us the Body and Blood of Thy most dearly beloved Son; so that we receiving them according to Thy Son our Saviour Jesus Christ's most holy institution, in remembrance of His death and passion, may be partakers of His most precious Body and Blood'. The Forbes and Falconar Book used the word 'become' instead of 'be unto us', and omitted the petition 'that we receiving them . . .'.

Other changes were that the 1764 Book put the Epiklesis after the rehearsal of the institution and the Words of Christ: 'This is My Body. This is My Blood.' This remains in the present Prayer Book (of 1929) to the bewilderment of many not unskilled in liturgy. In the 1637 Book the Epiklesis comes before the rehearsal of the Institution and the Dominical Words. The other change was in the position of the Prayer For the Church. In the 1637 Rite it is said before the Prayer of Consecration; Rattray and Falconar placed it after. This may yet be altered; at the moment of writing the old sequence has in some churches been revived, the Prayer For the Church coming after the Creed and before the Offertory.

In both Books the Communion is given with only one sentence:

'The Body of Our Lord Jesus Christ which was given for thee – The Blood of Our Lord Jesus Christ which was shed for thee – preserve thy body and soul unto everlasting life.'

The 'Take eat, and feed on Him in thy heart, by faith, with thanksgiving' and 'Drink this in remembrance that Christ died for thee and be thankful' are omitted.

Whatever the details of difference between these forms of the Scottish Liturgy, that between Scottish and English is more significant. Her Liturgy conveys the mind of the Church on this most Holy mystery. The Consecration lay in the whole prayer, not in the Words of Institution alone. The Eucharist was one tremendous act, a sacrifice, an intercourse between earth and heaven.

And all this glory was witnessed in the humblest surroundings, often in a cottage or a barn, a store, or on the Highland hillside. In the bad days it must be celebrated secretly, with one keeping watch. Afterwards the worshippers, fed and renewed with the Body and Blood of Christ, might go peacefully home, or they, especially their priests, might be taken prisoner. They were very brave, very faithful those people of the Faithful Remnant.

For a long time they walked softly.

'I am a member of the suffering and Episcopal Church of Scotland – the shadow of a shade now,' Peter Pleydell told Colonel Guy Mannering; but he took his guest to Greyfriars' kirk, not to the Episcopal chapel in Carubbers' Close.

The fear of a return of the Stuarts faded, and with it the virulence of persecution. George III was tolerant and he was, on the whole, respected. In 1788 Prince Charles Edward, once, so long ago, the bonnie, valiant prince and king of the Highland hearts, died in Rome; the King, *de jure*, leaving no lawful issue. His sole heir was his brother, the Prince Cardinal Henry of York. It was the end of the old song of loyalty, the long dream. The most loyal Jacobite could now pray for King George.

In 1792 the Penal Acts were repealed, all but one. This one disability was to hamper the Scottish clergy for some seventy years yet. No priest, unless ordained by an English or Irish Bishop, might accept a charge in the Church of England. Otherwise the Church was free if impoverished, weakened, almost drained of life. Bishop Mitchell has given some details: in 1689 she held two-thirds of the people of Scotland with six hundred clergy; now she had four Bishops, forty priests, and only a twentieth of the people.

# 2

# The Church Set Free.
# Bishop Jolly

Some had lapsed, through apathy, discouragement, or lack of the means of grace; some, where the ministry of their own Church was lacking, turned in a generation or two towards another, and in the 1840's joined the Free Kirk of Scotland, less from belief in its Calvinistic doctrine than from sympathy with its resistance to any form of State control or patronage. But still Episcopacy lived, coming out of the shadows, a poor creature in material things but free, guarding her faith and order, cherishing her sacraments.

Her membership was still most numerous in the north-east, and for the first three decades of the new century all her Bishops came from that region. Aberdeenshire was the centre of Episcopacy, most of her priests were alumni of her University, either of King's or of Marischal College. There were still divisions among them. Even if there were no longer non-jurors refusing allegiance to King George, the old Scottish tradition was strong: opposing that, especially in the south, was the Anglicizing party who worked for complete conformity with the Church of England. There were also some 'qualified' congregations who, in the dark days, had made themselves secure by taking the oaths demanded of them and placing themselves under the rule not of the diocesan but of an English Bishop; and some clerics had come or intruded from over the border, forming a congregation without deference to diocesan authority. These have lingered into our own day in some places.

One of the conditions of relief from the penal acts was that the Scottish clergy should subscribe the Thirty-Nine Articles, which was done only in 1806 and after much controversy. These Scottish priests looked back not to the Reformation but to the primitive Church, and preferred to affirm primitive doctrine rather than to repudiate accretions or corruptions. They disliked, in particular, the Calvinism of the 17th Article. Thanks largely to the influence of Bishop Skinner, son of the poet-priest, the Articles were finally accepted at the Convention of Laurencekirk.

The road to freedom had been long and hard. Greatly to the credit of the Established Church of Scotland, her leaders had urged the repeal of the Penal Acts; equally to the discredit of the Church of England, most of her Bishops had been singularly unhelpful. The chief opponent of repeal had been Lord Chancellor Thurlow. Suspicion of Scots Episcopalians lingered, although their good defender, Lord Kinnoull, described them as: 'a decent, quiet, respectable body of people who, in the most trying time, had always behaved in a very becoming and exemplary manner.' A like defence of their brethren from the Episcopal Bench would have been as becoming as it would have been valued.

A delightful picture of a Scots Bishop in those early years of freedom is given by John Gibson Lockhart in his youthful novel *Reginald Dalton*, which appeared in 1823. It is not a good novel, the young author was trying his hand at a form in which he was not adept, but it has charm, especially in the recollections of Oxford. Reginald, on his way thither, falls in with a friendly, loquacious and inquisitive Scot, who announces himself a Master of Arts of St. Andrews, which Reginald has heard of as 'one of the Scottish Archbishoprics'.

'Did ye really think we had Bishoprics and Archbishoprics in our country?' asks the Scot; and Reginald, standing his ground, replies:

'I understood that you still had an Episcopal Church remaining there.'

'Ma certy, we have an Episcopal Church, no doubt, and a bonny like Church it is, I warrant ye, and very good Bishops too, sir – most apostolical chields, reverend and right reverend Bishops, too, wi' their tale, man – although I'm thinking ye wadnas maybe think vera meikle o' them, if ye saw them!' He then tells Reginald the story of the Countess of Sutherland's flunkeys. They were on their way to Dunrobin with the Countess and her husband, and, in the small town where they lodged one night, heard that the Bishop of the diocese was coming for a Confirmation. Picturing to themselves the entry of a magnificent prelate in coach and four with footmen and outriders and other attendants, they begged permission to wait and see the procession.

'My leddy, she was up to the joke in no time; and to be sure, they got leave to stay and take their glower at the Bishop, puir creatures.' In good time to avoid the crowd, they went to the end of the town and lined themselves along the road; but no crowd was there to be avoided, only 'a wheen o' the town bairns that had come out to look at their ainsells' – flunkeys in livery being a sight hitherto unknown.

'At last and at length up comes a decent, little auld manny, in a black coat and velveteen breeches, riding on a bit broken-kneed hirplin' beast of a Highland powney, wi' a red and white checked napkin tied round his neck, and a bit auld ravel of a spur on ane o' his heels, and the coat-tails o' him pinned up before wi' twa corkin' preens to keep them from being filed with the auld shelty's white hairs coming aff.'

This rider one of the men approached, asking with some civility but more condescension: 'My good man, can you have the kindness to inform us if My Lord Bishop's likely to arrive soon; for we've been waiting here ever since breakfast to see him make his entrance?'

'Fat's that ye're saying, folk?' is the reply. 'Troth, if ye've been waiting for the Bishop, ye may e'en gang your wa's hame again now; for I'm a' ye'll get for him.'

And so this not particularly proud prelate 'on he joggit, saddlebags and a', puir body.' Reginald, when asked what he thinks of the Scottish Bishops now, replies with sense and truth that their poverty is no reason for their not being worthy Bishops, that their earliest predecessors were even poorer than they.

The picture is hardly exaggerated. The Church was poor, her Bishops and priests in this dawn of her freedom had all been born and bred in penal times, most of them knowing poverty; if they had not themselves suffered for their faith they were close to those who had.

Alexander Jolly was born during the darkest period, in 1756, in Stonehaven. His father had been in business but had given it up for teaching, for which he would appear to have had as true a vocation as his son had for the priesthood. The boy never faltered. He was prepared by the Reverend Alexander Craig who had been imprisoned in Stonehaven Gaol along with a fellow-priest, Mr.

Troup. They held services in their cells and Mr. Troup used to play Jacobite airs on his fiddle – though not during the service. Young Jolly proceeded to Marischal College, was tutor, for a time, in an Episcopalian household, read for Holy Orders and in 1776 was appointed deacon by Bishop Kilgour of Aberdeen; in the following year he was priested, and given the charge of Turriff. Eleven years later he moved to Fraserburgh where he was to spend the fifty years of his long, succeeding life.

'Fat a cheepin' body 's that 't the Bishop's sent us?' demanded one parishioner. Jolly's voice was weak and thin, but his preaching was strong and full. He gained the love of his flock and of many others besides.

'My haun winna keep from my cap', one man declared in defence of his own deference. The laity were increasing in numbers and devotion, but the clergy were still few. Services were austere and life was of a Franciscan poverty. Jolly had, for parsonage, a cottage barely furnished except for a wealth of books. In Turriff his sister had kept house for him, but as his biographer, Dean Walker, cannily puts it, she 'was said not to have possessed his meekness of temper', and in Fraserburgh he lived alone. A neighbour woman came in to clean the house, cook his dinner, and sometimes admit, but more often repel visitors. Jolly faithfully visited his flock but was not over-eager to welcome callers who might interrupt his studies. His curate, Mr. Presslie, had a key to the cottage and used to come and go freely; otherwise Jolly's life was almost that of a recluse, certainly that of a scholar, monastic in regularity. The peat fire on the kitchen hearth was smoored at night, perhaps with one of the old blessings; early in the morning, about four o'clock, he came down to stir it to flame, to make his porridge and begin his day of study and prayer. The daily Office was said. On Sunday he conducted service in the bare little church: matins, Litany, and ante-Communion. The Eucharist was celebrated five times a year: at Christmas, Easter, Pentecost, and twice during Trinity-tide. On those occasions the church was full of devout communicants. The Rite was celebrated with the utmost reverence, the Elements were brought to the altar and offered up with prayer, but there was no Elevation, no genuflection. The Sacrament was reserved in an aumbry, for the sick, but not for adoration. Every Sunday Jolly himself received it, after reading the Collect, Epistle and Gospel, but without celebrating the Liturgy or giving Holy Communion to the people.

It must appear strange to us, especially after studying the profoundly sacramental belief and teaching of the Church, to find these celebrations so rare. Even a monthly Communion was then, and for years to come, unknown. What was the reason? Not apathy, but an awful devotion, a sense of unworthiness; the act was so tremendous, the privilege so immense that, to the mind of those reticent worshippers, it should not be too easily accessible. That was, in part, the reason; in part, no doubt, there was also a residue of caution after years of being proscribed, harried and penalized. Many still recalled meeting in secret, with one to keep watch and give warning lest the meeting-place be invaded, the Liturgy interrupted, the Sacrament perhaps desecrated. There had been a real danger for both celebrant and communicants. Both this practical caution and the spiritual reserve and awe were deep in the minds of the people. Then there was nowhere any habit of frequent Communion. Few if any parish churches in England had, as yet, a monthly Celebration; Roman Catholics must, by canon law, celebrate or attend Mass on Sunday, but very few of the laity, even the most devout, communicated oftener than two or three times a year.

At those rare Eucharists in the bare little church in Fraserburgh the Scottish Rite was followed. Many of the congregation would have their wee bookies; some may have used the Book of Bishop Falconar and Bishop Forbes of 1764. There was also a later edition of the Prayer Book, published in 1787, including private prayers before and after Communion: reticent, devout, dutiful. The prayer to be said at the almsgiving accords well with our modern idea of stewardship:

'I acknowledge, O Lord, that all I possess is the effect of Thy bounty. It is from Thee I have received it, and to Thy Holy Name be the praise. Accept of this free-will offering from my hands as a testimony of Thy right to all I enjoy, and as an exercise of that love and charity to my brethren which Thou requirest and art pleased to take as done to Thyself. Lord, grant that I may always dedicate a part of what Thou hast bestowed upon me, to the maintenance of Thy clergy, to the support of Thy divine service, and to the relief of the poor; and so influence and dispose my heart that what I shall apply to these ends may bear a just and due proportion to what I enjoy, and so be acceptable in Thy sight, through the merits of Him who gave Himself for me.'

In 1796 Jolly was consecrated Bishop, as Coadjutor to Bishop Macfarlane of Moray, Ross and Caithness. Two years later, when Moray was disjoined from Ross and Caithness, he himself became Diocesan. He remained priest in charge of Fraserburgh in the economy of the period. He visited his diocese once in every three years when he held a confirmation in every church. These were few and widely scattered. Boards and committees did not exist, organization and administration were at a minimum. A Diocesan Synod was called at the discretion of its Bishop, a right which Jolly rarely exercised; he never once delivered a charge. He communicated with his clergy chiefly by letter. He was a true Father-in-God to them, benevolent, charitable, sending them, in need, money out of his own small income, but he rarely if ever consulted them or asked their advice. What it seemed good to him to do, that he did. Paternal authority was very much part of his episcopal mind, as well as fatherly loving-kindness.

In his visitations as in his way of life he was humble, travelling, if not on a Highland shelty or pony, in a hired chaise. Life in the parsonage at Fraserburgh was very different from that in an English episcopal palace.

By his fellow Bishops he was named *Cunctator* for his over-cautious attitude to change and development. The idea of a General or Provincial Synod did not commend itself to him, and the proposal of the reforming Bishop of Brechin, Gleig (of whom more will be told), that Presbyters as well as Bishops should attend, deliberate and vote, he found almost an attack on the authority of the Episcopate. Gleig urged the holding of a Synod in 1820 to revise the canons. Jolly protested:

'It is stability that gives strength . . . mild firmness is the life of authority. Our strength in such case is to sit still.'

Gleig and his supporters had, no doubt, another word for 'stability' and for 'mild firmness'. A saint Jolly undoubtedly was in his devotion, humility and charity, but in some ways 'a sair sanct' for the Church, for those who were looking forward rather than backward.

But the sanctity was clear. A lady recalled for his biographer her first sight of him on a visit to Fraserburgh. There was a cry: 'Here's St. Jolly,' and the Bishop, old, benign, holy came along, leaning on the arm of his curate. Others felt the holiness. Young Jonathan Christie, son of the parson of Fyvie, rode, as a boy of fourteen, eleven miles across rough country to visit the Bishop and receive his blessing. A newly married couple went off, it was assumed on their wedding journey, but really to Fraserburgh for the same blessing.

There are pleasant glimpses of him in his later years. He wore a wig long after other men had reverted to their own hair, and an old-fashioned wig at that, with rows of curls six or eight inches deep. When George the Fourth came to Edinburgh, and the Church, through her Bishops, sent him a loyal welcome, it was feared that the Jolly wig might overcome His Majesty. But the Bishop wore a new one for the occasion, and the King was impressed by his venerable appearance. In 1823 the Bishop of New York, Dr. Hobart, came to Aberdeen and met Jolly whom he declared to be: 'one of the most apostolic and primitive' men he had ever met; to meet him had alone been worth the journey from New York.

Three years later Robert Chambers of the young and flourishing firm of publishers, historian of the Forty-Five, not himself an Episcopalian but sympathetic with the Faithful Remnant, came to Fraserburgh, called on the Bishop, and described 'the beautiful old man, for he was beautiful' who sat 'in his neat, old-fashioned black suit, buckled shoes, and wig as white as snow, surrounded entirely by shelves full of books, most of them of an antique and theological cast. Irenaeus or Polycarp could not have lived in a style more simple. The look of the venerable prelate was full of gentleness, as if he never had an enemy or a difficulty or anything else to contend with in his life. . . . His passion apart from the church was for books, of which he had gathered a wonderful quantity.'

The historian John Hill Burton said of him that, in his holy poverty, which was beneath that of all but his poorest parishioners, his only link 'with this nether world' was his passion for books.

He died in 1838, full of years and peace and holiness.

'No human eyes beheld his departure,' so it is recorded in

George Grub's *Ecclesiastical History of Scotland*. It was said of him that his character was 'formed upon the model of the primitive saints', that 'the spirit of primitive and apostolic piety seemed to be revived in him'. He had grown like those saints whose lives and works had been his study; it was as if he had entered their world and spoken with them, bringing back news of the dawn of Christianity. 'Death was to him but the removal of the veil which divided him from a world in which he had for years habitually dwelt in habit and in mind.'

That night he had insisted on being left alone. In the morning he was found dead, his body meetly composed, even, it was said, his arms folded on his breast. The Fraserburgh folk declared that the angels had come, thus to lay out his body. And so he 'passed into that world for which, as he had said a few days previously, he was longing but not impatiently'.

A Cambridge cleric reported a talk he had had with him on prayers for the dead; the Bishop, while repudiating 'the Romish doctrine of Purgatory' had commended prayers for those 'awaiting in Paradise the consummation of all things'.

He left a memory, a tradition, a book, still classic, on The Eucharist, and his library which is part of the Church's treasure; his name missed, only by its unsuitable allusiveness, one form of fame. When The Spalding Club was formed for the publication of books of Episcopal interest it was proposed that it be called 'The Jolly Club'; but this was decided to be suggestive of other interests and was rejected.

The new age of Scottish Episcopacy was beginning as this valiant defender of her faith was departing. In the first quarter of the century the somnolence of the Church of England was stirred by the Evangelical Revival. This was hardly needed by 'the long-persecuted and well-instructed Episcopal Remnant in Scotland', but here too were signs of new life: a looking forward and around as well as to the past, an active evangelism as well as a steadfast loyalty. When Jolly died, the Oxford Movement was very new, very exciting, startling indeed to most English churchmen: to the Church in Scotland it was only a bringing forth of treasures long hidden, the emerging into daylight from the shadows of neglect of the tradition and doctrine that the Faithful Remnant had known and taught. The Oxford Movement was to have an influence, was to help the renewal and growth of Scots Episcopacy, but it was no revolution.

The Tractarian leaders restored, in the Church of England, that emphasis on the Eucharistic Sacrifice which the Scottish divines had always taught. Jolly made it the heart of his treatise: *The Christian Sacrifice in The Eucharist* (which he dedicated to Sir William Forbes of Pitsligo, one of a great Episcopalian family, grandfather-to-be of the greatest of nineteenth-century Bishops, Alexander Forbes). The title of the book is significant. Jolly taught that the Eucharist, at once Sacrament and Sacrifice, derived its value and glory from 'that grand Archetype, the Sacrifice which Christ Himself offered and perfected upon the Cross'. He stressed the application, in the Eucharist, of the Sacrifice of Calvary 'for the salvation of men as long as the world lasts'. The Memorial or Remembrance – *Anamnesis* – was more than a human and subjective remembrance; it was that which brought the Sacrifice of Christ before God; it was a pleading, an act. 'This Do' meant 'Offer This' – the Bread and the Wine – to show forth and to bring before God Christ's Passion and Death; they were 'the Representative Body and Blood of His Son'; then, after the oblation and invocation or Epiklesis they were returned to the worshippers by God as Christ's 'life-giving, virtual or efficacious Body and Blood, for the preservation of our souls and bodies unto everlasting life'.

The Elements became the vehicle of the benefits of Christ's Sacrifice through the sanctifying power of the Holy Ghost: through Him, 'the Sanctifier, the Author of all benediction and grace' came their supernatural virtue and effect. Jolly maintained, with the Fathers of the Church, that the Invocation of the Holy Spirit was 'the third and consummating degree of the Consecration'; the others being the Oblation and the Words of Institution: all three essential. He saw in the Epiklesis a repudiation of the doctrine of transubstantiation, but he was very far from the Protestant, receptionist theory:

'We ought reverently to look beyond the veil which is, indeed, substantially bread and wine, to the inward and spiritual significance and efficacy, even the Body and Blood of Our Lord Jesus Christ.' And on the part of the communicants there must be an active reception, a response of faith and will. The bread and wine became the Body and the Blood 'in spirit and in power, for the communication of conveyance of pardon, grace and glory, upon condition of true repentance, lively faith, and persevering obedience. To these three heads, pardon of sin, increase of grace, and pledge of glory may be reduced all the blessings and benefits purchased for mankind by the death of Christ . . . All these blessings are conveyed to the well-disposed and well-qualified believer by this mystery of love and goodness'.

The Real Presence lay not in the substance of Christ's Humanity 'which the heavens must receive till the time of the restitution of all things', but in His Divine Power and Virtue present through the operation of the Holy Spirit.

This doctrine of the Sacrament and the Sacrifice was supported by 'three infallible signs – antiquity, universality and consent'. The Sacrifice was a gift to God, the Sacrament a gift from God. The Bread once consecrated became 'in virtue and effect, though not in substance, the thing which it represents': the Church had always offered Bread and Wine as 'the divinely constituted representatives of the Body and Blood of Christ'.

The doctrine had been clearly revealed. 'The *modus* or manner of its operation transcends human reason; the angels themselves desire to look into it, but cannot comprehend it.' Here is echoed Scougal's phrase about the heavenly company who stand about the earthly altar. Belief in the Real Presence brought a vision of all the hosts of God.

# 3

# The Church in Freedom.
# The New Age Begins

Bishop Jolly's biographer, Dean Walker, has written of the Church in the north-east in the first decade of the nineteenth century, of its austerity, its simplicity of worship. There was still little to tell whether a church were Episcopal or Presbyterian, for both were plain – that is, when the Faithful Remnant had a church at all and not merely a room in a house or other building. This had been safer in the penal days; a church or chapel could be and often was destroyed by Government forces, whereas the meeting-place which was part of a dwelling, a store or other secular building, must not be damaged. Within the church or chapel there was no separation of chancel from nave; the pulpit, sometimes a three-decker, was as conspicuous as the altar which was set in front of it, and the altar itself was unadorned. The clergy preached and celebrated the Eucharist in black gown with white bands, like their Presbyterian brethren: when the surplice or 'white gown' was introduced it was worn only at the altar and it was slow in coming into favour. The laity disliked it. 'Is that the corp himself?' one man asked at a funeral, regarding the surpliced clergyman with disfavour. Some of the older clergy were reluctant to wear it.

Morning service consisted as a rule of Matins, the Litany and Ante-Communion; Bishop Jolly called this 'the dry service' – *Missa Sicca* – commending it because it could 'keep the devout soul hungering and thirsting after righteousness' and strengthen 'the spiritual appetite for the fulness of God's house and table'. The service ended with the Nicene Creed and the sermon, no light diet of worship even if the sermon did not reach Presbyterian magnitude. A psalm or psalms might be sung in metre in addition to the recital of the psalms for the day in the Prayer Book. Evensong was according to the Book of Common Prayer.

Sermons were doctrinal, following the model of the great

Anglican preachers of the seventeenth and eighteenth centuries, and often, as Dean Walker puts it, 'likeness became identity'. One cleric, when complimented on his discourse, replied: 'I'm glad you liked it.' – 'Aye, sir, Bishop Horne writes good sermons.' The congregation listened patiently, but a Bishop might exercise his authority by interrupting a meandering discourse, or by bidding a priest 'go straight to the General Thanksgiving'. One Bishop had forbidden a cleric to begin the service before his arrival but was disobeyed.

'Oh, you're at your auld tricks again,' was the episcopal comment.

Even while officially opposed, Episcopal and Presbyterian clergy were often on happy terms with each other, good neighbours, agreeing to differ and to let sleeping dogs lie quietly by the fire of friendship. In one parish in Aberdeenshire the minister, named Cock, and the Episcopal priest, one Pratt, were both ardent violinists and used to play together in amity and with mutual admiration. When Paganini came to Aberdeen, Cock had the fortune to hear him; and to a neighbour's comment: 'Magnificent!' replied: 'Man, if you heard Pratt and me!'

In the parish schools which were under the rule of the Presbytery, the Church Catechism was taught as well as the Shorter Catechism, and with equal strictness, punishment falling impartially upon the young Pisky who failed to define the nature of a Sacrament and upon the Presbyterian who broke down among the Reasons Annexed.

Among Jolly's contemporaries was John Skinner the younger, son of the poet-priest of Linshart. His life, too, has been recorded by Dean Walker. He was born in 1744 and as a boy shared his father's imprisonment. At the age of thirteen he went to Marischal College, Aberdeen, and graduated at nineteen. He was ordained at nineteen, much under the canonical age, because of 'the inexorable no-law of necessity' which compelled the Scots Bishops to ordain 'beardless boys'. This boy was given the charge of two congregations, at Chapelhall and Bernie, near Ellon, Aberdeenshire, with a stipend of from twenty-five to thirty pounds a year. At twenty-one he married, bringing his wife to the rented farmhouse which served as parsonage. His two chapels were fifteen miles apart, but he conducted services in both every Sunday.

His next call was to Aberdeen, to the congregation of St. Andrew, which as priest and Bishop he was to serve for the rest of his life. There he began work in true pastoral fashion by visiting his flock whose numbers were soon doubled. 'If they did not hear him on Sunday they would see him on Monday.' He took a house in Longacre, making a large room on the upper floor into a chapel; there, in 1782, he was consecrated Bishop Coadjutor to the Diocesan, Bishop Kilgour; and there, two years later, these two, with Bishop Petrie, consecrated the first Bishop of the Church in America, Samuel Seabury. Alexander Jolly was present and wrote afterwards that he had 'scarce recovered from the pleasing dream-like joy which the late extraordinary occasion had thrown him into.' Along with the Apostolic Succession the Scottish Church bestowed upon the American her Liturgy. The American Book retains the Epiklesis in this form:

'And we most humbly beseech Thee, O merciful Father, to hear us; and of Thy mighty goodness vouchsafe to bless and sanctify with Thy Word and Holy Spirit these Thy gifts and creatures of bread and wine; that we receiving them according to Thy Son Our Saviour Jesus Christ's holy institution, in remembrance of His death and passion, may be partakers of His most blessed Body and Blood.'

So this chapel, this upper room became the threshold of a great house of God; for Seabury's consecration 'opened the door of access' to the churches of the future overseas. He was 'the first of a long line of Anglican prelates who have gone out into all lands'. Even before she herself was freed from penalties and disabilities, the little Church in Scotland knew the liberty of mission. The door from the Church of England was not opened until two years later, by an Enabling Act which permitted the consecration of Bishops for any part of the Anglican Communion without regard to political adherence. It might indeed be claimed that the idea of the Anglican Communion was conceived that day in Aberdeen.

On Bishop Kilgour's resignation in 1786 Skinner succeeded him as Diocesan. His episcopate was to see the new freedom, the beginning of growth and transition. While he saw the end of persecution he knew also, unhappily, some internal dissension. Desire in some quarters for closer conformity with the Church of England led to many disputes, for it meant a breaking away

49

from the Scottish tradition so dear to Skinner and others. The north held by the old ways, the south looked towards England. Skinner defended the Scottish Liturgy but he was not a rigid conformist. He had been brought up in strict orthodoxy of doctrine, but with comparative ease about details of liturgy. In his youth the services had been varied, the wee bookies used; the clergy had not held themselves strictly bound by rubrics.

They provoked the disapproval of a fellow Bishop whose election was long opposed by Skinner: Gleig of Brechin. A liturgical scholar himself, he urged uniformity of worship. Of him more will be told.

Skinner's was truly one of the most eventful episcopates of the Church. He joined in the consecration of Bishop Seabury, he brought about the acceptance of the Thirty-Nine Articles which ensured the relief of the Church, he helped to bring freedom and external peace. He was however still surrounded by problems and difficulties. One of the worst was that of intruding clerics from England, who refused canonical obedience to the Diocesan, giving it instead to an English Bishop. Part of the argument for signing the Articles was that this would help to bring those wilfully separated brethren into the Scottish fold. In some cases this proved a valid plea. Three English priests in Edinburgh, Sandford of St. John's, Alison of the Cowgate Chapel which became St. Paul's, York Place, and Lloyd of Leith submitted to the Bishop, Abernethy Drummond. Some years later St. George's also came in, and was to unite with St. Paul's and become the church where Sir Walter Scott worshipped. The incumbent who submitted was something of a squarson in dress, wearing breeches and hessian boots.

Other English and qualified congregations however held out; and not only in them but in others, although Scottish in background and allegiance, the English Office was used, the Scottish rejected. The difference and antagonism grew.

At the Synod of 1809 the canons of the Church were revised, with a renewal of discipline: the clergy of one diocese were forbidden to receive direction from the Bishop of another; no Bishop might interfere in a see other than his own; the rubrics must be obeyed unless the Bishop permitted some departure. These canons imply an existing liberty or licence. The new discipline was the result of the new freedom. The Church set free must put her affairs in order. The canon against the interference of one Bishop in another's diocese reflected the old controversy between the College Bishops who had referred all matters to the exiled King, and the Diocesans who had demanded spiritual freedom. It was partly the result, too, of the custom, made necessary by poverty, of a Bishop's retaining his priestly charge as well as his episcopate. That might be in another diocese.

The Synod of 1811 formed itself into two chambers, the first of Bishops, the second of Deans and other representative clergy. The full assembly of presbyters was to be formed in the future, as was the representation of the laity. At this Synod a most important act gave primary authority to the Scottish Office, while ratifying the use of the English where it was desired by both priest and people. The Scottish Book thus authorized was the edition of 1764, by Bishops Falconar and Forbes. Other canons enjoined the regular recital of Morning and Evening Prayer; forbade people to leave their place of worship without reasonable cause; ordered all incumbents to live within their charge, and bade them celebrate the Eucharist so often that everyone might communicate at least three times a year, of which either Easter or Pentecost was to be one.

One of the new rights and duties which fell to Bishop Skinner was the nomination of candidates for the Snell Exhibition, the result of an effort to regain for the Church an old legacy. In the seventeenth century, while Episcopacy was still established, John Snell, a native of Glasgow living in England left an endowment to train college-bred clergy for the Church in Scotland. He devised the bulk of his estate to provide scholarships or exhibitions at Balliol College, Oxford, for young Scots nominated by the University of Glasgow. These exhibitioners were bound, under a penalty of £500, to take Holy Orders and return to serve the Church in Scotland. This was in 1679. Within ten years the testator's purpose was frustrated by the Revolution and Disestablishment. The Trust was administered by the Fellows of Balliol who accepted nominations from Glasgow but imposed no condition of taking Holy Orders or of returning to Scotland and to Scotland's disestablished Church. The exhibitioners were brilliant young classical scholars and many of them followed secular careers. Lord Medwyn (a Forbes, and father of a future Bishop) took the matter up. He did not win a reversal of the injustice, but he did win for Skinner who was now Primus, the right to nominate exhibitioners. Skinner chose well: one of his nominees was George Gleig, son of the Bishop who was his antagonist at some points; another was Jonathan Christie (who had ridden to visit Bishop Jolly and have his blessing) also the son of a Scottish cleric; a third was John Gibson Lockhart, son of a Presbyterian minister, a brilliant scholar and the future son-in-law and biographer of Sir Walter Scott.

Of these three only one took Holy Orders: Gleig, and he served the Anglican Church well, although not in her Scottish Province. He went into the army and served in the Peninsular War, from which experience he wrote *The Subaltern*, an excellent documentary novel. After taking Holy Orders he became a military chaplain and was finally Chaplain General to the Forces. Christie became a lawyer. He was one of Lockhart's most loyal and most loved friends, and played a part almost ruinous to himself in the miserable affair of the duel with John Scott. Lockhart's career is beyond the scope of this history, but he became, perhaps because of those friendships, sympathetic with the Church. As editor of *The Quarterly Review* he published many articles on Church matters, particularly on the Oxford Movement and its results: he showed considerable knowledge of Scots Episcopacy, which held his father-in-law's allegiance, and he was to have an indirect connection through his son-in-law, James Hope, for the latter was one of the founders of the new Scots Episcopal school and college, Glenalmond.

Bishop Skinner died in 1816, only two years beyond the three score and ten. Jolly and Gleig were long to outlive him, but his life had seen many and major changes: the Forty-Five with its bitter aftermath, the French Revolution and the long war with France, the American War of Independence and the sending forth of the American Bishop. A small child when Culloden was fought, he must have heard many a living memory of that tragic battle. In his last year he heard the rejoicings after Waterloo, saw the candles lit in the windows, the bonfires kindled on the hills. There was no King Over the Water now, and the Corsican Tyrant was driven into exile. The Bishop who had shared his father's imprisonment and had known what it was to worship in secrecy, had seen the Church come out of the shadows into light: a dim light of dawn, so far, and her vitality was still low, but she was free, and as the light strengthened so did her vigour.

His son William was elected his successor in the diocese; and he, with Jolly, Gleig and the other Bishops went to Edinburgh in 1822 to present a loyal address to King George IV, the occasion for which Jolly bought a new wig; and so came the end of an auld sang of loyalty and suffering.

The story of the Church in the nineteenth century could almost be entitled *Battling Bishops*. When the need for defending their flock against Government marauders was over, they found cause of offence in each other, and laid about them stoutly with their crooks. The hungry sheep looked up inquisitively, were fed and cared for, and often joined in the fray with bleatings and buttings. These Bishops were, and had need to be, men of strong will and character intensified by native thrawnness which no grace could eliminate. They held firmly to their opinions and had little notion of an objective approach to any question. 'I'm not arguing with you, I'm telling you' was their response to contradiction.

Jolly, indeed, was not of this type. If he annoyed his brethren, which he did somewhat in his latter years, it was as a *cunctator*, not as dictator or antagonist. But between Skinner and Gleig battle frequently raged. The latter is one of the great warrior Bishops.

William Walker, that gentle but not dim-sighted biographer of Jolly, has compared him with Gleig. They were almost of an age, Gleig born in 1753, Jolly in 1756, both of the north-east and within the same region: Gleig was a native of Arbuthnott near Stonehaven. Both went to college in Aberdeen, Jolly to Marischal, Gleig to King's. Both knew, by living tradition, the Church of the penal days, both were scholars to the bone. Brother Scots, equally devoted to the Church, with Jacobite loyalty in their blood, both steeped in learning they might appear to be very brothers; but beyond the resemblances lay a gulf of difference in temperament. Jolly was humble and gentle, 'primitively pious', somewhat too much of the recluse, with a mind receptive rather than productive, lacking in energy, in knowledge of the world. Gleig, to quote Walker's pleasant understatement, was not

adorned by 'a meek and quiet spirit' and was less perfect as a
pattern of primitive piety than Jolly. He was energetic, versatile,
alert to present needs, full of wordly wisdom: an administrator,
he can easily be imagined in a modern diocese, whereas Jolly
cannot be moved beyond his own time.

The most brilliant student of his year in classics and philosophy,
George Gleig was given a class to conduct before he had graduated, and might have had a Chair, but he could not subscribe
the Confession of Faith of the Church of Scotland, which was
then demanded of all Scots Professors. Ordained in 1773, he was
appointed to the charges of Pittenweem and Crail. He lived in
Pittenweem, riding over to Crail every third Sunday. In neither
place was there a church; that in Crail had been burned down, in
Pittenweem the meeting-place was the upper flat of a dwelling-
house and so had been spared destruction.

Gleig's stipend rose to £30, paid partly by subscriptions, partly
by the collection on Sunday. He added to his income by writing;
as a contributor to *The Monthly Review, The Gentleman's Magazine*,
and *The British Critic*, his articles on church matters made the
Scottish Church better known over the border. In one of those
he noted the decline of Jacobite fervour among Episcopalians; it
was only a sentiment now, no longer a passion or a principle;
the shadow of a shade. In another he criticized the sermon preached
by Bishop Skinner at Seabury's consecration; this he found 'in
unity of subject and perspicacity of thought . . . so miserably
deficient that although I have read it again and again, with the
closest attention, I can only hazard a probable conjecture what
are the main doctrines its author means to inculcate'.

This might be called miserably deficient in tact, courtesy and
charity, however perspicacious in thought and expression, and
the mildest of men, such as Jolly, might well have resented it.
Skinner was not mild, it was not his nature.

'This critique probably cost Mr. Gleig twenty-two years exclu-
sion from the Episcopate.'

There was no lack of invitation. In 1786 he was elected Bishop
of Dunkeld by the Presbyters of that see, but the election was
quashed by the College of Bishops, dominated by Skinner. Fuel
was added to the flames of mutual resentment by Gleig's attempt,
before 1792, at having the Penal Laws repealed. He would have

conceded prayers for King George, and to this the College were rigidly opposed. The Bishops still prayed for 'Thy servant, Charles our King' – the King Over the Water, and over this stumbling-block the attempt at repeal fell and broke. From this came the bitter and continuing opposition of Lord Chancellor Thurlow and of the English Bishops; and from this a deeper enmity between Skinner and Gleig.

The presbyters of a diocese had, at this time, little power: they could elect their Bishop, but the College could overturn the election without giving a reason. It was easy to indulge private prejudice or enmity, and in this case both were apparent. The gulf between north and south was opening; in a Church so poor, so harassed, any dissension was dangerous. It was as if a family having barely survived shipwreck should fall to wrangling. The north followed the non-juring tradition and cherished the Scottish Liturgy, the south desired conformity with the Church of England. There were other differences. Some of the northern clergy were Hutchinsonian, tinged with those peculiar views of Hutchinson which rejected, or appeared to reject, the orthodox doctrine of the Eternal Generation of the Son. The men of the south, including Gleig, were, on the other hand, accused of Pelagianism because of their violent denial of the Calvinist teaching on sin and grace and justification. Opposed in matters of liturgy and theology, Skinner and Gleig were still more antagonistic in temperament. Neither of them suffered opposition meekly or felt any need to make concessions.

'The Bishop, like most Bishops of those days, was very sensitive to public criticism, and the presbyter was a watchful and trenchant critic.' So Gleig was kept out of the Episcopate for the best years of his life, and for years in which he would greatly have helped the slowly reviving Church; and Dunkeld was for five years without a Bishop.

In 1787 he was called to the charge of Stirling which he held for the rest of his long life. It was a pleasant place. Stirling, according to Dean Walker, not only had 'almost every natural advantage' but enjoyed 'in a high degree the advantage of intellectual and well-cultivated society', including Ramsay of Ochtertyre, Lord Woodhouselee (father of the historian Fraser Tytler) and Sir William Stewart of Allanton. Here, as in Pittenweem, the congregation still met in an upper room, a large one, thirty feet long, which had been divided into five compartments with glass partitions so that the congregation could be separated into small groups and meet in numbers which kept the letter of the law. It included some old ladies who long after the King Over the Water was dead, used to slam their Prayer Books shut and yawn audibly during the prayer for King George.

Gleig, a faithful and diligent priest, soon doubled the congregation, uniting to it a qualified congregation in the town. He found time for writing and contributed articles to the new edition of the *Encyclopaedia Britannica* and later became editor. Aberdeen gave him the degree of LL.D.; that of D.D. could not be conferred without acceptance of the Westminster Confession. In his private life he was happily married, and his youngest son, that Snell Exhibitioner who became Chaplain to the Forces, inherited his full share of the paternal intellect.

In 1792 he was again chosen to be Bishop of Dunkeld and again rejected by the College in favour of another, Jonathan Watson. Against this second disappointment might be set the solace of seeing the Penal Laws revoked, of having his own church built, of bringing out the new edition of the *Encyclopaedia*, and of publishing a volume of sermons. Again and again he was brought forward for the Episcopate, again and again thrust back. Proposed for Edinburgh, he was rejected for his own proposer, Daniel Sandford; for Dunkeld, a third time, on the death of Bishop Watson who had a brief reign, he was passed over for Patrick Torry. But at last came triumph. In 1810 he was elected Bishop of Brechin, and this time there was no opposition. Skinner imposed only the condition that he accept the Scottish Liturgy. On the feast of St. Simon and St. Jude he was consecrated by Bishops Skinner, Jolly and Torry, and proceeded to be a reforming, indeed a battling Bishop.

His battle-cry was Conformity. Liturgic observance was still casual, the wee bookies still in use, the English Prayer Book adapted, at least by the northern clergy, as they chose, with prayers interpolated at discretion. Gleig urged its unqualified use, as a 'collection of the most perfect liturgical offices that ever were used in the Christian world'. Skinner opposed him but without acrimony. The canon of 1809 bidding the clergy obey the rubrics and make no change, unless by permission of their Bishop, was in effect a triumph for Gleig. He wrote to Skinner:

'There never was a Church since the days of the Apostles and never will be till the millennium totally free from the party spirit. I am perfectly convinced in my own mind that nothing has done so much injury to our Church as the useless alterations which are made by many of the clergy in the daily services. You and I have often pleaded the cause of Catholic unity and I hope we shall both do so again; but I do not see how we can do it with any effect if we set I know not what patriotism in opposition to uniformity in prayer. I see not why we may not adopt the daily service of the English Church verbatim.'

There was no doubt a degree of patriotism or nationalism, of loyalty to a native tradition and heritage behind the devotion to the Scottish Liturgy: but the devotion went deeper than that; it followed a theological tradition, primitive, Orthodox, Catholic, which was expressed more clearly in the Scottish than in the English Rite.

Gleig was supported by John Skinner the younger, son of the Bishop, and himself the incumbent of Forfar: he was later the Dean of Brechin. The controversy between the supporters of the rival Books went on long after the death of the two warrior Bishops. They were reconciled with each other before Skinner died in 1816: his elder son, William, succeeded him as Bishop, Gleig as Primus. When Bishop Macfarlane of Ross and Argyll died, Bishop Jolly refused to have that see added to his own of Moray, so David Low was elected Bishop of Ross and Argyll. He was Gleig's successor, at one remove, at Pittenweem, had been greatly helped by him in his preparation for Holy Orders and might be called Gleig's spiritual son.

Dean Torry, son of the Bishop, has left a picture of Gleig at home in his study, with its book-laden shelves, picking out the volume he wanted, blowing off the dust and replacing it after consultation. None of his household dare dust the books unless he were absent for some time.

He used to walk about Stirling in a short cassock worn over breeches, with silk stockings and buckled shoes, wearing a shovel hat and carrying a gold-headed cane. On his triennial tour of the diocese he drove in a gig, wearing grey breeches, a heavy travelling coat and shabby old top-boots: not a glass of episcopal fashion, but a little more point device than Lockhart's Bishop. Obedient to the apostolic injunction to hospitality, he used to serve his guests with strong London porter in a large silver loving-cup handed round the table, himself taking 'a long and a strong pull'.

In his time the Church grew considerably. At the Synod of 1824 there were signs of change and development. Dean Skinner proposed a canon making a regular Synod obligatory, and further proposed the admission of the laity. This shook the Bishops who saw the proposal as an invasion of their authority. It came, but not yet. The first proposal was, however, carried four years later when it was enacted that Diocesan Synods be held every year, General or Provincial Synods every five years. Every new law or canon was to be submitted first to the Diocesan Synods and approved by a majority before being taken to the General Synod.

An event which linked the Scottish Church with the wider world occurred in 1825. Matthew Luscombe, an English clergyman living in Paris, sought consecration as a Bishop with pastoral care of Anglicans on the continent, especially in France and Belgium. There were now thirty-five British residents in France and many American: they were served by a chaplain in Paris or by one in Caen, and there was another in Ostend, Belgium. Among such a flock a Bishop would have strictly defined authority: he would be chief pastor and Father-in-God: he would confirm, if necessary ordain, but would have no jurisdiction beyond the Anglican faithful, make no attempt to proselytize. His duties would, in Gleig's definition, be 'to preserve among the British in France a just veneration for the doctrines and constitution of the Church of England'. There were difficulties about his being consecrated by Bishops of the Church of England: this would make it appear too official, too much an action by the State, and there was fear of arousing the jealousy of French Catholics. The Scottish Bishops, with their tradition of purely spiritual authority independent of the State, understood the position, were sympathetic and had power to act. So, like Seabury some forty years earlier, Matthew Luscombe came to Scotland, to Stirling, where, on Palm Sunday, 1825 Gleig, with Bishops Sandford of Edinburgh and Low of Ross and Argyll, laid consecrating hands upon him. The promise of canonical obedience to him made by the chaplains in Paris, Caen and Ostend was taken as the valid equivalent of election by presbyters. The deed of consecration declared:

'He is sent by us, representing the Scottish Episcopal Church, to the continent of Europe, not as a diocesan Bishop in the modern or limited sense of the word, but for a purpose similar to that for which Titus was left by St. Paul in Crete, that he might set in order the things that are wanting among such of the natives of Great Britain and Ireland as he shall find there, professing to be members of the united Church of England, Ireland, the Episcopal Church in Scotland, and the Protestant Episcopal Church in America. But as Our Blessed Lord when He sent out His Apostles commanded them, saying: 'Go not into the way of the Gentiles, and into any city of the Samaritans enter ye not, but go rather to the lost sheep of the house of Israel'; so we, following so divine an example which was certainly left on record to the Church to guide her conduct in making future converts to the faith, do solemnly enjoin our Right Reverend Brother, Bishop Luscombe, not to disturb the peace of any Christian society established as the National Church in whatever nation he may chance to sojourn, but to confine his administrations to British subjects and such other Christians as may profess to be of a Protestant Episcopal Church.'

This admirably temperate, tolerant and unintrusive document was the beginning of a new chapter in the story both of Scottish Episcopacy and of the Anglican Communion.

The years were fleeting past and the Primus was growing old. He asked for a Coadjutor and would have chosen Michael Russell, incumbent of St. James's, Leith, but the other Bishops opposed this. It might lead to difficulties if a Coadjutor were not, after the death of his Diocesan, chosen as successor. Russell was elected Bishop of Glasgow in 1837, when that diocese was disjoined from Edinburgh.

Gleig became difficult in age; increasingly deaf, increasingly obstinate, increasingly autocratic. The burden of hearing complaints and keeping peace fell upon Torry of Dunkeld. At last he persuaded Gleig to resign the office of Primus, in which he was succeeded by Bishop Walker of Edinburgh. He remained Bishop of Brechin until the end of his life and in his last years some gentleness crept in. The old lion ceased to roar. He was much venerated in Stirling and the place where he used to walk, about half a mile out of the town, was long remembered and is marked by The Bishop's Stone. His end was in peace. Dying in 1840, aged eighty-seven, he could look back on a long, faithful service of the Church in her shadows and her daylight. His son wrote of him:

'I know that his brethren feared more than they loved him; but he was a true man, and if hasty at times and somewhat impatient of mediocrities, he was generous and even tender in his feelings' – a true sketch of many Scotsmen.

Gleig's junior by half a generation, David Low, like him a son of the north-east, carried the story into mid-century. He was born in 1768, went to Marischal College, Aberdeen, and like Gleig was a man of letters. Ordained in 1787, he was appointed to Pittenweem which he found a pleasant place. He was at ease with the gentry, most of them Episcopalian, and used to stay for a week or two at a time at one of the mansions in the neighbourhood. There he met some of the influential men of the day. Like Gleig he was himself a man of the world, perhaps one of the first to return to the long secluded Church.

The charge grew under his care. In 1805 a church was built within the precincts of the old Priory of Pittenweem and part of the Priory itself made into a parsonage unique among Scottish clergy-houses. In 1819 he was consecrated Bishop of Ross and Argyll, in 1820 made a Doctor of Laws by Aberdeen. His first episcopal tour was made in 1823.

Argyll had suffered much at the Revolution. *The Records of the Diocese of Argyll and the Isles* published by J. B. Craven are significant and terse. Of the clergy at the disestablishment, some conformed to Presbyterianism, some deserted, some were faithful. Of these last many were deposed 'for contumacy' or 'deprived for not praying', which does not mean failure in devotion but merely refusing to pray for William and Mary instead of King James. Two or three of them went to Ireland. One entry is laconic: a Presbyterian minister in North Uist was 'ordained, intruded, drowned'; the drowning it may be assumed was accidental, not vengeful. Of one spirited priest it is recorded: 'Refused to conform; died 1728 much esteemed; marched out Presbyterian intruder.'

A Faithful Remnant kept and transmitted their faith and now, under Bishop Low, they grew in numbers. It is recorded that in 1808 the only clergy were the Bishop and the Dean. In 1838 there were seven priests, and fifteen years later there were fifteen, and eighteen congregations. The people's part is shown in a petition to the Bishop in 1837 for a church and resident priest in Skye. There had been a visiting priest who had been received 'not only with the hospitality which characterizes all Highlanders, but also with that love and affection which is always evinced by sound churchmen towards a regularly ordained clergyman, towards a legitimate ambassador of the Apostolic Church. He found many families and a number of individuals scattered here and there who are sounder churchmen and better versed in our tenets than in many other places where they are blessed with the ministry of a clergyman. They allow no Sunday to pass but they assemble in groups, and offer up their petitions to the Throne of the Deity in the unexampled Order of our Common Prayer.'

The Prayer Book was used in family worship and parents gave their children sound Church teaching. The Bishop visited Skye in 1838 and appointed William Greig as incumbent of a chapel in Broadford.

Congregations in Appin and at Ballachulish, with other scattered groups were served by the Reverend Paul McColl, known as 'Mr. Paul', an itinerant priest who lived chiefly at Ballachulish. He had the Gaelic and at festivals he used to preach from the outside stair of the church which was then too small to hold the congregation. People came from far, fasting, to receive Holy Communion. He claimed to have baptized, during his ministry from 1810 to 1828, ten thousand souls, some of them babies who were brought to him on his journeys, brought to no church but to a mountain stream. His successor built a new and larger church. It may have been here that a visiting English clergyman 'was astonished to see a neat chapel and enclosed ground, in which, at the very moment of his passing, a Bishop, with several clergy in their canonicals, were perambulating the churchyard in the act of its consecration. . . . The impression was as pleasing as it was remarkable'. Ballachulish cherished its Communion Vessels from the days of Establishment: from the Chalice men had received the Wine before going out to fight for King James at Culloden.

Bishop Low's journeys were not only diocesan. He represented the Scottish Church at the consecration of St. Saviour's, Leeds, one of the earliest Tractarian churches. He went to Paris to stay with Bishop Luscombe. When he proposed making a formal call at the British Embassy his host offered to take him in his carriage, but Low insisted on having his own carriage for the dignity of his office and the honour of Scotland.

In him the Church begins to go out into the world while going out also among the scattered faithful at home. He cherished and renewed the tradition of the past and did much to shape the future. His building of the new church and parsonage at Pittenweem from the ruins of the old Priory is symbolic. He gave generously to the founding fund of Holy Trinity College, Glenalmond; and when at his urging Argyll and the Isles was made a diocese separate from Ross, he gave what was then the immense endowment of £8,000.

Much to his pleasure he was given the Doctorate in Divinity by two American Universities, a link with the Church across the Atlantic which he valued. He died in 1855. Lord Lindsay of Balcarres described him as having the look, air and manner of a French Abbé of the old school; and the Bishop used to tell a story of the poet-daughter of the House of Balcarres. When Lady Anne Lindsay was writing *Auld Robin Grey* she found invention fail for a moment. What further disaster could she bring upon her heroine?

'Steal the cow, Sister Anne,' advised her young sister. The cow was stolen and the lass in the poem married Auld Robin Grey who was a kind man to her.

# 4

# The Church in Perth.
# Patrick Torry

Patrick Torry, a contemporary of David Low, born in 1763 in the parish of King Edward, Aberdeenshire, is one of the great Bishops of the old school. He was fortunate in his biographer, J. M. Neale, who, in an amply documented *Life*, gives a history of the period as well as of the man, a record of the age of transition.

Torry came of good, middle-class stock, mostly farmers, of what in Scotland are called 'bien folk'. His grandfather was one of the first three in the parish to own a tea-kettle (which was then a status-symbol!), the other two being the laird and the minister. Patrick was brought up officially a Presbyterian, his mother being one, but he absorbed both Episcopalian teaching and Jacobite tradition from an uncle who had been out in the Forty-Five. When the boy went to school at Lonmay he became a friend of the Episcopal priest there and also of Skinner of Linshart. He was confirmed, soon discovered his vocation, and read for Holy Orders. At nineteen he was appointed deacon by Bishop Kilgour and put in charge of the congregation at Arradoul, Banffshire. A year later he was priested. For lack of a church he used to hold services in his kitchen. In 1789 Bishop Kilgour invited him to become his assistant at Peterhead, and on the old Bishop's death, Torry held the charge alone for many years to come.

Late in life he wrote to his friend Lord Forbes about the days of his youth. He could remember the hurried, secret gatherings to worship in a barn or a kitchen. The Faithful Remnant had then 'no place wherein to celebrate the Divine Worship but the seclusion of a thicket, the kitchen, the barn or the hut, as it might be, of some of their adherents. . . . To this day persons of the highest rank think it no disgrace to worship God in a damp and miserable hovel.'

Yet the Remnant never lost their awareness of being the

representative in Scotland of the one Holy, Catholic, and Apostolic Church. Now, emerged from the shadows, Episcopacy was 'putting forward her genuine claims to the affections of the Scottish people'. Torry remembered the 'extemporaneous manner of worship'. He told how Bishop Kilgour used to hold a service in private houses as often as twelve or fourteen times on a Sunday. When young Torry came to Peterhead he found a 'qualified' congregation as well as his own; it was under a cleric, Laing, who had been ordained by the Bishop of Down and Connor. On Laing's death the breach was filled: the schismatics became part of the regular congregation.

The young priest settled down happily if not opulently. He married and reared a family of seven children, two of his sons entering the priesthood. An idea of his stipend is given in an appeal he made in 1802 on behalf of the clergy in general. Their stipends came from collections, pew rents, altar offerings and in some places subscriptions. Torry had £8 1s. 8d. from rents, £36 10s. od. from collections, £10 from altar offerings: a total of £54 11s. 8d.

'It will readily occur to you all that this sum or any sum near to it, is far short of a decent competence in these times, to the clergyman of such a numerous and respectable congregation as this.'

His diplomacy was rewarded: his congregation raised their donations. That he cared for his people more than for their payment was evident when he was offered the charge of Dundee with a stipend of £150 a year. He chose to stay at Peterhead, and it is pleasant to know that Peterhead rewarded him. A new church was built, the old chapel was made into dwelling-houses, and the rent was paid to him. By that time he was Bishop of Dunkeld, elected and consecrated in 1801, and it was as Bishop that he consecrated his own new church in another diocese. In this connection there is a most interesting letter written by the Bishop of Aberdeen to Torry on his election:

'I hereby formally declare you and your congregation in Peterhead, in terms of the ninth Canon of our Church, to be exempt from my jurisdiction as Bishop of Aberdeen.'

Peterhead would appear to have become Bishop Torry's own private charge which may have been the custom in such cases. Another Bishop, Macfarlane of Ross and Argyll, gave the new prelate some details about confirmation. This was administered only on a Bishop's infrequent tours of his diocese: Bishop Petrie had confirmed infants after their baptism, in the tradition of the Orthodox Church. Bishop Petrie had also received ordinands in his own house for instruction. This letter is a record of the old ways. Torry was to see the transition to the new: the founding of a Theological College, the building of a cathedral, the liturgic revival, the beginning of ceremonial, of ritual and the wearing of vestments. The surplice was now more commonly worn and Bishops were beginning to assume robes like their English brethren. A benevolent friend offered to procure for Torry the robes of the late Bishop Horsley, a warm friend and defender of the Scottish Church whose own son was now one of her priests. Bishop Gleig and Bishop Sandford (of Edinburgh) had their robes: 'As your diocese is situate contiguous to theirs, and many persons of rank residing in it, they naturally would conceive it strange that you should be visiting your clergy in a black gown when the neighbouring clergy were otherwise arrayed.'

The murmured appeal to snobbery is agreeable.

Another offer, from Mr. Bowdler of Eltham, came of help for any poor chapel in need of repair; Mr. Bowdler made the proper and prudent reservation that he would 'pay no debts, nor contribute towards ornaments, nor assist those who are able but not willing to repair the chapels they may attend'. Gleig had no high opinion of Torry's notion of dress. When the Bishops were preparing for their audience with George IV, in Edinburgh, he wrote to William Skinner of Aberdeen:

'We are to appear before the King in our gowns and cassocks, but should the King receive us on his throne, which is very little probable, we must appear in lawn sleeves. But perhaps what may be necessary for you to tell the Bishops Jolly and Torry is that we must not appear at Court without buckles on our shoes' – or appear in an M.A. gown. And of course there was the problem of Jolly's wig. Jolly himself wrote to Torry:

'If we must go forward on this astonishing journey, I beg that your fraternal kindness will take me in charge, and make me sharer in your plan, sending me the earliest notice. God grant that all may aim and end well, I take comfort in our mutual prayers.'

It was a far cry from the book-lined attic in Fraserburgh to the royal pomp of Holyrood. To the old Bishop and recluse the troubles of the penal days must have seemed no heavier than these present forebodings. His prayers were heard and all ended very well in Royal benignity. Like many another man of speckled character, like his lively predecessor Charles II with Bishop Ken, George IV had the sense and grace to recognize and honour pure goodness. He listened and responded graciously to the loyal message of the Church conveyed by her Bishops:

'We must beg leave solemnly to declare in your Royal presence, that viewing in Your Majesty's sacred person the lineal descendant of the royal family of Scotland and the legitimate possessor of the British throne, we feel to Your Majesty that devoted attachment that our principles assure us are due to our rightful sovereigns; and that should evil days ever come on Your Majesty's house (which may God in His infinite mercy avert) the House of Bruns-wick will find that the Scottish Episcopalians are ready to suffer and endure for it as much as they have suffered for the House of Stewart, and with heart and hand to convince the world that in their breasts a firm attachment to the religion of their forefathers is inseparably connected with unshaken loyalty to their King.'

The winds of change were indeed blowing, sometimes, as here, with mellow freshness, sometimes with a snell blast which led to a hurried shutting of episcopal windows, as when John Skinner the third – the Dean of Brechin – proposed and was refused the admission of the laity to Synods. He accused the Church of lethargy: other churches had begun to look outward, to know the stir of new life, but in the Episcopal: 'the churchman has been doing nothing beyond the precincts of his diocese, if a Bishop, or, if a presbyter, beyond the weekly routine of pastoral duty.'

This criticism was not well received. The Synod of Laurence-kirk in 1828 did, however, begin to set things in order, appointing regular meetings of Synods and ordering that Morning and Even-ing Prayer be said regularly by both Bishops and presbyters. Less admirable, to the mind of the northern clergy, was the canon which gave the Bishops power to set aside the Scottish in favour of the English Liturgy. The first blow at the primary authority of the Scottish Book was thus dealt. Unpopular too, with the older clergy, was the Church's now styling herself the *Protestant* Episcopal Church.

Younger Bishops were taking office, the older men clung to the old tradition: Torry stood in the midst. In his sixties, now, he was young and vigorous in the eyes of his seniors who appealed to him for help and intervention. Jolly relied upon him as upon a son. And in the difficult business of persuading the aged Primus, Gleig, to resign at least that office, he was left to bell the cat. Jolly, himself old and feeble, pleaded for gentleness; he begged Torry to make a fair copy of his letters:

'There let me stop, for I am unable to proceed,' he ended one; 'of which, had you seen me this morning, you would have had ocular demonstration. My blots are shameful. If you copy, keep them out.'

Torry had the gentle touch:

'Do then, my dear Sir,' he wrote to Gleig, 'allow yourself to be persuaded to make a voluntary resignation' – and so be relieved of a heavy burden, be spared future urging and earn the respect and gratitude of his brethren. Gleig answered mildly that he would willingly resign as Primus but must retain his diocese. Having now given up the charge of Stirling he would be a shepherd without a flock. He asked again that he might be given a coadjutor, and this was granted, though reluctantly. David Moir was consecrated and in time succeeded Gleig in Brechin. Bishop Walker of Edinburgh became Primus. This was formally intimated to Jolly as the senior Bishop.

'In point of age I rub shoulders with the oldest of your number,' he wrote to Torry. 'There, ready to sign the canonical deed, let me stick; only let love be our universal cement. Kindly now send copy of letter (blots excepted, your hand still serving you well, *De.Gr.*) to our very active brother of Aberdeen. I know that you will tenderly interpret what I thus confusedly write.'

The new reign began and the new Primus sent a loyal address to the young Queen Victoria. The diocesan pattern changed. Dunkeld and Dunblane were joined to what had, for a time, been called the diocese of Fife and now regained its old title; Torry was now Bishop of St. Andrews, Dunkeld and Dunblane. He resigned his charge of Peterhead where the congregation had increased to twelve hundred. Three of the old Bishops died within three years of each other: Jolly in 1838, Gleig in 1840, Walker in 1841.

Bishop Walker had also been Pantonian Professor of Theology under the Trust of Miss Kathrein Panton, a devout lady of Bishop Jolly's flock, who in 1810 had bequeathed the endowment of 'a Seminary of Learning or Theological Institution for the Education of Young Men desirous to serve in the Sacred Ministry of the Scottish Episcopal Church.' Bishop Walker lectured to ordinands in his own house: the College existed and fulfilled its function, although then and for six years after the Bishop's death it had no settled habitation. Walker was followed as Bishop by Charles Terrot, as Primus by William Skinner. Torry was now the oldest Bishop, but still vigorous in mind, still an ardent defender of the Scottish Liturgy.

His letters give glimpses of his private life. One, to his son, refers with reticent love and grief to the death of his daughter:

'Isabella's conciliating manners and the general benevolence of her heart gained for herself friends wherever she was, and that without any effort on her part, her amiable qualities sitting so easy on her' – a charming phrase. 'To those, therefore, who have long been acquainted with me and with her, it can excite no surprise that she had got such a strong hold of my heart.'

In another letter he recalled his youthful excursions into verse:

'As my muse seemed more inclined to lash the follies of my neighbours than to correct my own, I had the sense to see that it would be an act of wisdom to restrain her.' He still cherished an ambition to write a long poem on a sacred subject:

'But alas, with me, planning and creating are very different things. I have not yet written a single line of it.'

So an unborn poem drifts away like a dream and what we have lost we shall never know.

These were years of strife in the Presbyterian Church of Scotland, chiefly about lay patronage and any form of intrusion by the State. It came to a head in the Disruption of 1843 when a great body of ministers and laity left the Established to form the Free Church of Scotland. Some Presbyterians came over to Episcopacy in search of peace.

There were many of these converts in Torry's diocese, and he was consulted about their being admitted to Holy Communion before being confirmed. His counsel was to assume that they were desirous of Confirmation and having received the Sacrament of

the altar, would, with some instruction, then offer themselves for
this other rite.

'All therefore who apply (not of doubtful character) may be
admitted with the understanding above stated. We must not
narrow the door of admission so as to prevent the entrance of
those who are desirous of going in and there abiding, nor must
we widen it further than is consistent with the faithfulness which
we owe to our Heavenly Father.'

These new-comers must therefore be earnestly advised to receive
Confirmation, 'because the reception of one ordinance does not
make up for the want of another'. If they refused, the gravity of
such refusal must be shown them, the hazard laid upon themselves; but even so, they should not be denied access to the altar,
because:

'People in these days are held by a very slender cord, easily
snapped asunder, and because we know not what allowance God
may make for inveterate prejudice.'

Little did they know, those peace-loving Presbyterians, how
many squalls were disturbing the haven they wished to enter.
The Episcopal Church was preserved from schism but she came
very near it, and had to endure many schismatic members. The
intruding clerics buzzed like fretful midges. One in Edinburgh,
D. K. Drummond, resigned his charge in order to form a congregation of his own and was paid in his own coin by his curate's
starting a schism within this schism. No Presbyterian sect could
do better than that. In Aberdeen, the Rev. Sir William Dunbar,
ordained in England, refused obedience to his Diocesan Bishop,
who then formally pronounced him to be no longer a presbyter
of the Scottish Church, declaring his ministerial acts void and
without authority. This virtual excommunication caused no small
stir. Other clerics followed this bad example. The English Bishops
might deplore such acts but made no formal protest or condemnation. Their disloyalty to their brethren in Scotland is more
grievous than any Presbyterian animosity. Episcopalians in
America on the other hand were warmly sympathetic with the
Scottish Church. The schismatics rejected the Scottish Liturgy,
and the rejection spread unhappily among the loyal. There was
dissension, too, between the Bishops. Torry defended the Scottish
Book with all the ardour of his heart and force of his mind,

proclaiming it 'our chief glory and ornament, the only badge of our being an independent, a national and not a colonial Church. It recognizes, moreover, the truth of the primitive Eucharistic doctrine and the warmth of primitive piety beyond any Office now in use in the Christian world'. Of the English Rite he declared: 'Its doctrine was made less explicit, its arrangement less orderly, and as a barrier against transubstantiation it was and is less powerful.'

The Primus was with him, Low, Russell and Terrot against, Moir neutral. In his own diocese Blair Atholl applied for permission to use the English Book: this was refused and the congregation appealed to the College of Bishops. The Primus urged Torry to yield, which he did for the sake of peace, but with a protest: 'I permit myself to be thus concussed into a compliance with that measure.' What an excellent word, here, is 'concussed!'

Perth had a troubled history. Canon George Farquhar, in his *Episcopal History of Perth*, commented: 'It has been so ordered by Providence that whatever trials beset the Disestablished Church of Scotland at large, they should appear in the acutest form in Perth.' He quoted some pungent examples of Presbyterian disapproval. One minister declared that those who read prayers worshipped the Devil. 'I defy all the world to show me where the Scripture commands us to read prayers; therefore they who read prayers worship the Devil.'

There would seem to be a flaw in logic as well as in courtesy about this, but it is a fine, sappy statement. The Prayer Book gave scandal. Canon Farquhar found that 'Episcopacy without the Prayer Book had been bad enough, but Episcopacy with the Prayer Book was far worse'.

The deposed Episcopal clergy had been uncompromising. They declared:

'They are properly intruders in the Scriptural sense of the word who thrust themselves into the ministry without a legal mission or canonical ordination.'

Perth had its part also in the internal dissension, adhering to the party of 'Non-Usagers'. This strife died out but it left a legacy of trouble.

Bishop Rattray had brought a measure of reconciliation and left a legacy of liturgic learning and a code of canons. He renewed the worshipping life of the Church, but after the repeal of the Penal Acts there came a lethargy, due no doubt to exhaustion, and with it that irritability which is another symptom of weariness. Congregations continued as well as they could, but the sense of diocesan unity was lacking. Farquhar quotes an anonymous writer, travelling through Perth to Forfar, thinking of and deploring the schismatic English chapels:

'What a pity, said I to myself, to see so many fine houses inhabited by intelligent people, without a single one that I am aware of being occupied by a member of the Scottish Episcopal Church. That all who attend what is anomalously called "The English Chapel" are ignorant of Episcopacy I cannot allow myself to suppose. I can even imagine that some of the best informed among them would not be hostile to an indigenous Bishop were their present state fairly and fully brought before them. . . . Just as I was about to contemplate in imagination the pleasing spectacle of a Confirmation in Perth, the guard of the coach desired the passengers to replace themselves'; and on the next stage of his journey he fell asleep so deeply that 'nothing but the dirl of the coach on the streets of Forfar had the effect of awakening me'.

The pleasing spectacle was truly to be witnessed, but the dissidents continued, and the indigenous Bishop Torry did not win full loyalty. Indeed the Faithful Remnant in Perth were absorbed by the English congregation in 1808.

At Muthill the congregational history went back beyond the disestablishment. Here, the feasts and fasts of the Church had always been kept, the Eucharist celebrated on the great feasts, daily prayers recited in Passion-tide. The Church accounts for 1703 (given by J. H. Shepherd in his *Episcopacy in Strathearn*) include such details as: 'Nails to fix the [Communion] Table' and soap 'to wash the table cloaths'. The old meeting-house, burned down in the Forty-Five, was repaired: in 1771 a new one was built of clay and thatched, with a fire-place and a window at each end, deliberately made to look as little like a church as possible. The incumbent at this time for over fifty years (from 1732–1783) was the Reverend William Erskine; his second son, also William, became Lord Kineddar, a Lord of Session and a friend of Sir Walter Scott to whom he transmitted his love and knowledge of Scottish Episcopacy. The tradition was strong in Muthill, where the Episcopal Church was regarded as a refuge, a place of peace. Even in mid-nineteenth century critics of the parish kirk would say:

'Weel, an it gets muckle waur, I'll just gang back to my granny's kirk' – and some of them may have been among the converts of whom Bishop Torry wrote.

Erskine was succeeded by the Reverend George Cruickshank, who would appear to have met some trouble. A letter to him from George Gleig – at Pittenweem – offers good advice:

'I need not tell you that your flock are far enough removed from what was lately denominated High Church; they are in truth what neither you nor I would wish them to be.' Cruickshank should be gentle with them, not violent in sermons, not harsh in discipline: 'Were I in your situation, I would yield to my people in every-thing not essential, and for a time at least, I would see as if I saw not their tendency to go anywhere for a good sermon.' The trouble apparently was with the qualified clerics. 'Be earnest to demon-strate to them that the difference between us and the juring clergy-men in this country does not consist in a political tenet, in itself of little certainty and of less importance, but in the unity of the Church. An Episcopal presbyter without a Bishop is like a body without a head.'

Cruickshank, himself a strong Jacobite, conformed in 1788 and prayed for King George; but one of his flock, Oliphant of Gask – father of Carolina the poet, who became Lady Nairne, objected, forbade Cruickshank to enter his house as chaplain to conduct family prayers and sent back his gown. At Gask the Prayer Books had the names of the exiled Royalties substituted for those of the Hanoverians. 'The auld hoose' was very steadfast. The laity indeed were stiffer than the clergy about the change of allegiance.

The services were very simple: the Eucharist was celebrated only at Christmas, Easter, Whit Sunday and once during the autumn. The surplice was not worn. The metrical psalms were sung. Tokens, small metal discs, were given on the previous Sunday to intending communicants. One Roman Catholic con-trived to have one, not for its proper use but as evidence in court of having attended a non-Popish service. He was discovered and deprived of the token.

Cruickshank was succeeded in 1834 by his grand-nephew

The Right Reverend Alexander Jolly,
Bishop of Moray, 1798–1838

The Right Reverend George Gleig,
Bishop of Brechin, 1810–1840

The Right Reverend James Walker,
Bishop of Edinburgh, 1830–1841

The Right Reverend Charles Wordsworth,
Bishop of St Andrews, 1853–1892

Alexander Lendrum, who had been priested by Bishop Torry and became almost his grey eminence. A new church was built in proper ecclesiastical style, with the altar at the east end. Lendrum was a zealous priest, a passionate Episcopalian, a fervid Scot. He urged the Bishop to new schemes. A revival was needed.

The Bishop was cautious:

'In regard to weekly Communions at Perth,' he told Lendrum, 'we cannot hope to revive primitive faith and zeal all at once. Such a change, however desirable, must, under the Divine Guidance, be a work of time and require more previous instruction and preparation. It therefore appears to me the preferable arrangement to begin with monthly Communions.'

There was however a mission in the city and Lendrum found the missioner, a priest called Chambers who held frequent services in an upper room, began a school, held Confirmation classes. The poor people came, thus disproving the assertion that Episcopacy was merely the religion of the gentry.

A more ambitious scheme, one of almost startling grandeur to those long held in poverty, was that of building a cathedral in Perth. It was the Bishop's dream, but Lendrum helped to bring it into reality. There was much opposition. The Primus expostulated: 'Your most active advocacy of this scheme forms a serious ground of complaint against you. All of us admire and applaud your zeal in the cause of the Church, but would be glad to see it with somewhat more of prudence and discretion.' That good friend of the Church, Lord Forbes, favoured the plan, but according to the Primus had 'been urged to press it forward by yourself or some equally zealous friend'.

The core of this opposition lay in the concern of the Primus and others for a cherished scheme of their own, that of founding and building the College of the Holy Trinity, Glenalmond, to be a school and a theological college, the seminary or place of learning for which Miss Panton had left endowment. This (of which the story will be told in the next chapter) had been already begun in 1847. The Primus feared that the Perth Cathedral and the Perth Mission would deflect funds from the new College.

'By all accounts, Mr. Chambers' mission is likely to prove a failure, and I was really shocked to hear from Dean Ramsay that he had been dunned by them for 60 Bibles, for 100 Prayer Books, for the maximum allowance for clerical income, and for a grant to fit up the Chapel, while their collection for the year is returned at 28/1. Now this is too bad, and not to be encouraged.'

Lendrum continued to encourage and to urge his Bishop in all his hopes and plans: for the mission, for the cathedral, for a residence in Perth. The cathedral was begun in 1848, and in 1850 the completed nave was consecrated by the young Bishop of Brechin, Alexander Penrose Forbes, who had become a spiritual son to the old Bishop Torry. They were of one mind in devotion to the Scottish Church and her Liturgy. More and more in his last years Torry turned for help to Forbes who was to him what St. Timothy was to St. Paul. Forbes used to take confirmations for him.

'Although I can still do much at my desk,' Torry wrote to his son in 1848, 'my locomotive powers are sadly diminished. But I am thankful that God has raised up for me a friend who is not only willing, but expresses himself delighted to be able to act for me on every necessary occasion.'

The new cathedral, St. Ninian's, was the first to be consecrated in Scotland since the Reformation and the second in Britain after Wren's St. Paul's. J. M. Neale was the preacher. The Scottish Liturgy was used: all the Scottish Bishops were present and English and Irish prelates came to represent their Churches. They and the diocesan clergy walked in procession through the streets of Perth, a strange sight for the multitude, a symbolic procession as well as an actual, the Church so long hidden coming into full daylight.

It was the fulfilment of a dream for the old Bishop. In his other campaign, for the Scottish Rite, he had won a troubled victory. There was a strong desire, among the northern clergy at least, for a Prayer Book to be used without alteration or variation: the 1764 Book of Robert Forbes and Falconar was that which had been authorized and given primacy of honour, but other editions with variations had been published and were in some places used. Many of the clergy desired a Book with rubrics providing for Reservation of the Sacrament for the sick, the use of the Mixed Chalice, the signing with the cross in Confirmation, all of these being among the old usages. Among these clerics were the Bishop's son now Dean, Lendrum, and Chambers. They petitioned the Bishop for such a Book; Lendrum helped to prepare it, the Bishop gave it his approval and it appeared in 1850.

'The Book of Common Prayer . . . according to the Use of the Church of Scotland.' Other rubrics permitted the celebration of the Eucharist with only one communicant, and enjoined the departure of non-communicants after the Creed. This was a return to the primitive discipline of bidding catechumens depart before the celebration of the Holy Mysteries. In baptism the parents were permitted to be sponsors. The Kalendar included the Celtic and Scottish Saints: Ninian, Columba, Kentigern, Patrick, Adamnan, Cuthbert, Serf.

The storm broke in a new Battle of the Books, fiercer than any already waged between the Scottish and the English Liturgy. This new Book was attacked by many who were loyal to the Scottish tradition. It was condemned by the Episcopal Synod, Forbes of Brechin alone dissenting. Another and more painful blow was dealt the old Bishop by some of his own clergy who presented a memorial or protest, not attacking himself directly but accusing his advisers of making him appear to act illegally, uncanonically, inconsistently with his own practice, uncharitably towards his flock. To this he replied:

'I have resolved, at whatever disadvantage to myself individually, not to recall the Scottish Prayer Book lately published. Should violent measures be followed out, I shall receive them as a portion of my cross, and beseech God to make them instrumental towards my greater happiness hereafter.'

He told his fellow Bishops:

'It ought never to be forgotten that the Episcopacy of Scotland is a Diocesan and not a College Episcopacy.' He declared their condemnation to be illegal. The Bishops replied, Forbes again dissenting, that in matters of discipline and form of worship the decision of the majority must prevail. They entreated him to remember his own subscription to this rule and to withdraw his commendation from the Book. At the same time they issued an Address to All Faithful Members of the Episcopal Church of Scotland, counselling them against the use of 'the said pretending Prayer Book' which had no synodical or canonical authority, and they wrote in like manner to the English Bishops repudiating the Book.

Lendrum fought joyfully on his side, defending not only this Book but the Scottish Liturgy in whatever form or edition. He saw Dean Ramsay as the worst enemy and attacked the increasingly English tendency in the Church, one not untinged with a new gentility:

'St John's or St. Paul's, Edinburgh, give the tone, and hence the National Office is considered good enough for the poor, but entirely unsuited for the potentates of the earth who take their tone from St. George's, Hanover Square, London. It is not the merits or demerits of the Office that influence them, but simply fashion.'

To have the Scottish Office used in the new cathedral would give it dignity 'even in the eyes of unthinking religionists', and would 'disarm opposition, promote unity, and at the same time maintain our independence'.

He accused Dean Ramsay of hostility and duplicity:

'Had the National Office not been used there he would have acted very differently, but he knows that its position will be strengthened by the success of the Mission and the erection of the cathedral, and he therefore means to try, while it is yet in its tender infancy, to crush the whole thing.' Defending the mission he announced that this congregation had given £100 to the Bishop's Endowment, £174 13s. od. to the Cathedral Fund. The congregation of a hundred and fifteen members was made up of forty-six from the schismatic chapel, nineteen converts from Presbyterianism and fifty new-comers. There were fifty-four communicants.

The old Bishop had his own way of defence. In a Pastoral Letter he recalled his own youth when all but one of some fifty-eight congregations used the Scottish Office:

'The only one now in use in the Christian world that fully recognizes the Scriptural and primitive doctrine contained in Christ's blessed institution.' He found the English Office imperfect through lack of a full Oblation and Invocation, the Roman and the Eastern laden with accretions, although of the Eastern Orthodox Rite it must be said he knew very little.

'Unless we in Scotland are faithful unto death, retaining what we hold and not preferring the worse to the better, we sadly obscure our hopes of ultimate approbation from our final Judge, and shall probably, even in this world, have the mortification of seeing our expected gain turned into loss by the gradual diminution and at last the entire frustration of our hopes.' The argument for one particular Prayer Book can never have been put with quite such a mixture of solemnity, sincerity and *naïveté*. The vision of Divine disapproval of those who forsake the Scottish Office comes near the Presbyterian minister's opening prayer: 'Lord, Thou hast said, and rightly said . . .'

The controversy was to flare up recurrently for many years to come. J. M. Neale has suggested that this particular phase, about Bishop Torry's Book, would not have occurred had the Scottish Church been ruled by an Archbishop, Metropolitan of the Province. This office came near being restored in 1811 but the mind of the Church was against it. An Archbishop would have pronounced in favour of one Book or the other. Whether this would have prevented or ended strife at this crisis and at another which was to come, which concerned Bishop Forbes, remains matter for debate.

The middle decade of the century indeed saw much trouble in the Church on both sides of the border. In Scotland the schismatics continued to harass lawful authority. That turbulent priest, Sir William Dunbar, being deprived of his office by the Bishop of Aberdeen for canonical disobedience, brought an action against him in the Court of Session and had his appeal upheld. But dramatic retribution followed, in a schism within his own schismatic congregation as had happened in that of Drummond in Edinburgh. Dunbar sought refuge in London but the Bishop of London, loyal to his Scottish brother, refused to institute him to a living. (London, with Canterbury and one or two others, supported the Scottish Bishops.) Dunbar was compelled to submit to his Diocesan, to crave pardon and restitution.

This was the counterpart of the troublesome affair in the Church of England of the Gorham Judgement in 1850, when a clergyman, Gorham, being refused institution by his Diocesan, the Bishop of Exeter, because he would not profess belief in Baptismal Regeneration, appealed to the Privy Council and won his appeal. The Scottish Bishops wrote in formal sympathy to their brethren of London and Exeter in this act of State interference, and at the same time published their own defence of the doctrine.

Torry had realized two dreams, in his cathedral and in his Prayer Book. Both were to prove a noble but a troublesome legacy to his diocese in the next few decades. The Battle of the Books continued with acrimony; the other Bishops indulged in unedifying disputes. But the old Bishop of St. Andrews was beyond the strife. He was content to have seen a renewal of the old, strong Scots Episcopacy, refreshed by the spirit of the Oxford Movement whose leaders taught, as he and his spiritual forebears had, the doctrine of the Eucharistic presence and Sacrifice.

George Farquhar wrote of him that he represented 'the vessel of our old, non-juring divines which had sailed through so many stormy seas' and now came into calmer waters and felt warmer breezes from the south.

Lendrum, like his Bishop, links the old tradition with the new devotion. Comment on him was tolerant.

'He juist took up with these Puseyite notions.'

The line was continued. Lendrum's curate was John Comper who, as Rector of St. Margaret's Aberdeen, carried the Catholic revival further and directed the way of one of the early religious communities in Scotland.

The old Bishop was drifting away from the ever-changing and expanding life of the Church he had served so long. He lingered now in her heroic past, hardly able to comprehend or enjoy her freedom or to admit new liberties. Like Jolly he deplored the idea of admitting the laity into the Synods:

'I am quite bewildered when I think of it,' he told Forbes, admitting humbly: 'I do not think my advice would be considered otherwise than as an old man's dream, who thinks nothing wise that deviates from the track in which he had been accustomed to move through the long period of more than sixty years of ministerial life in the service of the best of Masters. My wisdom, therefore, seems to be to "sit still" and submit quietly to the decision of the majority, and pray God to direct them.'

His last years were spent in study and prayer, with much letter-writing. On an old envelope he noted: 'Unable to take any concern in the future matters of the Church.'

He died in October 1852 and was buried in his cathedral. Bishop Forbes conducted his funeral service, commending his faithful soul to God.

# 5

# Scholastic Interlude.
# Glenalmond

The school and college of Holy Trinity, Glenalmond, may be said to have begun in Fraserburgh, for the endowment left by Miss Kathrein Panton, one of Bishop Jolly's congregation there, to found 'a Seminary of Learning or Theological Institution' accomplished, in time, even more than that good benefactress planned. The Pantonian Trust established after her death appointed, as we have seen, Bishop Walker as Professor of Theology, and before, during and for six years after his day, the College was peripatetic, meeting in one house or another in Edinburgh. In 1847, by the energy and generosity of a group of laymen, the College of the Holy Trinity was founded at Glenalmond in Perthshire, to be both a Theological Seminary and a school on the model of the English public schools. Among these founders were Mr. Gladstone, always a good friend to the Scottish Church, and James Hope, later Hope-Scott, husband of Charlotte Lockhart, and grand-daughter and heiress of Sir Walter Scott. The Hopes were to be received into the Roman Communion in 1852, but at this time they were devout Anglicans of the Tractarian school.

Glenalmond's own historian, G. H. Quintin, places it with two other schools of contemporary foundation, Radley in England, St. Columba's in Ireland, both founded by another Tractarian, William Sewell, with the same purpose as Glenalmond: 'to provide a public school education with special attention to the inculcation of Church principles.'

The idea was first mentioned in 1840 in a letter from Gladstone to Archdeacon Manning, as he then was: he did not 'Romanize', to use Lockhart's word, until twelve years later, along with James Hope. Gladstone wrote that the idea was to found 'a college akin in structure to the Roman seminaries in England; that is to say, partly for training the clergy, partly for affording an education to children of the gentry, who now go chiefly to the Presbyterian schools or are tended at home by Presbyterian tutors'.

A year later a formal proposal was circulated, signed by Gladstone, Hope and Dean Ramsay and approved by the Bishops. The first subscribers included the Dowager Queen Adelaide. By 1846 subscriptions amounted to £33,000. The site chosen for the new college was on the banks of the Almond and was bought from a Perthshire laird, George Patten. Many years later Gladstone described the event to Hope's daughter, Mary Monica Hope-Scott:

'We were, I do not say assisted, but cheered up in fastening on it, by a luncheon which Mr. Patten the proprietor gave us, of grouse newly killed, roasted by an apparatus for the purpose on the moment, and bedewed with what I think is called "partridge-eye champagne".'

The building had begun in 1847, the architect being John Henderson. In 1846 the foundation stone of the chapel, consecrated by the Primus, was laid by Sir John Gladstone and in that year the first Warden was appointed. This title was taken from Winchester where he was a master. He was the Reverend Charles Wordsworth, nephew of the poet and son of Christopher Wordsworth, Master of Trinity, Cambridge, by his marriage with Priscilla Lloyd of Charles Lamb's well-loved Quaker family. Charles's brother Christopher became Bishop of Lincoln; his nephew (and biographer) John, Bishop of Salisbury; his niece, daughter of the younger Christopher, was the delightful and only amusing member of this most serious family; and Elizabeth was the first Principal of Oxford's first college for women, Lady Margaret Hall. The new Warden was decidedly of the Establishment in the modern as well as the traditional sense of that word, English of the English, steeped in the atmosphere of the public school.

He was born in 1806 at Lambeth where his father was then chaplain to the Archbishop. As a schoolboy at Sevenoaks he showed his strong talent for Latin verse and for cricket. Somewhat delicate, he was sent, not to Winchester like his brothers, but to what his biographer calls 'the milder discipline of Harrow' where among his friends were Henry Manning, the future Cardinal, Richard Trench, future Archbishop of Dublin, and Charles Merivale who called him 'king of our cricket field'. Young Wordsworth played in the Eton and Harrow match in 1822, the

Harrow and Winchester one in 1825 and he brought about the first Oxford and Cambridge match in 1827. He himself went to Oxford, to Christ Church, where he worked and played with equal fervour and success, taking a First in Greats, arranging the first Boat Race, and playing tennis as well as cricket. Golf did not attract him until about sixty years later, at St. Andrews, when he was eighty-four. After tutoring for a time, with James Hope and Gladstone among his pupils, he went to Winchester, to become a Wykehamist of Wykehamists. He married happily but the happiness was brief: his wife died in childbirth. For her he wrote an exquisite and moving epitaph:

> I, nimium delecta, vocat Deus; I, bona nostrae
> Pars animae; maerens altera, disce sequi.

His second wife was a niece of the Warden of Winchester, Barter. He was a close friend of the Headmaster, George Moberly, and brought one of his sons with him to Glenalmond. So he came north, enveloped in the mantle of William of Wykeham which he tried to drape round the shoulders of young Scots.

School opened in 1847 with fourteen boys. The first to arrive was Lord Henry Kerr, later Marquess of Lothian, who came a day early and was pressed into service by the Warden, helping him to unpack sixty cases of books. Among the others were two sons of Bishop Ewing of Argyll, and a grandson of Bishop Torry. There were four masters. The curriculum was much like that of the English public schools with a larger amount of divine learning added to the humanities. Modern languages were also taught. The fees were £70 a year.

Wordsworth's Latin Muse was inspired by the laying of the foundation stone of the chapel:

> Nactus honore proprio cognomine laetus,
> Fundamenta domus Virque Lapisque iacit,
> Quem Laetus-Lapis ipse iacit, lapis auspice laetus
> Stet, stet in aeternum mactus honore novo.

The prayer of dedication ran:

> Deus unus, unis in trinis, fac nos et
> Amare et intelligere et esse, unum et simul
> Fiamus alter alteri, atque unum Tibi.

In his *Annals of My Early Life* Wordsworth gave his rules for the new school. Chapel was compulsory and surplices were worn on Sunday and other holy days.

'In wearing them the boys will bear in mind what is meant by the pure white garment, and why it is required for their presence at such times in the House of God.'

Among Presbyterian neighbours a legend grew that those rags of prelacy were worn for cricket.

'Every boy on coming into his place in chapel will kneel down and say a secret prayer' and he was solemnly enjoined 'to say or sing, audibly and devoutly, all those portions of the service which are required of the congregation'. The boys must kneel and bow the head in reverence, 'remembering how they would behave if they were admitted to a palace and suffered to address an earthly king'; but they must not think that 'mere lip-service will be acceptable to God'. There must be the obedience of a life lived in faith and fear.

The rules proceed to domestic matters. It was punishable to exceed the weekly laundry allowance of three shirts and cravats, three pairs of stockings, one night-shirt, one night-cap. In school the boys wore gowns: outside they must not be seen without a hat or a cap, the hat on Sundays. When the gown was taken off for games it must not be thrown on the ground but be hung up in the owner's study. Wellington boots were forbidden.

House discipline was strict; noise on stairs or in passages would be punished; boys were not allowed to visit each other's rooms except on the last day of term when discipline was relaxed. In the dormitories, divided into cubicles, 'all violation of each other's privacy by looking over the partitions' was forbidden; there must be no sudden appearance of a night-capped head! The boys must be in bed, their lamps out, half an hour after going upstairs. No one appears to have seen the danger of those small portable lamps. Prep must stop as soon as the bell rang for bed and 'the time of study was to be strictly devoted to the school business', with no other reading, however excellent in itself.

The cult of games, now at its height at Rugby and developing rapidly at Winchester was not yet followed in Scotland, although boys played heartily enough. The Warden tried to inculcate this new form of high seriousness but the young Scots persisted in playing for fun, while some preferred other activities, such as walking and climbing. There were rules about games: no football between breakfast and chapel: all games to stop when the class-bell rang: bows and arrows were forbidden and there must be no snowballing in Quad and no stone-throwing anywhere. Gardening was encouraged but tools must be put tidily away in the shed. In summer the boys bathed in the river, but 'no boy who is not an officer will be allowed to bathe more than once a day'. Bird-nesting and tree-climbing in the College plantations were forbidden, and even more alarming than stone-throwing was the use of gunpowder which had to be prohibited. Out-of-bounds rules were strict, and no shops must be visited but the one kept by the Manciple who was 'authorized to keep on sale, for ready money only, such articles as are necessary or allowed'.

Finally: 'All dealings with vagrants is strictly forbidden.' Were these last two rules interrelated? Had some boys suborned or did the Warden think them likely to suborn an amiable vagrant to smuggle in forbidden goods?

So much for boys in health: as for those in sickness or going *aeger*:

'When a boy is poorly in the morning and wishes to be absent from first school, he must speak to the bed-maker as he rings the bell along the dormitory, and desire him to apply for permission from the Sub-Warden. He will then be visited in his bedroom by one of the authorities before breakfast, who will determine whether he is to remain *aeger* during the day.' (And heaven help malingerers!) A boy only slightly *aeger* must be up by nine o'clock: if really ill he was sent to bed in the sickroom.

Life was austere, the school was deadly cold, the heating apparatus inefficient, almost theoretical, and the day was long, beginning at half-past six with an hour of study before breakfast at eight. That meal was meagre, consisting of bread and butter with tea or coffee, unless a hamper from home provided sausages and other delights. Dinner was substantial enough, tea a repetition of breakfast, and supper in those early days did not occur at all. The boys spent nine or ten hours in study, with only one half-holiday in the week.

The Warden believed in the virtue of games:

'I did not consider it beneath my dignity to teach in the playground'; but the boys were not always apt pupils. As an angler and a skater he won their respect, but he was a solemn, remote and formidable figure. They nicknamed him 'Grumphy' or 'Grunter' from his habit of coughing before delivering an admonition.

One of his punishments was inflicted upon three boys who were found frying eggs and herring for a picnic in the woods, on the vigil of the feast of St. Simon and St. Jude; a sin against both ecclesiastical and scholastic discipline and so 'rebukit sair' like the auld Seceder cat, and set to translate a portion of Ecclesiasticus into Latin.

Wordsworth's poetic talent found frequent outlet. He was moved by the sight of the surpliced choir in chapel:

> Hark! 'tis the white-robed choral band,
> See where in order meet they stand
> Each answering each on either hand;
>    Except the Lord
> Shall build the house 'tis vainly planned,
>    Vain work and word.

The Prayer Book controversy reached Glenalmond. Which was to be used in chapel, the Scottish or the English? The Bishops being divided in opinion, they reached a compromise: each Book would be used alternately.

Wordsworth's brief Wardenship had its storms and stresses, a warning prelude to his stormy episcopate. One quarrel was with a parent, Major Sharp, who disregarded rules: he refused to kneel in chapel when visiting the school, failed to provide his son with the proper outfit, and worst of all he adhered to the schismatic congregation of St. John in Perth. As a schismatic he was refused Communion in chapel. It was a brief but violent struggle, discreditable to both antagonists.

The school grew in numbers and the Theological College was opened in 1851 with thirteen students. In 1854 Wordsworth (now Bishop of St. Andrews) resigned; he was succeeded by Dr. Hannah, an Oxonian, a Fellow of Lincoln, but with some experience of a Scottish school. Since 1847 he had been Rector of Edinburgh Academy. He found Glenalmond finances in a bad condition and dealt capably with them. Gladstone declared that he would have made a good Chancellor of the Exchequer. Hannah was formidable in energy and the boys called him 'The Grue' which became the official or hereditary nickname for the Warden. 'The origin of the title' according to G. H. Quintin 'is lost in the dim obscurity of the ages which have clothed it with reverence.' The interpretation most favoured is that 'Grue' being the Scots for greyhound was a suitable name for one of Hannah's swiftness of mind and movement: he pursued the boys as a hound does a hare. Both numbers and fees increased in his reign and new building was begun, including the Hall. This is all to his credit but greatly to his shame is his dismissal, under pressure from Wordsworth and Trower, Bishop of Glasgow, of William Bright, lecturer in theology, one of the greatest of contemporary theologians and author of the much-loved Eucharistic hymn:

> And now, O Father, mindful of the love
> That bought us once for all on Calvary's Tree.

The Theological College, unlike the school, did not greatly flourish. The theological course was for two years, with fees of £40 a year. The entrance examination was in Biblical History, the Gospels in Greek, and Paley's *Evidence of Christianity*, with translation from set books of Cicero and Demosthenes, and a Latin prose. Candidates must have taken a degree or at least attended the course for a degree: a concession was made to Old Glenalmonds of not less than two years' residence at the school who were 'duly qualified in literature'. The Warden was *ex officio* Pantonian Professor; the Sub-Warden, by a later endowment, Bell Lecturer. Graduates wore a hood, designed by Bishop Forbes of Brechin, of black silk lined with green in the same shade as that of the Order of the Thistle. Among those early students was Joseph Lyne who as Father Ignatius founded the Community of Llanthony Abbey, was among the leading ecclesiastical eccentrics of his age and later submitted to Rome.

The whole college had a distinctly seminarian discipline. The Report on Education in Scotland by Her Majesty's Commissioners, in 1867, gave the hours of attendance in chapel as three hundred and ninety-two in the year: at Rugby they were only a hundred and eighteen. The Commissioners doubted the efficacy of so much chapel-going. There were then ninety-five boys in the school, mostly of the upper class: 'There is less mixture among them than at any school which we have visited.'

The verdict was on the whole favourable, Glenalmond being found to have 'much of the freedom and manliness of the English Public Schools, something of the genial, healthy tone and *esprit de corps* of these great institutions'.

Dr. Hannah resigned in 1870, was succeeded by Dr. Thornton, and he, three years later, by Dr. Robinson. The curriculum was enlarged to include a mathematical side. There were now two half-holidays in the week: the vacations were seven weeks in summer, two at Christmas, five at Easter. Fees were now ninety guineas for boys over twelve, eighty for juniors: for sons of the clergy £50 and £40. Singing was taught as part of the curriculum; instrumental music and drawing were extras. The boys' outfit consisted of one black suit, two morning suits, a dressing-gown, ten shirts, four silk cravats, ten pairs of stockings, six night-shirts (but no longer any night-caps), four pairs of boots or shoes, one hat or cap, six towels and one large brown holland bag.

In 1875 a fire destroyed most of the Theological College, and the students, with the Pantonian Professor, Dr. Dowden, moved to Edinburgh. This move proved permanent and salutary.

In the same year a Rifle Corps, the first in Scotland, was formed. *The Church Directory* of 1878 stated its advantages: not only that of preparing candidates for the army but for others 'whose prospects are of a peaceful character, a continual lesson of order and discipline, and prompt obedience to command'. Cadets were filled with *esprit de corps*, they were taught the use of fire-arms, and acquired 'an upright, soldier-like carriage'. The uniform cost £3 10s. od., the rifle £2 10s. od., but this could be resold when a cadet left school.

In 1876 the first *Glenalmond Chronicle* appeared and in 1877, at Commemoration, the *Carmen Glenalmondense* was first sung in public. The Warden in the 1880's was W. J. Richmond, formerly Dean of Keble, who was succeeded in 1888 by Warden Skrine from Uppingham, who guided the school into the new century.

Games had by this time been developed. Warden Richmond introduced compulsory rugby. These footballers were tough. An Old Glenalmond has left an account of a match against Loretto in 1885. The Glenalmond Fifteen left by coach early on a wet November morning for Perth, thence by train to Burntisland, across a stormy Forth by ferry to Granton, and finally by train to Loretto. The match began at three o'clock on a misty afternoon, and Loretto won by five goals. After tea Glenalmond took a train to Edinburgh, thence back to Perth, reaching home about midnight.

Equally energetic and more regular were the labours of the modern side who helped to repair the Old Dam on the river, cleared the woods of fallen trees, drained the football field, laid out a tennis court and helped to repair a road. In the winter of 1886 the College was cut off by snow, and boys and masters had to dig their way out and make a road for delivery vans.

Life was still austere. Food was plain: it was not forbidden to buy cake and jam but Warden Richmond disapproved of this 'consumption of what is, in schoolboy language, called grub'. Such luxuries were unnecessary and 'in those who are weak enough to be liable to such temptations, they lead to the growth of a sickly and unhealthy appetite'.

Life, however, was not all work. The Richmonds were musical and fostered a love of music in the boys. There was a school orchestra and concerts were given; plays too were performed. The music master, A. H. Black, composed the Glenalmond March and School Anthem and a *Reverie* for piano, violin and organ, with the plaintive title: 'Thy sweet, sad face, Glenalmond.' His successor preferred Jacobite songs as more suited to a place of Scottish Episcopal foundation.

Its situation made Glenalmond secluded, almost monastic. Richmond, if not positively allergic to parents, was at least irresponsive to their pressure. He rarely wrote to them or they to him, which made for a certain peace and detachment. Few if any of those parents appear to have thought their offspring unusually gifted, sensitive, or in need of special care: if they did they kept their views to themselves. Physical ailments were treated when necessary. Two boys were sent to Edinburgh to have their tonsils removed but their parents were not informed: the operation over, the boys returned in the evening to Glenalmond. Yet The Grue did care for them, individually and collectively. Richmond had learned from the great Thring of Uppingham a respect for the average boy, and Skrine continued to show it. The school was not a forcing-house: it was a preparation for life.

Skrine was at heart romantic and something of a poet. He loved the atmosphere of Glenalmond:

'The distinctive character, the secret of Glenalmond is too marked to escape the eye of a new-comer. Placed where it is, amid wild and beautiful country, with moors to roam over and streams to fish in . . . Glenalmond seems called upon to escape the narrowing influences which are sometimes deplored in the mill-round of the common school athletics, and to give the scholars a versatility and initiative, a range of mind and a habit of observation which elsewhere can be taught with difficulty, but here should come of themselves. . . . No one can know Glenalmond and not recognize in her a "sweet nurse" for that generous, chivalrous order of sentiments which was the glory, amid many defects, of the older public school training.'

Warden Skrine made conditions more comfortable with a decent heating system. He was still young in office at the Jubilee of 1891, dating from the issue in 1841 of the circular letter which led to the founding of the school. Of the signatories, Dean Ramsay and Hope-Scott were dead, but Bishop Wordsworth and Gladstone were still in vigour: they attended the celebrations and Gladstone laid the foundation stone of the new building. The Warden wrote a poem which was set to music by the choirmaster. Both the Bishop and Gladstone made speeches. The Bishop's, by doctor's orders, was brief; Gladstone's lasted for three-quarters of an hour. Lord Lothian, who had been the first boy, gave some reminiscences. And here, although Victorian Glenalmond has still nine years to go, we may leave them in their jubilation.

The Theological College had developed, even before its removal to Edinburgh. *The Church Directory* of 1878 shows a number of Old Glenalmonds among the clergy, with T.C.G. (Trinity College, Glenalmond) appended to their names. The Council at the time of the move consisted of the Primus and the Bishops of St. Andrews, Edinburgh and Glasgow; the staff, of Dr. Dowden, James Montgomery who was Dean of Edinburgh as Lecturer in Pastoral Theology, and John Cazenove, Lecturer in Apologetics. Students attended, in addition to their own courses, the class in Metaphysics or in Moral Philosophy at the University. They spent

The Right Reverend Anthony Mitchell,
Bishop of Aberdeen and Orkney, 1912–1917

The Right Reverend Alexander Penrose Forbes,
Bishop of Brechin, 1847–1875

St Adamnan's Parish Church, Kilmaveonaig, Blair Atholl, Perthshire

The Cathedral of the Isles, Millport

two sessions at College: the fees were £12 a year, with £4 4s. od. extra for University class fees. There were bursaries and scholarships to help payment, and one of these, the Luscombe, was a legacy from the first Bishop to be consecrated for work on the continent.

Almost from the first the College had a devout and friendly rival or brother. The College of the Holy Spirit, a Collegiate Church, was founded in 1849 on the Isle of Cumbrae by the Honourable George Boyle, who became Earl of Glasgow. Dean Perry, in his *History of the Oxford Movement in Scotland*, has written delightfully of 'the young Cathedral builders' at Oxford in the late 1840's: Lord Forbes at Oriel, Boyle at Christ Church. They both had a share in the building of St. Ninian's, Perth, and Boyle now made his own foundation.

His idea was to found a community of clergy and laity, 'a monastery in spirit and in purpose' to use Dean Perry's phrase, with a church, a college and a home for aged clergy. Its chief end was to be 'the worship and service of Almighty God by daily prayer and frequent celebration of the Holy Communion'. The old priests could help to maintain the worship although they no longer had the strength for active pastoral work. There would be younger clergy in the college too, who would serve the Church in Argyll and the Isles where priests were so few, and who would relieve other clergy in sickness or other need. Ordinands would be prepared especially for work in Gaelic-speaking districts. Graduates would attend for one session, others for two. Men might come there during the university vacation to read theology. The idea took effective shape. In 1874 this Collegiate Church became the cathedral of the Isles. It followed the Tractarian tradition; Keble said it would be his refuge if he were driven out of the Church of England. The Bishop of the Isles, Alexander Ewing, was less well disposed. He detested the Oxford Movement and its followers, and under his episcopal rule Cumbrae was not altogether an isle of peace.

The list of expenses in 1878, to take only one year as illustration, gives £2 2s. od. a week for board and lodging due by the Provost, Canons and other resident clergy: ordinands paid £95 a year; students being prepared for one of the universities, £125 a year; and undergraduates resident during university vacation paid

£3 3s. od. a week, which included tuition. Visitors paid £2 2s. od. a week, but this was reduced for visiting clergy. The cost of single meals was: 2s. od. for breakfast, 1s. od. for luncheon with meat, 6d. without meat (probably bread and cheese), 6d. for tea, 2s. 6d. for dinner. There was a choir school with fees of £12 12s. od. a year.

Cumbrae from the first held a holiness, something of the atmosphere of Iona, of the Western Isles where in the dawn of the Christian faith in Britain Columba and his followers had brought the good news.

The Church was beginning to train lay teachers as well as clergy; from mid-century, teaching was becoming more and more of a profession. In 1850 a Training College or Institution was opened in Edinburgh, first for men: fifteen years later women were admitted 'owing to the great decrease of male candidates', and it became and remained a women's college. The Board of Governors included a clerical and a lay representative from each diocese; the Bishop of Edinburgh was Visitor, the Principal was a clergyman. The rest of the staff was female, except for two French visiting masters.

Candidates were aged from eighteen to twenty-five and were trained and examined in religious as well as secular learning. Latin, French, German, music, needlework, domestic economy and school management were included in the curriculum.

Most of the students had been pupil teachers. They paid an entrance fee of £5 or £10 according to their status as Queen's scholars or pupil teachers, and paid in advance for their books and stationery. They were then 'set free from all further charge for the two years' training, including board and laundry and medical attention'. There were sixty students and the College was in Dalry House.

In the second half of the century there were many Church schools for what the Victorians frankly called 'the lower classes'; there were fee-paying schools for the more prosperous and genteel; the public school pattern, followed by Glenalmond, was copied also, though with variations, by Loretto. Of these and of the teaching work of the revived religious orders a later chapter will treat.

# 6

# Edinburgh and the South

Edinburgh is unique among Scottish dioceses in her foundation which is post-Reformation. Its founder was Charles I, who gave the Bishop precedence immediately after the Archbishops of St. Andrews and of Glasgow. The first Bishop was William Forbes, of whom Charles said he was worthy to have a see erected for him. His was a brief episcopate, for he died in 1634, the year of his consecration, and was buried in his cathedral, now the High Kirk of St. Giles. The succession continued through the storm of the Civil War and the changing fortunes of the Church. In 1685 Charles's son bestowed upon the Bishop, John Paterson and his successors, the dignity *ex officio* of Chancellor of the University. Bishop Paterson was translated to Glasgow as Archbishop in 1687, and was succeeded in Edinburgh by William Rose who had the fateful interview with William of Orange. He lived until 1720, aided in his last years by a coadjutor, John Fullarton. Among later successors were Falconar the liturgical scholar, translated from Moray, and Abernethy Drummond, translated in 1787 from Brechin. The latter resigned in 1805 and was followed by Daniel Sandford, with whom we come into the age of elegance.

Daniel Sandford was born in Dublin in 1766, the son of a clergyman of the Church of Ireland who was also an English squire, Sandford of Sandford Hall, Shropshire. He died young and the children were brought up by their mother, who took them to England, to Bath. She was a friend of Mrs. Delany and of the Bowdlers whose most eminent member gave his name to an expurgated edition of Shakespeare and added a verb to our language.

Young Daniel was a serious boy. 'To his early introduction into polished and intellectual circles, Mr. Sandford owed much of his literary taste, as well as his elegance of mind and manner,' so his son and biographer has recorded, adding that the Bishop dearly cherished his memories of boyhood.

'He thought there was a closer affinity between high breeding and elevated sentiments than many men imagine, that ruffles and brocade were useful fences of society, and that what the present age gained in ease it lost in refinement – that late Georgian age which to us appears one of supreme elegance. He sometimes regretted that the days were gone when birth and breeding were preferred to wealth, when the gradations of society were definitely marked.'

Young Daniel and his brothers were educated at home with sufficient discipline; their mother used to shut them into their schoolroom every day until they had learned their tasks. This plan worked. When Daniel went up to Christ Church in 1784 he distinguished himself in scholarship, especially in Latinity, and in behaviour.

'At no time' according to his son 'did this noble college present a better opening to a young man of piety and conduct' than at this period under Dean Jackson. Our young man, whose piety and conduct were beyond reproach, lived in the best society, believing that there was no alternative but to have no society at all. 'He never sought the society of men of rank, but he was always found in it' – a most gratifying situation. Never idle or extravagant, he read, he botanized (for which he had a great liking), he rowed. 'He was a thorough Christ Church man, and he never discoursed more delightfully than when he spoke of its august walk and classic meadow, of its wits, of its awful censorship and venerable Dean.'

The best society was not limited to college. He often stayed with Mrs. Delany at Windsor, and more than once met King George and Queen Charlotte. The latter was particularly gracious and future preferment seemed probable. One way of pleasant eminence might have been that of a Fellowship, leading perhaps to the Deanery of his college, but for 'that common occurrence which spoils so many a hopeful academician'. He fell in love and married. His bride was Scottish, a Douglas, whose father had fought for Prince Charles in the Forty-Five, had followed him to France, and now lived in Bath. The marriage took place in 1790, in which year Sandford was appointed deacon. He was priested in 1791, and so strong was his emotion that he fainted at the altar. After a brief curacy in England he moved in 1792 to Edinburgh, as priest in charge of a small English congregation. They met first in a private room, then in the Charlotte Chapel in Register Street. They were a qualified, indeed a schismatic congregation, not giving canonical obedience to the Bishop of Edinburgh.

For the young English cleric it was a change to a new climate, a foreign region. Edinburgh still basked in the afterglow of her golden age. She was a city of wits, of poets and philosophers, clerics and lawyers, keen of brain and tongue, and of gentlewomen similarly endowed who still spoke the pithy and dignified Court Scots. They are portrayed in Scott's Mrs. Bethune Balliol in her silk gown of sober colour, rich quality and a style within bowing distance of fashion, her cap of Flanders lace, her diamond-buckled shoes, her jewels and her gold *bonbonnière* containing 'a few pieces of candied angelica or some other ladylike sweetmeat'. Mrs. Bethune Balliol had travelled widely and her outlook was far from parochial or provincial, but her speech was 'decidedly Scottish, often containing phrases and words little used in the present day'. Her pronunciation was also different from the contemporary utterance, and also from the vulgar, 'the Scottish as spoken by the ancient court of Scotland to which no idea of vulgarity could be attached.' It must, however, have been difficult for English new-comers like Sandford. He may have met the prototype of Scott's old lady and those fascinating and formidable gentlewomen whom Lord Cockburn remembered, one of them still coming to church in her sedan.

Edinburgh was much given to hospitality: less to formal dinners, however, than to ceremonial tea-drinkings and to suppers where other liquors were both lavish and potent. The speech might be difficult but the breeding and manners were of Sandford's own high standard: birth and background, talent and intellect mattered much more than wealth. Poverty was no disgrace and not even too harassing in a society which did not measure its members by status symbols. It is likely that the young clergyman and his wife, both of good family, were well received. Yet there was a difference from the equally well-bred society of Bath and that of genteel England in general:

'There, conventional rule was supreme: here it was little regarded; there, prescription was everything; here originality was the zest of conversation.' In England 'a crude or paradoxical opinion would have excited as much consternation as a breach in politeness; but in Edinburgh the drawing-room was more of an arena'.

This was the Edinburgh of the young Walter Scott who was that year called to the Bar, and who was as deep in the study of literature as of the law, collecting ballads, notable among his friends as a teller of tales. It was the Edinburgh into which the greatest of Scots Victorian Bishops, Alexander Forbes, would be born: his uncle, Sir William Forbes, was to have much to do with the building of St. John the Evangelist's where in 1818 Sandford moved with his congregation. Thirteen years earlier, in 1805, he had brought his people under the authority of the Bishop of Edinburgh: he had never been happy about intrusion. A year after this submission he was himself elected Bishop and consecrated by Skinner, Jolly and Watson: like them he continued to hold his congregational charge.

A scholar, he fostered scholarship, holding a class in Hebrew for ordinands. By his son's account he was serious and devout to a degree remarkable in a period when 'in general, vital religion was at a low ebb; if men were not sceptical they were indifferent'. He was not without humour and there is a pleasant note in his *Journal* about the Scots cult of preaching:

'The lower orders like sermons which are above their comprehension. They must be convinced that their pastor knows something which they do not know.'

He tells the story of a minister who used to quote the Scriptures in Gaelic to a Lowland congregation, calling it Greek: a Highland visitor complimented him on his good Gaelic and was implored to keep silence: 'My people would leave me at once if they thought I was not more knowing than themselves.'

Unlike the intruding English clergy and some of the anglicizing Scots, Sandford valued the Scottish Liturgy and the true Scots Episcopacy. A friend of Scott, he may have influenced Sir Walter's change from Presbyterianism to Episcopacy: he baptized three of his children: Sophia, Walter and Anne. Sandford defended Episcopacy (as Scott did) as nearest of all Churches to the primitive purity and tradition.

He died in 1830 and was succeeded by James Walker who has already been noticed as Pantonian Professor of Theology, and who as Primus sent the message of the Church's loyalty to Queen Victoria on her accession. Walker was a living link between the suffering and the restored Church, for he was born in the penal days in 1770: a north-easterner like Jolly, Gleig and Torry, and like them an alumnus of Aberdeen. Unlike them he was also a graduate of Cambridge and Cambridge made him a Doctor of Divinity. As a young man he travelled in Germany, being tutor to Sir John Hope of Craighall, and learned a good deal of German philosophy: he contributed an article on Kant to the *Encyclopaedia Britannica* of which he was, under Gleig, sub-editor. After being ordained he was appointed to St. Peter's, Edinburgh; his successor in that charge, Charles Hughes Terrot, was also to be his successor in the bishopric in 1841.

Terrot moves altogether away from the old Scottish line, being English by birth, of Huguenot ancestry, and born in India. His father, an officer, was killed in action and the family returned home to live with an uncle in Berwick. Charles went up to Trinity, Cambridge, to distinguish himself in scholarship and be elected a Fellow. Ordained in 1814 he was given the charge of Holy Trinity, Haddington, where he had leisure for study and composition. He wrote a prize poem on 'Hezekiah and Sennacherib', and a satire after the manner of the *Dunciad* on contemporary celebrities. From Haddington he came to Old St. Paul's, Edinburgh, as assistant to James Walker, followed him to the daughter-church of St. Peter and after that went to the other St. Paul's in York Place, a church in which three congregations had merged (St. Paul's, Skinners' Close, St. Andrew's, Carubbers Close and the chapel in Blackfriars Wynd). Scott and his family had worshipped in St. Paul's. This charge Terrot retained as Bishop of Edinburgh.

Like his predecessor and his fellow Bishops at this time, Terrot was a scholar, though in mathematics rather than in philosophy or theology: he was a member of the Royal Society of Edinburgh. Like those other Bishops, too, he was a forceful and forthright character.

Dean Walker in his *Reminiscences* describes him as a Johnsonian talker, loving argument, impatient of twaddle, himself precise and witty. Of this Dean Ramsay has given two illustrations. Terrot used to say that the two chief impediments to good conversation were humbug and humdrum, and once when asked whether he did not think table-turning and other minor efforts of spiritualism were of the devil he replied: 'It must be a mark of Satan being in a state of dotage.'

Pious twaddle he detested. To a Presbyterian lady who argued that the more infrequent a Celebration of Holy Communion was the more solemn it must be, he retorted that an annual or bi-annual Sabbath 'would be a very solemn ordinance indeed'. When asked by some of the godly to disapprove of a charity ball in aid of hospitals, he declared that he would dance a fandango in full canonicals, along George Street, if he thought it would help the poor patients. He disliked the title of 'My Lord Bishop'. In his latter years he had a coadjutor on whom he called one day to be told by a solemn footman that 'The Lord Bishop of Edinburgh was not at home'. He left a message that Bishop Terrot had called.

His choice snob-story was of his Haddington charge when he was churching the Countess of Wemyss. To the versicle: 'Lord save this woman Thy servant,' the clerk responded: 'Who putteth her ladyship's trust in Thee.'

Far from being a ritualist he reassured a lady who was perturbed by the new habit of clerics crossing themselves in church:

'I am so careful on this point that I never even cross my legs in the drawing-room.' There is a touch of schoolboy humour in his wit.

One of his most famous and delightful friends was Mrs. Carlyle, a friend since the days of girlhood in Haddington when as Jane Welsh she drew all eyes after her when she went up and down. In November 1834 he was in London and called on the Carlyles, newly settled in Cheyne Row. Jane, homesick for Scotland, wrote to her mother-in-law:

'When Mr. Terrot came in I sprang into his arms, and I believe almost stifled him with the ardour of my embrace. He returned it, however, with more sympathy than was to have been anticipated. I have wondered at my audacity ever since, for the thought of such an attempt in a cool moment would have made me quake.'

So the future Bishop shared a privilege with Leigh Hunt although he did not celebrate it in verse:

Jenny kissed me when we met,
Jumping from the chair she sat in.

Eleven years later Jane's reference to him was more serious, even sombre, though touched by irony. She was writing to her husband, absent in Scotland, in one of her moods of black melancholy, fighting the devil:

'But here on the table before me at this moment, one would say, lay means enough to keep him at bay for a while first:

Two series of Discourses
  on
1st 'Christian Humiliation.'
2nd 'The City of God.'
By C. H. Terrot, D.D., Bishop of Edinburgh;
  and secondly
a pair of pistols with a percussion lock.

Are not the Fates kind in sending me two such windfalls in one evening? When I have made myself sufficiently desperate by study of the one, I can blow my brains out with the other. Come what may, one has always one's "City of God" left – and one's pistols'.

She quoted the Bishop in a letter of 1862 written from Scotland to her husband in Chelsea:

'My departure from Nithsdale was like the partings of dear old long ago, before one had experienced that

> "Time will teach the softest heart
> Unmoved to meet, ungrieved to part"

as the immortal Mr. Terrot once wrote.'

Another friend was Mrs. Sellar, wife of the Professor of Humanity in Edinburgh. At one of her dinner parties a question of precedence arose. The Bishop and one of the Lords of Session, Lord Moncrieff, were fellow guests. Mrs. Sellar asked the latter whether he or the Bishop were principal male guest and who should take her down to dinner. Lord Moncrieff gave judgement that it was himself: the Bishop in Scotland was only a dissenting parson.

Like his predecessor at one remove, Bishop Sandford, Terrot declared himself to be a Scottish, not an English Churchman, but of 'the Edinburgh or trans-Forthian type'. He had no liking however for the Scottish Liturgy, or for the non-juring tradition. His opinions may be gathered from two of his Synod Charges in 1848 and 1857 respectively. In the first he deplored the contemporary vogue of sentimental medievalism and the cult of saints. Of that word he gave three definitions:

'In the Roman sense, a departed human being respecting whom that portion of the Church has dared to forestall the judgement of God'.

In popular meaning saints were 'men and women remarkable for their piety above the ordinary run of Christians'. In the Scriptural sense they were 'all those who, having been grafted into Christ by baptism, live in accordance with their baptismal promise'.

In the first sense the Episcopal Church had no saints 'because we dare not assume to ourselves the incommunicable prerogatives of God'; in the second 'it was not the ideal of the Church to possess only a few undefiled individuals'; in the third sense it was false to declare that there were no longer saints upon earth.

Continuing with definitions which pleased his mathematical mind, he defined the Church, which might be one particular Communion or the universal Church. The Scriptural meaning was 'the entire society of baptized believers' and this had once been truly the Catholic Church. The idea of 'essential unity is as true now as it was at the beginning'. The idea of formal unity must be received with caution. Truth was revealed in Scripture and must be accepted by reason and conscience, not because it was Catholic.

'The truth is in its essence, the Catholicity is accidental.' Acceptance by a majority did not prove a belief to be true.

In his advice to his clergy the Bishop dealt with the problem of refusing Holy Communion. They must repel, as the canon decreed, anyone of notoriously evil life. As for the admission of strangers, they should have an attestation from their former priest, but this, not always practicable, should not be enforced. He was thinking of English new-comers, duly confirmed; but what follows might well be held to include others, devout, unconfirmed, longing for the Food of the Sacrament:

'When an ordinance is held to be necessary to salvation, the great law of charity dictates that those who are entrusted with the dispensation of it should dispense it to all who apply for it, and are not manifestly incapable of profiting by it. And who are they who are incapable of profiting by it? Not, surely, all those who are erroneous in religious opinions or faulty in practice; for in that case, what man who knows himself would venture to approach the table of the Lord? No, it is the hardened sinner, the denier of Christ, the man who is living without God in the world. . . . Wherever there is spiritual life, there the Body and Blood of Christ work to the strengthening and refreshing of the soul.'

In 1857, in which year he became Primus, he spoke pungently about the attitude of the Church of England towards Scots Episcopacy. The Low Church party were especially hostile, accusing the Scots of being 'partizans of that movement towards Rome which unquestionably exists in the Church of England'. With this movement Terrot had no sympathy. But he did not blame the Scots. For any conversions to Rome, which he resented, he blamed the English!

'Every conspicuous perversion of a lay member of the Episcopal Church in Scotland has occurred under the baneful influence of some English clergyman.'

This attitude and accusation lack both courtesy and charity, but in that decade feeling was intense. There had been some notable secessions among the Scottish laity: James Hope-Scott and his wife, also the Marchioness of Lothian and the Duchess of Buccleuch who had both been benefactresses of the Church on the borders. Lady Lothian had given Jedburgh its Episcopal church, and the chapel at Dalkeith, on the Buccleuch lands, was a centre of Episcopal worship, one of the first in Scotland to have the regular Sunday Eucharist.

With regard to the Scottish Church, the Low Church in England was hostile, the High Church sympathetic but unhelpful; and indeed active help from that quarter might have proved harmful. The average member of the Church of England was simply indifferent, ignorant, insular, even parochial, unable to accept any other Rite than that of the Book of Common Prayer, unable to realize 'the spiritual sufficiency of a Bishop in whose appointment the Crown has had no share'. The Scots clergy were still barred from accepting an English charge. This final disability remained supported by ignorance and prejudice which the English Bishops did nothing to remove, while English clergy were permitted to intrude themselves into Scotland without obedience to the Scottish Bishops. This scandal was not yet removed.

Terrot found that the Presbyterian attitude varied between courteous friendliness and bitter intolerance. The latter was a bad legacy from the past:

'Up to the beginning of the eighteenth century there were no Churches and very few individuals who considered intolerance to be a sin. I consider it to be a great sin.'

Terrot was twice married: by his first marriage he had fourteen children, of whom six predeceased him. His eldest daughter went to the Crimea as one of Florence Nightingale's ladies. The end of his life was clouded by ill-health, first of the body then, even more pitifully, of the mind. He died in 1872 and was succeeded by Henry Cotteril.

His episcopate, like James Walker's, saw the growth of the Church in the south, an expansion visible in a rush of building. Churches replaced the small chapels or the upper rooms of the secluded years, many of them of considerable size and dignity. The Episcopal tradition might not pervade Edinburgh and the south-east as it did Aberdeen and the north-east, but some of the congregations had roots deep in the past and a life maintained since the Caroline Establishment. St. Peter's, Musselburgh, had been the parish church before 1688: its priest, Arthur Miller, refused to conform to the new Establishment, was ejected and deprived of his charge but promptly gathered a congregation of the Faithful Remnant, and in 1727 he was consecrated a College Bishop. Meanwhile he continued to live in his parsonage or manse until the General Assembly of the Presbyterian Kirk petitioned the Court of Session to compel the magistrates of Musselburgh to eject him. The congregation met where they could: in 1704 they risked building a church and paid for their temerity later in the century by having it burned by Cumberland's men. When the penal laws were quiescent though not yet repealed, another church was built which served them about eighty years.

St. James's, Leith, also had a long history and a strong Jacobite tradition. Its most famous incumbent was Robert Forbes who became Bishop of Ross and Caithness while still retaining his charge. He was out in the Forty-Five and left a singularly laconic account of the matter in the church baptismal register:

'Here a great interruption has happened by my misfortune of being taken prisoner . . . on Saturday the 7th of September, 1745, and confined in Stirling Castle till February 4th, 1746, and in Edinburgh Castle till May 29th of the same year.'

While in prison he collected many of the stories and memoirs which he afterwards put together in that incomparable record of The Rising, *The Lyon in Mourning*. From him Robert Chambers drew much of the material for his own *History of the Forty Five*. We have seen his work as liturgiologist.

His successor at St. James's, at some removes and nearly a century later, also became a Bishop while retaining the charge, one of the last to do so. This was Michael Russell, consecrated Bishop of Glasgow in 1837. The see of Glasgow, once an Archbishopric, had been held with Edinburgh since 1787. The newly disjoined see took into itself the border charges of Galashiels, Melrose, Jedburgh, Kelso, Selkirk and Hawick, an arrangement, odd geographically, which continued until near the end of the nineteenth century.

In the meeting-place of St. James's congregation the poet-priest John Skinner of Linshart had been baptized by the Episcopal Rite, he being a convert from Presbyterianism and uncertain of the validity of his Presbyterian baptism. In 1806 an English congregation joined St. James's and together they built a chapel: their growth was such that in 1849 they began to build a school, then a church and parsonage. The foundation stone of the church was laid in 1862 by Mr. Gladstone whose austere but benevolent presence appears frequently in Scottish Episcopal history. The plan by Gilbert Scott was in Victorian Gothic, the west front being, according to a contemporary account, 'pleasantly recognized by all acquainted with Scottish mediaeval architecture to be a highly successful adaptation of the west front of Dunblane Cathedral so much admired by Mr. Ruskin'.

It is among the minor troubles of the Scottish Church that her growth and prosperity occurred in an age of deplorable imitation. Had there been an architect inspired by a new vision rather than by a dream of the past, there might have arisen a truly Scots Episcopal style of church, plain but beautiful, holding the old simplicity and austerity and expressing the faith and spirit of the suffering and Faithful Remnant. But Gothic was the only style deemed truly religious.

Old St. Paul's, thus styled to distinguish it from the younger

St. Paul's in York Place, also remembered the days of persecution. The congregation, driven from St. Giles, met in a store in Carubbers' Close off the High Street. A chapel was built, for a time the only Episcopal chapel within the city walls, and here young Samuel Seabury, when a medical student in Edinburgh, came to worship. John Wesley was present on Good Friday 1772, and was much moved by the devout behaviour of the congregation, the solemn reading of prayers, the excellent sermon. This was a Jacobite congregation. Sir Walter Scott's friend William Erskine described the first service in which King George was prayed for by name:

'Such blowing of noses, such significant hems, such suppressed sighs, such smothered groans and universal confusion can hardly be conceived.'

Among the congregation were Lady Nairne, born Oliphant of Gask, William Edmonstoune Aytoun, and Sir Stuart Thriepland of Fingask, all of the old loyalty. The incumbent at this time of reluctant acceptance of the new allegiance was Dr. Charles Webster whose assistant and successor was his nephew John: together they founded St. Peter's, Roxburgh Place. When St. Peter's became an incumbency, later to move to Luton Place, it had as priests, two future Bishops, James Walker and Charles Terrot.

For a short time, before he moved to St. John's, Edward Ramsay was in charge of Old St. Paul's, an incompatible alliance for this moderate of moderates, anglicized and anglicizing, utterly out of sympathy with the tradition of the congregation. Then came a great priest, John Alexander, inspired by the fervour of the Oxford Movement. He held daily prayers, celebrated frequent Eucharists and began missionary work in the city. In 1846 he left Old St. Paul's to make a new foundation, St. Columba's by the Castle, which from the first was both Catholic and evangelical. For Old St. Paul's there was a period of difficulty and strife, complicated by attacks from without. The cry of 'No Popery' was loud and frequent. The resurgence of the congregation began in the 1880's with the building of the present church in Jeffrey Street.

St. John's flourished mightily. Dean Ramsay (as he became in 1846) was enough to ensure prosperity and gentility. He was well

born, cultivated, suave, humorous and of the centre in churchmanship. Other qualities less admirable will be mentioned in later
chapters. His name endures through his *Reminiscences of Scottish
Life and Character*, that treasury of anecdotes and pithy sayings
cherished by many public speakers. He deprecated the Oxford
Movement:

'The Romanizing tendencies so openly avowed in the Church
of England alarm me. I have made up my mind to a conduct and
demeanour in Church matters almost neutral. I positively will not
again mix myself up with party or even take part. I will confine
myself to St. John's and its duties. This is my line – hear what
everyone has to say, and keep a quiet, conciliatory and even tenor.'

His conduct in more than one controversy did not fulfil that
promise.

Among his congregation and devotees in the late 1840's was
that pioneer woman journalist Elizabeth Rigby, who, with her
mother and sister, lived in Edinburgh from 1844 till 1849, when
she married Sir Charles Eastlake. She contributed articles and
reviews to *The Quarterly Review* under John Gibson Lockhart's
editorship. When she chose, she could dip her pen in vitriol,
notoriously in her malignant criticism of *Jane Eyre*: her account in
her letters of Presbyterian services was tinged with the same fluid,
but when she wrote of the Dean she used only honeyed phrases.
He was all that was good: 'tenderly persuasive in the pulpit, in
private a delightful friend and host.'

Dean Perry in his excellent study of *The Oxford Movement in
Scotland* has described the churchmanship of Edinburgh and the
south as 'more colourless' than that of the north. The northern
clergy and laity were 'by conviction and sympathy, Tractarians
long before *The Tracts For the Times* were written'. The ritualistic
and aesthetic development came slowly there; it seemed comparatively unimportant, Catholic principles being so firmly held
already. The old simplicity remained. In the south, on the other
hand, as Episcopacy became favoured there was a desire for the
graces of liturgy and ceremonial. Some converts came into the
Church to escape the dreariness of Presbyterianism: they did not
ask for over-much theology.

'The policy of the south, therefore, was to preach a somewhat
harmless Gospel, and to win cultured people through the quiet

beauty of the Prayer Book services.' The strong, Catholic teaching of Keble and Pusey was tactfully omitted.

There were exceptions to this, notably in St. Columba's where both the outward form and the inward spirit of the Catholic Movement were found. St. Columba's was the first church in Edinburgh to return to the primitive practice of celebrating the Eucharist every Sunday, and there were celebrations also on Thursdays and on Saints' Days during the week.

Along with this worship went sound teaching, care for the poor and for children. St. Columba's had a school three years before Dr. Guthrie began his famous 'ragged schools'. It was held in the hall beneath the church. There were a hundred and forty poor children who were taught Church doctrine as well as secular learning and came to church every Sunday. Three times a week they were given a free dinner. The school was supported by subscriptions. A contemporary account of the consecration of St. Columba's refers to the antagonism its services had at first aroused, quelled by 'a singular reaction in its favour' due to the zeal of its priest and his care for the poor.

The church in Jedburgh (which in mid-century was in the diocese of Glasgow) was, like St. Columba's, Tractarian from its foundation. Lady Lothian had caused it to be built when she came to Monteviot in her fervently Anglican days. Keble, Hook and Wilberforce came to its consecration in 1844, the only church in Scotland in which Keble officiated, dearly though he loved and venerated Scottish Episcopacy. Jedburgh's neighbours were most of them built in mid-century: Melrose in 1849, Galashiels in 1853, Hawick in 1864. Peebles had come earlier, in 1833; Selkirk came later in 1869.

Glasgow's development began only about this time, the latest diocese in growth, but the growth was to be rapid. This will be noted in a later chapter. There was one congregation which went back to the penal days, although it had suffered no penalties, being a qualified chapel: this was St. Andrew's-by-the-Green built in 1750 for an English congregation which prayed for King George. The head mason was a member of the strict sect of the Original Secession and was excommunicated for 'the sin and scandal of biggin' ane Episcopal kirk'. Relations with the Established Church of Scotland proved mellower. When Glasgow Cathedral in the early nineteenth century discarded an organ as Popish, the instrument came to a Presbyterian, St. Andrew's, which was on friendly terms with its Episcopal neighbour and namesake and passed the organ to that congregation. Thereafter St Andrew's-by-the-Green was known as The Kirk o' Whistles from this organ or Kist o' Whistles. The church's most precious possession was a fragment of the high altar of the Abbey on Iona, set into its own altar.

One other church in the city, St. Mary's, dated from the early nineteenth century. This in our own century became the cathedral. Michael Russell's episcopate saw the beginning of growth, his successors saw its notable development.

# 7

# Sanctity and Strife.
# Alexander Penrose Forbes

With the great Victorian Bishops we come to a new phase in
Scottish Episcopacy. Their predecessors had known penalties and
poverty, a tradition of defensive seclusion, of primitive simplicity.
Torry had carried that tradition into the new age and had wel-
comed the beginning of the Tractarian influence and revival. His
young colleague in the Episcopate, his spiritual son, Alexander
Forbes, came under the direct influence of Oxford, bringing to
Scotland new treasure to add to the heritage of the native Church.

The Bishops of this first Victorian generation knew the old
ways by report rather than direct experience, and they knew a
good deal of the world beyond Scotland. They were strong personalities, varied, often antagonistic one to another, not con-
spicuously peacemakers. Some are very much of their period and
of their class; Forbes belongs to no set time; he would have been
the ideal Father-in-God in the first centuries of the Church and
would be equally so today. Many people today regard him as a
true if unofficial patron saint of the Scottish Church in general
and of the Episcopate in particular.

He was born in Edinburgh in 1817. His father, Lord Medwyn,
was one of the Judges of the Court of Session, his grandfather was
Sir William Forbes the banker, to whom Scott paid tribute in the
Introduction to the Fourth Canto of *Marmion*:

> 'Far may we search before we find
> A heart so noble and so kind.
> . . . If mortal charity dare claim
> The Almighty's attributed name,
> Inscribe above his mouldering clay:
> "The widow's shield, the orphan's stay!"'

Scott's friendship continued with the next generation, with
Lord Medwyn and his elder brother, the second Sir William with

whom the friendship had a certain poignancy. This Sir William married Scott's first love whose memory could pierce his heart to the end. She was Williamina Stuart Belsches, and her parents discouraged the romance with the young advocate whose future did not appear to have any special brilliance. How much she loved him no one can tell, or whether she was easily or with difficulty persuaded to make the excellent match with the wealthy young banker of such good family. What is certain is that she married a man of noble heart. When Scott's fortunes crashed, Sir William was one of his most loyal friends and a secret helper. When he died in 1828, Scott wrote:

'In him I feel I have sustained a loss which no after years of my life can fill up to me. . . . If I look back to the gay and happy years of youth, they must be filled with recollections of our departed friend.'

Lord Medwyn married Louisa Gordon Cumming, a lady of the type Scott knew and appreciated, and portrayed in his Mrs. Bethune Balliol. She used the dignified and pithy old court Scots and he must have delighted in her company. He was a frequent guest in her house.

Forbes had a goodly heritage of gentle blood and breeding, steadfast loyalty, sober piety. The family worshipped in St. Paul's, York Place, and Lord Medwyn had much to do with the practical affairs of the Church. He administered the Scottish Episcopal Fund which helped the poorer charges. On the spiritual side he was of the old reticent but unswerving devotion. When his sons were about to be confirmed he wrote them a letter of counsel about regular Communion:

'Times will come when all pleasure and warmth in prayer will be completely gone, and you will be apt to fancy that all your religion is going. It is not enough to trust in earnest prayer, but good religious habits will be to you like what a steady favourable tide would be to a ship which lies like a log when a breeze ceases. Therefore look upon regular attendance at Holy Communion as the most important of all religious habits. For surely there, more than anywhere else, we have Our Saviour beside us. . . . Do not trust your feelings . . . make and keep fixed religious habits, especially that of regular attendance at Holy Communion.'

Alexander went to school at the recently founded Edinburgh

Academy where a future Archbishop, Archibald Tait, was a fellow-pupil: he left at the age of fifteen to be coached by a tutor for the service of the East India Company. After a term at Glasgow University he went to the Company's College at Haileybury. He was a brilliant student in every class, including Sanskrit and Arabic. In 1836 he sailed for India, posted to the Madras Presidency, but his career was broken by illness. In 1840 he was sent home on a two years' furlough which was far from an idle convalescence. That autumn he went up to Oxford, to Brasenose, with a scholarship in Sanskrit: he was the oldest and much the most mature undergraduate in college.

This was the Oxford where the spell of the Middle Ages still lingered, intensified by the Tractarian Movement; a city of dreams and enchantment, for some a city of holiness. Forbes came under the influence of Keble and Pusey who were to be life-long friends; of Newman, too, then at the height of his power, 'the Chrysostom of the English Church', preaching his golden-tongued sermons in St. Mary's.

'Men hung in rapt attention,' Forbes recalled. 'Young men from the manor houses and parsonages of the country, from the streets and squares of the city (for Oxford then was still the privileged seat of education of the upper classes) came term by term under the spell of Oxford, and in many cases owed to Oxford their immortal souls. Boys tainted by the precocious vices of the public schools were won by a real conversion to God; while those more fortunate ones who left an innocent home to enter on their University career, were kept pure and unspotted to the end.'

Some absurdities and affectations did exist along with genuine piety: they always do. Tom Brown, fresh from Dr. Arnold's Rugby, was moved to indignant amusement by 'man-millinery' as he called it, and by other tokens of spikiness. The leaders of the Movement were imitated in small things, for 'a great movement among young men could not be without its side of unreality'; but a real desire for holiness underlay all the attitudes and 'if they assembled in each other's rooms to sing the Canonical Hours in Latin, during the season of Lent, it was not a mere exhibition of religious dilettantism. It was the outcome of a real devotion' – which was shown further in regular attendance at chapel and frequent Communions at St. Mary's, in fasting and abstinence by staying away from Hall on fast days, and in almsgiving. The colleges varied in degree of devotion. Christ Church, in reaction against Dr. Arnold's Rugbyism, was distinctly Catholic, 'the centre of the Romanizing school' which included Oakley and Ward. Trinity, under Isaac Williams, was steadily Anglican.

Forbes's latent sense of vocation awoke and developed. He gave up his career with the East India Company and read for Holy Orders. Appointed deacon on Trinity Sunday 1844 by Bishop Bagot, he was given title to a small country parish, Aston Rowant, ten miles out of Oxford. The vicar was ill and the new curate was given full charge. He found himself desolate: 'bookless, friendless and guideless'. This was a period of unhappiness, mercifully brief, ending when Pusey had him appointed curate to the Reverend Thomas Chamberlain of the parish of St. Thomas the Martyr, Oxford. This included the bargees on the river, also some of the worst slums in the town, and it was work after Forbes's own heart. His new vicar was of his own sort, a Tractarian, full of missionary zeal, with a passion for souls. They held daily services, had a barge on the river made into a chapel, worked unceasingly, cheerfully and devotedly and brought many souls to God. Forbes made another friend in the young Richard Benson of Christ Church who used to come to St. Thomas's. Forbes had started the Brotherhood of the Holy Trinity and to him Benson may have owed, if not the idea, certainly much of the inspiration for the Society of St. John the Evangelist he was to found.

This too was a brief curacy. Priested in 1845 Forbes was called back to Scotland in 1846, to the charge of Stonehaven. He came to the Church of his fathers bringing treasure new and old, the poetry, the mystical devotion of those golden Oxford days, the new wisdom and practical compassion he had learned in his service of the poor.

Stonehaven kept to the old ways. The people held firmly their belief in the three-fold ministry and in Apostolic Order, in the Offering and Sacrifice of the Eucharist and the Real Presence there: they used the Scottish Liturgy, but along with this fundamental devotion went indifference to externals. The surplice was rarely worn, there were no ornaments or symbols, the ritual was of the plainest. Nothing could be further from the devout culture of the young men in Oxford with their delight in ceremonial, their meticulous care for ritualistic details. These Scots had an equal horror of Rome as of Presbyterianism: they knew where they stood and had no mind to move aside in either direction.

Their new priest was prudent and did not impose changes; rather did he pick up the living tradition of the place, listening eagerly to stories of the penal days. He wrote a novel, *The Prisoners of Craigmacaire* (the Gaelic name of Stonehaven). This was again a brief phase in his priestly career but one in which he made many friends and formed the pattern of his priestly and episcopal life. In Stonehaven he began the custom he never gave up, of giving tokens – small metal discs – to intending communicants.

Within a year he was called by Pusey to the new Tractarian church of St. Saviour's, Leeds, which was very Anglo-Catholic, very poor and very unhappy, under the ban of the Bishop and of Hook, the Vicar of Leeds Parish Church. St. Saviour's was in the van of the long and often bitter fight between Anglo-Catholics and the conservative Establishment. Three of its clergy had already seceded to Rome. Besides this ecclesiastical unhappiness Forbes encountered again the misery of the poor. There was an epidemic of cholera. Conditions could not have been more wretched, but he was in his element. He visited, he taught, he administered the Sacraments, he brought peace.

This was the last of his brief phases or flashes of experience as parish priest. Before the end of a year he was again recalled to Scotland, and this time for good in the full sense of the word. Mr. Gladstone suggested him to his brother, Sir Thomas Gladstone of Fasque, as Bishop of Brechin, on the death of Bishop Moir, who had succeeded Gleig. Alexander Forbes was duly elected and on the Feast of St. Simon and St. Jude, 1847, he was consecrated Bishop in St. Andrew's Church, Aberdeen, by Bishop – and Primus – William Skinner and Bishops Terrot and Russell. The Warden of the newly founded Glenalmond, Dr. Wordsworth, preached the sermon. At the same time another Alexander was consecrated, Alexander Ewing, as Bishop of Argyll and the Isles.

The coincidence was irresistible to Wordsworth's muse:

Two Alexanders on one fatal day
Rose to the Church's throne, and pastoral sway,
Born to spread discord o'er the tranquil land,
One ruled the Eastern, one the Western strand.
Dark ebon locks dishevelled in the wind
Betrayed in each the tempest-loving mind;
While gentle speech and meekly winning ways
Disguised their aims, and won mistaken praise.

Unhappy lot that brought me here to dwell,
And bade me try the rising storm to quell;
Attached to both, fain would I both restrain,
A midway resident – but all in vain,
War ceaseless raged. Great Sandy, King of Greece,
Between two Sandies who can keep the peace?

The muse was unhappily a true prophet. Wordsworth called it a *jeu d'esprit* but it was a caustic play of wit. Both as Warden of Glenalmond and as Bishop of St. Andrews he was 'a midway resident' between the sees of Brechin and Argyll, and perhaps midway in churchmanship between the high Catholic teaching of Forbes and the distinct Protestantism of Ewing: but he by no means tried to restrain the two opponents; indeed he set them further apart. Far from keeping the peace he stirred up strife. War was to break out on a matter of doctrine, but there may already have been a latent antagonism between the two Alexanders: in a letter to his brother, during his Oxford curacy, Forbes referred to Ewing's 'intriguing to be made Bishop'. On the day of consecration, however, all was peace; the two Alexanders received the Apostolic Succession and went their separate ways.

The Church was still poor in the number of her clergy and Forbes held, along with his Bishopric, the charge of St. Paul's, Dundee, which still lacked a church or chapel. The congregation met in a large upper room in a bank house, furnished with green-baize-covered pews and an altar draped in red velvet. On 'Communion Sundays' the rail was hung with white linen; the Eucharist was not yet celebrated every Sunday. The pulpit and prayer-desk were as prominent as the altar, which would no doubt have horrified some of the Oxford young men. The congregation, numbering about three hundred communicants, ranged from the county gentry to the very poor, through the middle class which was increasing in numbers and variety. The Bishop visited all of them. By birth and breeding he was of the gentry and had many loyal and helpful friends among them, but he gave his heart to God's poor, of whom there were plenty. It was a grim and ugly poverty in Dundee. There was work enough in the jute mills, the ship-building yards, the engineering works, but wages were low and so was the price of whisky. The slums were appalling; in the tall blocks or lands whole families lived in one room, foul and bug-ridden, thick with stench, devoid of sanitation. The only escape was in the pub.

The Bishop entered every house. He became known simply as The Bishop and he was truly a Father-in-God. He visited non-Episcopalians as well as his own flock, making no attempt at proselytizing. An account of his work, written by one of his curates, George Grub, in 1871, is valid for any period of his episcopate and ministry, for he began as he continued and ended, the servant of the servants of God and of many who could hardly be said to serve Him.

'The short year of my diaconate was spent as near to the better world as is possible to mortal man': so George Grub recalled, with thankfulness, his time spent in surroundings which, to most observers, would seem nearer hell than heaven. One of the worst districts was known, with that irony which occurs in slum chronicles, as Paradise. Yet even there life was lived well and in the spirit of Christ. Some of the most faithful were found among the very poor. One cripple used to come to his Communion regularly on his crutches. Dundee, crowded, squalid, impoverished became to young Grub 'a city of wonderland and delight' almost as much as Oxford of the dreams and spires had been to Forbes himself.

The Bishop was Evangelical as well as Catholic: the two streams of devotion, too often separated, flowed together into the river of his faith and charity. Many stories are told of his goodness. One man of letters, fallen into wretchedness, recalled: 'His teaching has soothed my troubled soul . . . I hope his many prayers for me will be answered. His wine and his gold have been free to me. Many a bottle of port has he brought me in those big pockets of his.' Forbes came to this man to pray for his departing soul. He came to another in spiritual agony, prayed with him, taught, and saved him.

'The Bishop was the light and centre of all the mission work in the town.' He trained his curates well. One practical bit of advice he gave them was to eat a ginger biscuit before visiting fever patients: otherwise neither he nor they took any precautions and they came to no harm. He won respect for all the clergy. Young Grub recalled a visit to a dying man in one of the worst slums: the next room was full of rough types, but when he went in every head was bared and when he left one of the men lit him carefully down the broken stairs.

Forbes 'was equally at home with the highest and the lowest. He could lift rich and poor alike into the presence of their all-merciful Father and loving Saviour, and fill them with the comfort of the Holy Spirit', for he saw them all as children of God.

He was the first of the great social missionaries in the Scottish Church. The older Bishops had known and shared poverty among the fisher-folk and country people, but here in Dundee was a poverty degrading and dreadful.

'Poverty is one thing, pauperism is another,' Forbes himself wrote. 'Poverty is the momentary or even the permanent deprivation of the enjoyment of means; it is the state in which man is condemned to work for the necessaries of life; but pauperism is a chronic, normal, even fatal state of misery which hands over a notable portion of living humanity to moral degradation and physical suffering, while a small and privileged class live in the most unexampled luxury. And here is the awful fact that pauperism is measured by the advance of industry, and progress in wealth goes on side by side with progress in misery.'

Like Disraeli he was aware of the two nations in this island with a dreadful gulf between them. He saw the inordinate growth of industrialism, the separation between masters and men, the division and specialization in labour which made men more and more like machines.

This missionary zeal never overwhelmed his other gifts; he was still the scholar and theologian, 'the man of the world and the saint' in his curate's tribute. The balance and wholeness of his personality impressed many observers, including Matthew Arnold who noted the blend of worldly wisdom with profound religion.

Dean Plumptre found that his wide scholarship was combined with humility and spirituality, adding that his appearance, dark of hair and complexion, 'gave one the impression that he might serve as representative of the best type of the Italian ecclesiastic, say, specially, of the Society of Jesus – supple, subtle, courteous, and yet with an underlying thoroughness and gentleness of character'.

Living in voluntary poverty – the episcopal 'palace' a very modest house – the Bishop raised wealth for his diocese. In 1848 he began collecting money to build a church. Sir Gilbert Scott was the architect, the style, inevitably, Victorian Gothic, but modified, lightened, quickened by the Bishop's demands. A church should be, in his words, 'a builded prayer in stone and lime, a standing creed'; and he was well pleased with St. Paul's, opened and dedicated in 1855, consecrated ten years later: the Bishop's church, it was to become the cathedral of the diocese.

His episcopal duties were comparatively light, with, at first, only eleven charges in the see, and these took about a quarter of his time during the year: but his day was long and packed with work and prayer. It began at seven with private prayer and ended, if he were not called out to the sick and dying, at eleven at night. He always said Sext and Compline as well as the canonical offices of Matins and Evensong.

Much of his money was given to the poor, with ample supplies of food and wine. In his own house there were only two full meals a day, breakfast and dinner or supper. Lunch was a mere collation of bread and cheese and beer, afternoon tea did not occur.

The Church in Scotland was now growing in numbers and prosperity, with new dangers threatening – that of living sentimentally in the past, and that of forgetting her spiritual heritage and duty.

'We are indeed a scattered remnant,' Forbes said in a sermon preached two years after his consecration, 'for our sins brought very low. Attaching ourselves to the ill-fated House of Stuart, our fathers were driven into exile and obscurity; our religion was proscribed; banishment was the reward of administering the Sacraments; bonds the crown of preaching the Word. In upper chambers and with doors closed the Church dragged on a feeble existence, and but for His promise must have perished.' Now that we were free, 'righted in the eyes of our fellow-citizens if not in the estimation of our brethren' (was this an allusion to the unhelpfulness of the English episcopate?) there came the new danger, an insidious infection of the spirit.

'Can we conceal from ourselves that with all our supernatural graces there has crept over us a lethargy, a mortal coldness eating into the very heart of our religion? Is not the Church regarded as an easy religion, very creditable to belong to, the faith of the aristocracy of the country, not making any great demands upon our comforts, our purses, our principles?' That sermon cannot have been heard, it cannot now be read with any complacency. Forbes foresaw the still familiar reproach that Episcopacy is merely the religion of the gentry.

His zeal made converts, recalled the lapsed. In the first twelve years of his Bishopric three new charges were formed, communicants increased from seventeen hundred to two thousand three hundred souls, and churches and schools were built. He founded an orphanage and an agricultural school for boys working on the farms. J. M. Neale, visiting him in 1855, was impressed not only by the dignity of the new St. Paul's church – the finest he had seen since All Saints', Margaret Street – but by its full congregation, many of them poor people.

All this time, too, Forbes found space for reading, study and writing. A good French as well as a classical scholar, he translated a number of French devotional works, wrote a treatise on the Nicene Creed, compiled a catechism for children and a *Companion to the Altar*. At the heart of all his teaching lay devotion to the Sacred Manhood – 'the foundation of all true Christian worship, though the soul, after mastering this, will rise to the thought of the Godhead'.

True belief, right worship, good living were inseparable. He deplored any failure of the sense of worship, of awe, of holiness. A sermon preached at the consecration of St. Columba's, Edinburgh, in 1848, holds the essence of his belief and teaching:

'It has pleased God to bind together holy living and right believing. . . . Wickedness shuns the austere presence of truth. . . . He does not live well who does not believe aright, and a good life and true faith are linked together in a golden bond.'

The eighteenth century had lapsed into coldness through

imperfect faith in the Divine Nature of Our Lord: the present age held imperfectly the doctrine of His Sacred Manhood and could not comprehend 'the stupendous humiliation of the Incarnation' and could not contemplate Very God as Very Man. There was a tendency to regard the Incarnation and the Passion as events past, finished, separate from the Eternal Glory.

'Be it remembered that the Manhood of Christ is the instrument of the Godhead; whatever in the mystery of man's redemption has been caused by the Holy Trinity, has been effected through God the Son in His Nature as Man.' From that Manhood came every supernatural grace, through that Manhood the Communion of Saints.

The Humanity of Our Lord directed the mind to a proper adoration; the doctrine of the ascended and glorified Christ gave a right direction to worship. We adore the Body in which He was born, lived, suffered and died, now glorious in heaven but still a Human Nature comprehensible by the mind of man. Contemplation of the Incarnate Lord must kindle a fervent love of God, lead to the communication of 'Christ in you the hope of glory', to the communication of the Divine Nature through the Sacraments.

Forbes dwelt here upon the eternal priesthood of Christ: His priestly work, begun on earth, continued in heaven through His pleading His Own Sacrifice, continued on earth through his priests:

'He it is who consecrates in their Sacraments . . . As God, receiving worship, as Man, paying it; as God granting, as man, suing; at once, in an ineffable manner, the Deity, the Priest, and the Victim.'

This sermon is of great importance not only for its spiritual value, in which it is among the treasures of the Church, but for its clearness as prelude to a later utterance, Forbes's Charge to his clergy at his synod of 1857, which led to controversy and to trial. It is indeed so clear that one finds it difficult to understand how Terrot and Wordsworth, who heard it that day in St. Columba's, should have professed themselves startled and shocked by the teaching of the Charge.

Forbes, like Keble and Pusey, taught his people the Catholic doctrine of adoration of Christ in the Eucharist – as inseparable from adoration of the Sacred Manhood. Among both clergy and laity he found this imperfectly realized. Celebrations of the Eucharist were still, in the 1850's, infrequent; it was to emphasize the doctrine, to stimulate the devotion, to bring about frequent and regular Celebrations that he delivered his Charge, the first he had given since his consecration:

'The subject is one that transcends indeed the ken of angels and of other holy beings who adore round the throne on high. . . . The highest intellects have confessed their inability to understand it; the passions of men have been excited in its defence and attack; the axe and faggot of the finisher of the law, aided by the vindictive and bloody legislature of past ages have been used to enforce the fleeting opinions of the day concerning it; and that which was intended to be the symbol of the love of those who are one in Christ, has been the cause of the bloodiest wars and the bitterest dissensions that have ever polluted the earth.'

At the heart of this tragic controversy lay always the question of Christ's Presence in His Sacrament:

'Is He Himself, according to His own Word, truly present in the Holy Sacrament . . . or has He used a form of speech eminently calculated to deceive men, and are all these blessed words indicating union with Him mere figures of language, oriental expressions of exaggerated value to imply that effect upon our souls which a living faith in Him proclaims? Is the Sacrament of the Lord's Supper the partaking of the Living Christ or merely the memorial of the Dead?'

While rejecting the doctrine of transubstantiation, Forbes repudiated also the Protestant denial of the Real Presence, the Protestant assertion of these being 'only a memorial, not a mystery'. There were traces of such a doctrine in The Thirty-Nine Articles, which reflected the conflict at their drafting, but the Articles were never intended to be the sole or ultimate rule of faith: 'They are rather statements about truths than the truths themselves,' binding upon those who took office in the Church but not, in the strict sense, articles of faith. To ascertain the faith of the Anglican Church one must consult all the documents: Holy Scripture, the decrees of the first four Councils, the Catechism, the Liturgy: '*Lex supplicandi est lex credendi.*'

He deprecated the theory of development then so much in favour. Christianity was a revelation, not a progressive science, although its doctrines might, from time to time, be more clearly stated against heresies, and be renewed in warmth and life by the meditations of saints and mystics. The faith was there, once for all delivered to the saints. It was the function of the teaching Church to use all the resources of her heritage: no doctrine founded on one source alone, excluding the others, was binding on the faithful.

The Catechism was explicit that 'the Body and Blood of Christ are verily and indeed taken and received by the faithful'. The Liturgy expressed this belief, in prayer and exhortation and rubric. The teaching of Scripture was plain, that of the Fathers concordant. These made up a strong defence; but the Real Presence could not be apprehended only by intellectual argument:

'If there be one doctrine more than another that touches the heart and subdues the intellect and influences the will, it is that blessed one, that the Eternal Son of God, not content with taking upon Himself our nature in the Mystery of the Incarnation, has, by an extension of the same, found a way to communicate Himself to us. . . . What a tender delight, mixed with reverence and holy fear, does this truth infuse into Christian hearts.'

The Divine Sacrifice was for all time and all people:

'The objective Atonement made for us by the Life and Death of our dear Redeemer is here made subjective; all He did and suffered for the human race is here made over and sealed to us by an everlasting Sacrament. . . . We are in Christ and Christ in us.'

In Forbes the Catholic and the Evangelical devotion were perfectly fused. His rejection of transubstantiation was in line with Anglican teaching that this doctrine 'destroyeth the nature of a Sacrament' which has both an earthly and a heavenly part: whereas by transubstantiation the earthly part might seem to be banished. And he had the Anglican caution, the dislike of exact, intellectual definition:

'*Alii disputent; ego mirabor.*'

The mystery was so profound, so holy, it could not be expressed in words; it could not worthily be disputed. This repudiation was clear, yet such is the blindness of prejudice and antagonism that his adversaries accused him of teaching Roman doctrine.

Touching that precious tradition of the Scottish Church, belief in a Presence of grace and power, Forbes said:

'I would speak here with great reserve and tenderness' – and one can almost catch the hesitancy of voice, the tension in his hearers; but he spoke with decision. This doctrine was insufficient. The effect could not be greater than the cause. How could 'that which is not the Body of Christ produce the effect of the Body of Christ'. The theory was more difficult than the mystery; this teaching fell short of that of the Scriptures, of the Fathers, of the great Anglican divines of the seventeenth century, of the Liturgy.

'God ever does things in the simplest manner, and surely it is easier to believe, and more in accordance with His Truth that He should make that to be His Body which is to do the work of His Body, than that which is not His Body should produce the effect of His Body.'

Immensely far from any receptionist theory or from laying any stress upon pious emotion, Forbes recognized a subjective aware-ness, deeper than emotion, which was a direct and individual response to Christ in the Sacrament:

'You yourselves, my brethren, must have felt how that Divine Presence of which at times of Communion you were aware, was not only that of an influence but of a Person. . . . We, in spite of our manifold sins and infinite negligences, feel that it is no mere grace or effluence or energy that is received, but Christ the Im-mortal King, King of kings and Lord of lords, the holy, innocent, undefiled High Priest . . . the Redeemer Who has bought us with His own most precious Blood . . . the true Bread from heaven . . . How deep and incommunicable are the thoughts which this Mystery of Divine Love and Condescension suggests to the Christian soul.'

He came then to the problem of reception by the unworthy. Did they receive the Very Body and Blood of Christ? In truth they must, for the Sacrament was valid, unalterable, objective. Christ's Presence did not depend upon the worthiness or pre-paredness of the communicant.

'The Sacrament is what it is by the power of the Institution of Christ.' His Presence, His Life, were there, for the unworthy as well as for the good, but 'there can be no beneficial reception to those in a state of sin'. The Sacrament was not a charm or an act of magic. The wicked could not exclude Christ. He came, but He might come 'not to bless, but to judge. The wicked not only do not receive grace, but do receive judgement' and it were better for them that they did not approach this Holy Rite. This was a dark and terrible aspect of the Mystery, beyond our comprehension: 'It is enough to believe that in some sense the wicked do receive Christ to their condemnation and loss, for thus and thus only can they become guilty of the Body and Blood of Christ.'

From belief in the Presence must follow adoration: 'the prostration of the soul and spirit before the awful majesty of God . . . the incommunicable *latreia* due to the Very and Eternal God.' It must be the supreme adoration of the supreme Reality of God:

'If the Blessed Sacrament be really what we believe it to be; if the Body and Blood of Christ are verily and indeed taken and received by the faithful, that Body and that Blood, in supernatural mode, must be there really to be so taken. And if the Body and the Blood be there really (in as much as the Humanity of Our Lord, hypostatically united to the Divinity, is itself an object of worship) it follows that supreme adoration is due to the Body and Blood of Christ mysteriously present in the gifts which yet retain their own substance. The worship is due not to the gifts but to Christ in the gifts. How any belief in the Divine Gift in the Holy Eucharist can exist without this prostration of the soul and spirit, I am at a loss to conceive. . . . Either Christ is present or He is not. If He is, then He ought to be adored; if He is not, *cadit quaestio.*'

Forbes made much of the Sacrifice in the Eucharist. The Church had always taught that Our Lord's Sacrifice began at His Conception, continued through His Holy Life to His Passion and Death, 'consummated and slain upon the Altar of His Cross and now carried by Himself, as the Melchizedekean Priest within the veil, and perpetually pleaded and presented by Him there to the Eternal Father, and, in image, by the Church on earth in the Holy Sacrament. Christ *is*, not *was* the propitiation for our sins.'

There was one continuing Sacrifice, Act and Mystery; there was one Christ; Christ on the Cross, Christ in Glory, Christ in the Sacrament of the Altar.

'If, then, the Body of Christ, naturally in heaven, still pleads for us, and the same Body be, supralocally and mystically yet verily and indeed taken and received by the faithful at the Lord's Supper, if to be thus taken and received it must of necessity be present, then it will follow that, as is the Divine Gift, so is its faculty of impetration, and in proportion to the vividness of our belief in the Eucharistic Presence will be the firmness of our conviction regarding the Eucharistic Sacrifice.'

Our Lord, present in the Sacrament, must plead for us. 'If the Divine Gift be there It must act according to its own law. If there be an Objective Presence in the Sacrament, in contradistinction to a subjective Presence in the receiver, that Presence must effect its end.' Presence, Sacrifice and Pleading were inextricably one.

There was no repetition of the One Sacrifice on Calvary; there was a representation, an intercourse:

'As a natural and logical consequence of the Incarnation, there has taken place a *Commercium* between heaven and earth. The things of time are merged in those of eternity. The worship has blended in one united act. . . . Man now adores and is adored in heaven, for there the Son of Man is both God and Priest and Victim, and God now pleads on earth in the person of His ambassadors whose acts are as though Christ did beseech by them. The Cross of Calvary casts its blessed shadow across the floor of the Church below. The Sacraments belong not to time but are above it. There is no past nor future to the Supreme God, and it is God the Son who in the Christian dispensation is the Prime Agent in the Sacrament.'

Like Henry Scougal nearly two centuries before, Forbes swept his hearers up into his vision of the heavenly intercourse:

'The nature of man is now introduced into the deepest recesses of the heavenly choir in the Person of Jesus, both God and Man, while on earth every prayer is only accepted through Him; every thanksgiving only received in union with that thanksgiving which He is ever offering in His Humanity; and every praise in conjunction with that high and eternal laud which is made by all the saints and angels on high, and by the Eternal High Priest. . . . The same Lamb of God whom the rapt Apostle in Patmos saw in heaven "as it had been slain" is now mystically offered in the Church below . . . By virtue of the operation of the Holy Ghost our mystic sacrifice is now the Body and Blood of Him who offereth it. . . . In a Sacrament is the Lord's death shown forth in representation. "The very image" has taken the place of the "shadow". Full and sufficient is the marvel; for though it is given only to the eye of faith therein to discern the Lord's Body and to love It, yet is that Body "verily and indeed taken and received", and everlastingly under this image shown forth to the Father.'

The sequel to the Charge was a controversy which almost rent the Church. The attack was led by the Bishop of Glasgow, Walter John Trower, who had succeeded Michael Russell in 1848, and by Charles Wordsworth, now Bishop of St. Andrews: when the former retired, Wordsworth maintained the strife. The other Bishops acquiesced. Forbes told Gladstone:

'Wordsworth dominates over all the Bishops and gets them to do what he wills.' Even so, their somewhat passive acquiescence might have turned to tolerance had it not been stirred into activity by the wind of lay opinion. The laity almost at once joined in with loud and uninstructed cries of 'No Popery', and presented the College with a protest against Forbes. The Bishops then issued a Pastoral Letter, in 1858, addressed to All Faithful Members of the Church in Scotland.

They declared that Forbes's Charge forced upon them 'the painful duty of making known that we do not concur with our Right Reverend Brother in the views he has expressed'. The Charge having been published they saw 'no alternative but to declare our own dissent and to caution you against being led astray either by the teaching itself or by the undue confidence with which it is maintained'.

'Confidence' seems hardly the word to describe the humble and reverent devotion with which the Bishop of Brechin had spoken of the Sacrament. One feels the jealousy and resentment behind those brotherly comments. They would appear to have ignored what they chose in his arguments.

'He has pleaded for what has recently been called "The Real Objective Presence" in such a manner that the inference to be drawn from it, however doctrinally unsound, becomes as he represents it, logically inevitable; that is, Supreme Adoration becomes due to "Christ in the Gifts", and the Sacrifice of the Cross and the Sacrifice of the Altar become "substantially one" and "in some transcendental sense identical!"'

That he might be sound in theology as in logic they would not admit.

'Convinced as we are that neither of those conclusions is to be found in Holy Scripture or has been deduced therefrom by the Church, persuaded that the teaching of these has given rise to corruptions and superstitions, we feel it our duty to resist the attempt which has been made to press these conclusions upon your acceptance, and earnestly entreat you not to suffer yourselves to be disturbed or misguided by it.'

This may reasonably be held to come short of brotherly courtesy, let alone brotherly love.

There followed some instructions to the clergy setting forth the six Bishops' own sacramental belief:

1. 'You will continue to teach that the consecrated elements of Bread and Wine become, in a mystery, the Body and Blood of Christ, for purposes of grace to all who receive them worthily, and for condemnation to those who receive the same unworthily. But you will not, we trust, attempt to define more nearly the mode of this mysterious Presence. You will remember that as our Church has repudiated the doctrine of transubstantiation, so she has given us no authority whereby we can require it to be believed that the substance of Christ's Body and Blood, still less His entire Person as God and Man, now glorified in the Heavens, is made to exist with, in or under the material substances of Bread and Wine.'

(Their gift for ignoring what they did not choose to remember in the Charge was remarkable. Forbes had explicitly repudiated transubstantiation; he had spoken of 'the Body and Blood of Christ mysteriously present in the gifts which yet retain their own substance'.)

2. 'You will continue to teach that this Sacrifice of the Altar is to be regarded no otherwise than as the means whereby we represent, commemorate and plead, with praise and thanksgiving before God, the unspeakable merits of the precious death of Christ; and whereby He communicates and applies to our souls all the benefits of that one full and all-sufficient Sacrifice once made upon the Cross.'

(Forbes taught this very clearly.)

3. 'You will contine to teach that the Consecrated Elements, being the Communion of the Body and Blood of Christ, are to be received with lowly veneration and devout thankfulness.'

(Forbes had lifted up men's hearts.)

The reader not deeply versed in theology may well be puzzled to find any wide divergence between Forbes and his adversaries; certainly none so wide as to demand the lowering of a bridge across which they rushed to attack him.

Finally the Bishops stressed the reluctance with which they now took action against their brother after giving him opportunities 'to reconsider what he has written. But tracing, as we plainly do, in the teaching of this Charge, a tendency to undermine the great foundations upon which our Formularies rest, and to weaken our sense of gratitude and respect towards the holy men from whom we have derived them in their present state; and seeing also, on his part, an apparent determination not to surrender the position he had taken up; we have felt ourselves constrained to deal with the matter as we have now'.

And so, as controversy stamped in by the door, charity flew out of the window. How much principle and how much resentment underlay the Bishops' action may still be debated. That there was high temper with implacability on both sides is almost certain, and between Forbes and his three active protagonists there was some personal antagonism of temperament. 'I do not like thee, Dr. Fell.' For the six Bishops it may be conceded that they were pressed upon by the clamour of the laity, and that many Episcopalians were suffering from a fever of resistance to the contemporary Roman fever. Rome was in the full flush of her second spring, as Newman called it, her life enriched by many notable converts. Those who remained within the Anglican fold while holding and teaching Catholic doctrine were suspect. Scots Episcopalians in particular were aware of such suspicion on the part of their Presbyterian fellow-countrymen. They were hypersensitive in self-defence. The heat of individual Episcopal tempers was intensified by the general warmth of atmosphere.

Forbes did not take it meekly. He was wounded, especially by the accusation of going against those holy men of the past whom he revered: his own father blamed him for this. It was, however, more than a personal hurt, it was an affront to his office as Bishop and teacher. Those other Bishops had arrogated to themselves an authority to which they had no right, almost an infallibility in defining doctrine. He made a formal protest: no Episcopal Synod of the Church of England had ever attempted to define doctrine or to determine how far the teaching of individual Bishops conformed with it. The Scottish College were exceeding their powers: their proceedings were 'null, void and inept', a contravention of the canons, 'a violation of the recognized constitution and acknowledged practice of the Church'.

Keble came to his defence. Both he and Pusey had taught and preached in word and writing the same doctrine as Forbes. An edition of his book on Eucharistical Adoration appeared in 1857, the year of the Charge. Like Forbes, Keble found it illogical and impossible to withhold adoration from Christ in the Sacramental Gifts.

'All good Christians do so . . . whatever embarrassment many of them unhappily may have been taught to feel touching the precise mode of their adoration.' There was a good deal of this embarrassment, of shyness among devout Anglicans; their English reserve was profound; they feared the reproach of Romanism:

'The gift in the Holy Eucharist is Christ Himself, all good gifts in one.'

Keble too taught the Sacrifice in the Eucharist:

'If the Holy Eucharist as a Sacrifice is all one with the memorial made by our great High Priest Himself in the very sanctuary of heaven, where He is both Priest and Offering, by the perpetual presentation of His Body and Blood, then, as the blessed inhabitants of heaven cannot but be thought of as adoring Him in both His aspects of Priest and Sacrifice, so how should His Holy Church throughout all the world not adore Him in like manner? For there He is, in His Holy and Perfect Manhood, virtually present as our Priest and really present as our Sacrifice.'

Christ was the one Consecrator and all our Eucharists were a continuation of His Act at the Last Supper, 'the very image of that other and heavenly continuation of it which began on Our Lord's Ascension and will go on to the end of the world'.

Keble addressed an Open Letter to the six Scottish Bishops in reply to their Pastoral against Forbes. He found their teaching sound on the positive side, but on the negative there was much to deprecate. The Bishops seemed to doubt that Christ's 'entire Person as God and Man now glorified in the heavens' was present in the Sacrament: such a doubt was an approach to the Nestorian heresy which divided the Manhood from the Godhead. To accuse the Bishops of leading the faithful towards heresy was a deft thrust.

His reply did not, as he hoped, reconcile Forbes with his brethren: the struggle grew fiercer. Forbes told Gladstone that Trower was 'quite fanatical' against him, and that Wordsworth showed 'a bitter animosity which has almost grown into fanaticism'. Again and again the flames might have sunk to embers but there were too many folk, both lay and cleric, ready to huff and to puff and to blow them into a blaze. Dean Ramsay, a fox in sheep's clothing, persuaded nineteen other clerics to send an address to the Primus approving the Bishops' Pastoral against Forbes: a group of laymen, headed by Lord Wemyss, presented a memorial accusing Forbes of heresy. He had two fellow-victims.

One was Glenalmond's greatest teacher, William Bright, against whom Wordsworth burned with a hard flame. Dr. Bright had declared his agreement with Bishop Forbes; his own great Eucharistic hymn – 'And now, O Father, mindful of the love . . .' conveys the same doctrine.

It holds, as in a crystal, the whole Eucharistic belief and worship: the Memorial, the Sacrifice, the Presence, our pleading, intercession, self-oblation.

In a frenzy of antagonism Wordsworth procured his dismissal. Bright went to Oxford to become Professor of Divinity, much to the honour and enrichment of Oxford and the equal disgrace and impoverishment of Glenalmond and the Scottish Church.

The other victim was Patrick Cheyne, incumbent of St. John's, Aberdeen. In 1857 he preached and published a course of sermons on the Eucharist, teaching a doctrine like that of Forbes and of Keble, but expressing it in what Forbes found 'a hard and irritating manner . . . more apt to startle than to convince'. It was hinted that Cheyne published his sermons less as an act of devotion than as one of provocation. He had hoped to be elected Bishop of Aberdeen instead of Thomas Suther, and he may in any case have been addicted to trailing his coat.

He defined the Real Presence as 'the whole Christ, God and Man, truly and substantially present under the form of bread and wine. The Sacrifice in the Eucharist is substantially the same as the Sacrifice of the Cross because the Priest is the same in both and the Victim is the same in both. . . . What we offer is the Body and Blood of Christ under the form of bread and wine. That is the substance of the Sacrifice'.

The offending words were 'substance' and 'substantially': words comprehended by few but a scandal to many, and they stimulated anti-Roman fever in many Episcopalians. Three of Cheyne's fellow priests indicted him, and Bishop Suther gave judgement: he absolved Cheyne from the charge of teaching the Roman doctrine of transubstantiation but he deposed him from office. In this the Bishop was upheld by the College. For a time Cheyne continued to function as a deacon, but as he still taught the offending doctrine – or the doctrine in offending words – he came under further suspension. In the end, after he had offered explanation, apology and submission, he was reconciled and reinstated.

His turbulence had poured oil on troubled flames and Forbes was now presented (accused or indicted) to the Episcopal Synod or College by one of his own clergy, Henderson of Arbroath. Again there is a hint of rancour; Henderson had been proposed for the Bishopric in opposition to Forbes. Forbes's own brother George, a priest in the diocese of St. Andrews, urged him to withdraw his published Charge, and Gladstone begged him to consider his views more fully. This Forbes did in a statement which clearly rejected transubstantiation and conveyed his regret that any faulty expression should have caused misunderstanding of his opinions. The Primus, Terrot of Edinburgh, tried to reconcile the adversaries, but he failed. In February 1860 the Bishop of Brechin was formally summoned to trial by his fellow-Bishops in the Freemasons' Hall, Edinburgh.

Keble came up from his parish in Hampshire.

'It is a great thing to have written *The Christian Year*,' declared a sympathizer. 'It is almost greater to have come down at this season to stand by his friend.'

Early on the morning of the trial Forbes, Keble and two other friends, one of them being his Counsel, Professor Grub, went to the chapel of the House of Mercy in Lauriston Lane:

'There we celebrated the Divine Mysteries, and received that Lord for whose honour we were at that moment in unhappy antagonism with the other Bishops of the Church.'

Forbes read his own defence, a hundred pages already lodged

with the Synod. He accused his accuser of wilful misrepresenta-
tion. Henderson, whose indictment was 'a poor hash of Protestant
commonplace' had so much difficulty in proving his case that he
had to warn the Synod against taking into account the high
character and devotion of the accused. The case was adjourned
until March. At this second and final session Wordsworth spoke
for three hours, which might be held punishment enough for a
heretic, let alone a guiltless defendant. Forbes repeated his belief
in 'the real, supernatural Presence of the Body and Blood of
Christ, yea of Christ Himself, my Lord and my God, in that Holy
Sacrament. This I believe, that the Church in which God has
placed me, first as a member of Christ and of His Holy Catholic
Church, and since, unworthy as I am, as a Bishop, believes and
teaches. This chief scene of union with Himself, my Saviour and
my God, is, I believe, one chief portion of her inheritance. Him
I hope in my last hour thus to receive. This belief, if I were to
cease to confess – may my tongue cleave to the roof of my
mouth. . . . *Credidi, propter quod locutus sum*'.

He pointed out that he had asked only for toleration of his
views, not for the right to impose them.

The verdict now given, by its very mildness, brought out the
fatuity of the proceedings against him. It was no more than 'a
declaration of censure and admonition'. A mouse from a mountain, but the upheaval had done a deal of harm!

On the lighter side it is recorded that Keble spent the evening
after the first trial, not in discussion with his friends but in playing
with the children of his host. And Professor Grub celebrated with
a parody of the song *Bonny Dundee*:

> 'The Primus, douce man, said just "E'en let him be,
> For the Synod's weel rid o' that deil o' Dundee."'

Forbes wrote to his own people:
'As to the dilated Charge I had, in a great degree, the reunion
of Christendom in my mind when I wrote it. . . . I believed that I
was stating things in a way that might tone down the acerbities
of polemics, and induce men to look upon the most mysterious
and blessed doctrine of the Holy Eucharist in a devotional and
uncontroversial way.'

Shocked though he was by the strife and wounded by the

censure of his brethren, he could yet reflect that good might come out of this ill: 'A truth suffers more from being neglected than from being controverted.' The result might be 'a higher standard of faith in these supernatural verities'.

The wound went deep for all that. His own people brought the healing balm of love and loyalty. Messages of sympathy came in profusion, one of the most valued coming from over five thousand workers in Dundee, of every denomination.

'Of all classes of the community I specially honour the working man,' the Bishop had said. 'I believe there is a special benediction upon the condition of the working classes, since it was in that lot of life that our Blessed Lord condescended to be born.'

The wound was assuaged but not yet healed, and salt was rubbed in freely by more than one hand. There was an imperfect sense of honour among his opponents. The Bishops let it be understood that he had repudiated some of his first statements, not merely repeated his original repudiations. Dr. Bright urged him to deny this publicly but Forbes kept silence. Then Dean Ramsay spread a rumour, in malice or in silliness or in sheer love of gossip, that the conclusion of the trial had been pre-arranged between Wordsworth, Keble, Pusey and Forbes himself. At this Forbes spoke out. Ramsay apologized and withdrew his story, but it had already circulated.

And what good came of it at last? Was it nothing but a wanton tearing of the seamless robe of Christ, a wounding of His Sacred Heart? Or was it, as Forbes could see, a trial which would strengthen faith and devotion? The Church today is perhaps richer in Eucharistic worship because of that approach to martyrdom of her great Bishop; but he, Keble, Pusey, and Bright himself may well have uttered that prayer in Bright's hymn:

'And so we come. O draw us to Thy Feet,
  Most patient Saviour, Who canst love us still',

and teach us to love others who are unlovable.

In some men the wound would have festered and led to Roman fever which Pusey dreaded for Forbes.

'He has fled headlong to Rome,' he lamented when the Bishop failed to arrive on a visit to him at Christ Church. Forbes presently appeared; it was only that the train was late.

Oxford was a spiritual refuge and so, even more, was Hursley, Keble's country parish. Forbes went there for peace and comfort 'in the midst of the strife of tongues', and recalled that and many other visits with affection:

'Gradually as you approach the vicarage, cottages and houses of well-to-do persons line the road; and at last a gate on the right-hand side leads you into the shrubberies of the trellised and flower-vested residence of my dear friend' – a gem of Victoriana. There, Keble continued his scholarly life with his wonderful power of concentration and withdrawal.

'He had a great knack of writing important letters or carrying on his literary work in the sitting-room with Mrs. Keble and any guest that was with him. . . . It was quite wonderful how men in high position wrote asking advice from that tiny parsonage.'

Mrs. Keble, delicate and refined almost beyond all earthliness, used to go about her housekeeping with a French or Italian book in her hand. Keble held a Bible Class every Sunday in his study:

'Quite a sight – that beautiful and refined soul cheerfully lowering itself to the wits of the Hampshire peasantry', a slightly jarring note, unexpected in one who was so devoted a Father-in-God to his poor folk: he admired in Keble what he took for granted in himself.

At Hursley Forbes met Charlotte Yonge whose 'charming fictions were, in an indirect sense, greatly influenced by Mr. Keble's words and works', but not only in an indirect sense. She submitted her manuscripts to his and his wife's criticism. Her novels reflect the Oxford Movement in its influence upon English gentlefolk; they distil its essence which they conveyed to a wider public than were influenced by tracts or sermons. These 'charming fictions' are so vivid that it is the lasting sorrow of Scots Episcopalians that our Church produced no such novelist, and that Charlotte herself did not come to Scotland or take up the story of the Scottish Church.

Keble's vicarage used to be filled with boys from Winchester as well as by older guests. The young Moberlys, the Headmaster's large family, came there frequently. Forbes recalled a Harvest Thanksgiving at Hursley, a service still unknown in Scotland, which impressed him by its symbolism and fitness in that rural parish. The church was decked with flowers and corn, two great sheaves lying before the altar. Afterwards came a feast 'with much mirth and rural sport'.

When Keble died in 1866 Forbes wrote:

'The work for which he lived – the spread of Catholic truth, the adornment of the sanctuary with the spirit of beauty, the consecration of all that is lovely at the foot of God's altar, the reunion of Christendom and the moral and dogmatic restoration of the Church of England – lives on and prospers.'

The Church in Scotland was sailing into wider and somewhat calmer waters. In 1864 she was granted her final freedom with the removal of the last disability; her priests could now hold a charge in England. She began to look and to move beyond Scotland. In 1866 the Primus, Eden of Moray (who sounds like the hero of a ballad) went to Russia on a mission to the English colony in St. Petersburg. It meant a renewal of friendship with the Orthodox Church. He took with him as a gift a translation into Greek of the Scottish Liturgy. Forbes warmly approved this visit as 'a stretching forth from our narrow and insular position to a wider field of thought and a longer range of interests'. He himself was reaching out to Latin Europe and the separated Roman brethren, through his kinsman, Count Charles Forbes Montalembert, whose mother was a Forbes, the devout and liberal Catholic; and through Dr. Döllinger who was moving so close to his Anglican brethren and who understood the Anglican position; through many of the French clergy, too, who held Gallican views, and through the Benedictines of Monte Cassino.

In 1866 he visited the monastery and wrote an account of his impressions. In the town itself there sat, at doors and windows, 'gorgeous brown women twirling their distaffs, looking like nature's nobility'. Children, ragged but happy and beautiful, played in the streets, and little black pigs 'called *con rispetta, la bestia vera* (it is not possible to speak more definitely) are tethered in the sunshine to the walls of the houses, and seem to enjoy themselves'. The pilgrims rode on donkeys up to the abbey:

'On the left is an orchard-garden with a little fourteenth-century chapel. Above is the blue sky; beneath, the valley lies hushed in tranquil beauty.'

They were welcomed by one of the monks, Padre Tosti, to whom Forbes had a letter of introduction, and by him were presented to the Abbot. Forbes was impressed by the sense of tradition and continuity; the habit was a form of the peasants' dress in the time of St. Benedict and was altogether a continuance and transformation of the old Roman way of life. The visitors saw the library and printing press, attended the Offices in chapel, dined in the refectory. It was like dinner in hall at Oxford except that, as it happened to be a fast day, there was no meat. After dinner came recreation in the Abbot's room, with plenty of good talk and wine, and then the siesta. Forbes was presented with a copy of the Abbey Press's fine edition of Dante, produced for the sixth centenary. It was Eastertide and on Low Sunday the peasants came to Mass in the church, the women kneeling devoutly and telling their beads; 'some very beautiful, after the beauty of those pure races'.

The monks had a school for boys, a semi-novitiate in which the boys wore a habit. Learning and holiness flourished together. Forbes was convinced 'not only that here the Church of Rome exhibited herself in one of her most attractive and dignified manifestations, but that there is probably a mighty future in store for Monte Cassino . . . suiting itself to the progress of the world, and throwing itself heartily into the development of the human spirit, yet retaining the simple, undoubting faith of the days of its founder'. Forbes was aware of the need for *aggiornamento*. He repaid the courtesy of Monte Cassino by rousing the interest and sympathy of Gladstone and of Lord Clarendon, who had influence enough to prevent the secularization of the Abbey at the crisis of the unification of Italy.

The call of the cloister was not momentary. The religious life for men, newly revived in the Church of England by his old friend, Richard Meux Benson, attracted the Bishop. Lord Halifax recalled the beginnings of The Society of St. John (or Cowley as it was and is familiarly called), 'with which George Fox, Father Benson, the Bishop of Brechin (Dr. Forbes), Father Grafton (afterwards Bishop of Fond-du-Lac), Father O'Neill, who died as a missionary in India, were connected'.

George Lane Fox had, like Forbes, visited Monte Cassino; he and Halifax (then Charles Lindley Wood) had become acquainted with the Bishop; and he and they attended a meeting in the rooms of the Reverend Reginald Tuke, curate of St. Mary's, Soho. The idea and ideal of a religious community for men, both clergy and laity, were discussed. Benson and Grafton were strongly and positively decided in favour of such a community. 'The Bishop of Brechin seemed to share their wishes, but was doubtful how far his circumstances would prevent their realization.'

The society was begun with three members, Benson, Grafton and O'Neill: of these, Father Grafton came from and returned to the Church in America. That small meeting in the Soho rooms brought together three strands of Episcopacy: the Church of England, the Church in Scotland, the Church in America. Circumstances – his duties as Bishop, his ill-health among them – proved too difficult for Forbes; he did not fulfil his strong desire to enter the Community though in heart and mind he was so truly religious in the strict sense of the word. Perhaps some fulfilment came when, in 1871, he brought a Sisterhood to Scotland.

This began very quietly in Dundee where a small group of ladies working among the poor lived together in one house. In 1870 the house was presented to the Bishop's church, St. Paul's, by one benefactress, while another presented a chapel; Forbes laid the foundation stone, and a year later consecrated the chapel and installed a Mother Superior, with nine Sisters in her community, which was dedicated to St. Mary and St. Modwenna. He gave them their rule.

In his last ten years he paid many visits to France and Italy, spending one winter in Florence in the ample manner of the Victorians abroad. It seems, today, an incredible amplitude of leisure, but his ill-health was the main reason. And his was a very full leisure. Having made a special study of the Roman position he wrote an Explanation of the Thirty-Nine Articles with a dedication to Pusey in which he set forth his intention of aiding reunion. He saw the Anglican Church as one that could reach out to the Protestant bodies on one side, to the Roman and Orthodox on the other – and on that side his instinctive sympathies lay. In his explanation he minimized the differences, to return to the essential.

'The basis of reunion must be on that which is ruled *de fide*, and of this nothing is to be assumed as such but the contrary of what is published under anathema.'

Dr. Döllinger pronounced this book 'the best and certainly the most Catholic commentary on the Articles.' In France it was approved by Archbishop Darboy, among others, and Forbes was given letters of introduction to prelates in Rome. There, however, his ardour was chilled. The frigid attitude of the ultramontanes disillusioned him, and the First Vatican Council, under Pius IX, ended all hope of reunion with Rome. His own sympathy, at its most ardent, had remained unfevered. He gave sound advice to a young cleric in Dundee, the incumbent of St. Mary Magdalene's, who had caught the fever badly. Admitting the Anglican difficulties, the Bishop pointed out that they were nothing compared with the Roman; the convert would have to choose between the Gallican position in which he would keep his reason but come under persecution, and the ultramontane, 'Manning's party', in which he might come into favour but would have to give up his reason. Forbes quoted approvingly Döllinger's division of converts into three classes:

1. The intellectual like Newman, aware of latent infidelity in themselves, who chose 'to place themselves under lock and key'.

2. The materialistic ritualists who loved form, ceremonial and vestments.

3. Those who were 'concupiscible rather than irascible', who wanted the luxuries of Rome for which they would have to fight in the Church of England and who wanted 'the spoils of victory without the conflict'.

The young man listened and wavered, but he was impatient, arrogant and intolerant. His congregation aggravated his fever by an element of Orange Protestantism: he, in return, thrust his new practices upon them, failed to distinguish between ritual and religion, became a burden to his Bishop and almost started a schism in the congregation. Finally he resigned and departed to London, to seek counsel from Manning who bade him forget all he had ever learned and be taught anew, like a child. Duly received into the Roman Church he wrote an account of his conversion, vituperating the Church of his former allegiance: *quod saepe* if not *quod semper*. He had, however, the grace to respect Forbes.

In Forbes, intellectual integrity and respect for that virtue in others was fundamental. He deplored the Decree of Papal Infallibility as 'the aggression of the See of Rome into the jurisdiction of the Bishops. The Bishops have ceased to be judges of doctrine, and are now the Pope's curates or vicars'. For him it was essential to a Bishop to guard and teach true doctrine.

Father Benson recalled this defence of the intellect when, many years later, he wrote to a Religious about the claims of the contemplative life. He himself chose and advocated the mixed life, active and contemplative in his community. The contemplative alone had its dangers.

'I would have the contemplative side of the mixed life developed as strongly as possible. I am afraid that in what is called the contemplative life contemplation is very apt to be minimized instead of being promoted. . . . I fear it rather tends to intellectual stagnation than to the spiritualizing of the intellect. This was also Bishop Forbes's feeling.'

The Bishop never felt acrimony against Rome, either before or after the sundering Council. He urged his clergy to pray for those separated brethren. 'A family is not less a family because the members are not on speaking terms with each other.' They could all be on speaking terms with God.

This, 1871, was the year of young George Grub's curacy in Dundee which he found so close to Paradise, when he left his pen portrait of the Bishop: 'his tall, handsome figure, his long, dark, olive face, the plentiful iron-grey hair and searching eyes.' Some saw in that long, dark face a resemblance to James VII and II.

The Bishop's church, St. Paul's, had now the regular Sunday Eucharist at eight o'clock, with a second Celebration on the first Sunday of each month, and once a month the early Celebration was choral. Evensong was said on Sunday afternoon, sung in the evening, and in the afternoon there was a sermon or a catechizing. The sung Office was popular with the working people, who began their Sunday with the early Eucharist and ended it with Evensong; and many Presbyterians used to come, very devoutly. The Eucharist was celebrated also on Thursdays and on all Holy Days; Matins and Evensong were said daily. The Bishop used to give tokens to intending communicants and people came to him for Confession:

'They valued the absolution pronounced in Christ's Name by His priest, though the confessions were frequently of the simplest and most informal nature.' The Bishop was a great director of souls.

Dundee was part of the new industrial Scotland, with new needs and demands which the Church was meeting and fulfilling, but in many of the country places the old ways remained; time might have stood still. Young Grub went, once, to take the services in Lochlee during a vacancy. The congregation was chiefly of farmers and crofters; the choir, under a precentor, sat in the gallery; they sang the Tate and Brady metrical psalms, the congregation joining in heartily. It was a bare little church: altar, pulpit and reading desk were all set within the chancel.

'It was delightful to worship in this simple way with those representatives of the old days when the Episcopal Church still retained members of the gentry, farmers, fishermen and others who clung to the ancient ministry they loved.'

The phrase is worth noting: it was to this ministry, not to ritual, not even to one Liturgy, that the Suffering Remnant had above all been faithful. There was still a likeness to Presbyterian ways; the managers of the congregation were called elders and they signed the deed of presentation to the new Rector, William Presslie, who was instituted that year. The *Directory* or *Year Book* for 1878 describes this church as Grub saw it:

'A very plain, oblong structure with gallery at west end, built in 1810; three rows of pews separated by two passages, a portion of the east end railed off for chancel.'

By 1878 the congregation had acquired a harmonium and were saying the Psalms and singing *Hymns Ancient and Modern*. There were then ninety-five members, of whom sixty were communicants.

'I have always been glad to have been so near the days of persecution,' Grub reflected, 'when what people really cared about was to have a priest of their old faith to administer the Sacraments and preach the Word of God. The outward vestment mattered little while jealous eyes were watching to see that no priest of our Faith ministered to more than six persons at once in the same place.'

He himself wore the surplice that day, the first to be worn in that church. He was told by the priest of Brechin, James Crabb, who came to celebrate the Eucharist that before the last Celebration he had heard, in face of the congregation, the public confession of a man who had been guilty of mortal sin, and had given public absolution and restored the penitent to full communion.

The Bishop continued his life of devotion, scholarship and service, living as regularly and austerely as he would have lived in the Society of St. John the Evangelist. He gave lavishly to the poor, and he obeyed the apostolic injunction to be hospitable. There is a pleasant tale of his asking a guest what he would drink: the guest chose whisky and the Bishop sent his man to fetch it. The man was some time in bringing the bottle. 'Where did you find it?' asked the Bishop. 'In your lordship's bedroom.'

In 1872 the diocese celebrated his semi-jubilee as Bishop by giving him a pastoral staff. In his reply he said: 'The clergy don't make up the church. The laity are just as much part of the Catholic Church as the clergy are'; and he thought that temporal affairs were best left to them. He spoke of the 'magnificent future' of the Church in Scotland. The last echo of the old song of loyalty had died away. 'The beautiful old Jacobite flavour had vanished,' but there was a new valour, a new spirit, a new loyalty. The Church 'now wished to bring before Scotland earnestness, devotion, high sentiment, and above all, tenderness'.

Her membership was growing chiefly through the influx of professional men and of the new wealthy merchants: the middle class in all its divisions, its scope and intricacy, was enlarging what had once been the Church chiefly of gentlefolk and of the poor. And the Church had not forgotten her mission to the poor; she had gone down to the slums. Her priesthood had increased in numbers and with that increase had come a wider mission. The Bishop saw the mission spread beyond the seas: in 1873 the Episcopal Church in Scotland founded the diocese of Kaffraria in Africa, and sent forth the first Bishop – Galloway.

Forbes continued to write and edit his scholarly books, a Saint Book or *Kalendar of Scottish Saints*, and the Lives of St. Ninian and St. Kentigern. At the Church Congress of 1874, held in Edinburgh – the first to come to Scotland – and attended by English Bishops and by the new Bishop of Kaffraria, he was chosen to be preacher, but he collapsed in illness. The end of the chapter was near.

In December of that year, John Dowden, Principal of the Theological College and Pantonian Professor of Theology, preached for him at an ordination and was afterwards present at the Christmas Eucharist in St. Paul's. In 1875 Forbes paid his last visit to Pusey. On 21st September he laid the foundation stone of the new church in Stonehaven where nearly thirty years before he had begun his Scottish ministry. This was his last public appearance. He died on 8th October, loved and mourned far beyond his diocese, more than most men of his time. In his chapel at the Birmingham Oratory Newman said Mass for his soul. A French admirer wrote of *'cet aimable, respectable, et j'oserais dire même saint prelat'*. There are those today who would gladly have him canonized.

# 8

# Those Other Bishops

## I. EDEN OF MORAY

He sounds like the hero of a ballad, this Bishop from over the border who in his day helped to make the Church known beyond the border and beyond this island. He is one of the Bishops of the expansion of Scottish Episcopacy.

Robert Eden was born in 1804, a son of Sir Frederick Eden, grand-nephew of the first Lord Auckland and cousin to that gifted woman Emily Eden who wrote *The Semi-Detached House* and *The Semi-Detached Couple* (two slightly Austenish novels), and *Up the Country*, her Letters from India. From Westminster School he went to Christ Church where he was contemporary with his future fellow Bishop, Charles Wordsworth. Eden was an athlete as well as a scholar and was an especially good jumper. To this Samuel Wilberforce, Bishop of Oxford, referred at the dedication of Eden's cathedral in Inverness: 'His power of surmounting obstacles was just that of his ability at school to jump over anything that he could reach with his nose.' The episcopal nose touched many walls and gates.

Priested in 1828, Eden held curacies in Essex and was Rector of Leigh when he was called to the Bishopric of Moray, Ross and Caithness in 1851. He had already visited Scotland, having preached at the consecration of Bishop Trower of Glasgow in 1849. For an English cleric to come to a Scottish Bishopric was no worldly gain. Eden gave up a living of five or six hundred a year for an episcopal stipend of one hundred and fifty. The Scottish Church was still poor, and this diocese rivalled Argyll in poverty. At this time there were only eight incumbencies, with only two parsonages. The new Bishop was a builder and a missionary. Three years after coming to the diocese he visited the forlorn county of Caithness and revived the Church in Wick and Thurso. During his episcopate the number of clergy rose to twenty-three, of lay members from five to thirteen hundred.

The climax of his building and extension was his cathedral, dedicated to St. Andrew in Inverness. When he came in 1851 there was only a chapel which had once been a cottage. In 1854 he brought John Comper from Nairn to begin a mission and a school in Inverness. On the first day two children appeared – 'the nucleus of the now large congregation' as the writer of the Bishop's obituary in *The Scottish Guardian* was to point out some thirty-four years later. Already he had chosen Inverness as his seat, and he began raising funds for his cathedral. By 1866 he had raised £20,000 and the foundation stone was laid by the Archbishop of Canterbury, Longley, the first public occasion on which a Primate of All England had officially recognized the sisterhood of the Scottish and the English Church. He was a friend of the Bishop whose private friendships in the episcopate did much to break down the barriers of ignorance and ignoring. *The Times* regarded the Primate's brotherly courtesy as an insult to the majority of the Scottish nation and accused him of favouring dissent. 'And it is said,' added *The Scottish Guardian* in its obituary 'that the Archbishop's action was not kindly regarded in still higher quarters than Printing House Square' – presumably in Buckingham Palace, for Queen Victoria was no friend to Scottish Episcopacy. Far from feeling insulted most of the Scottish nation, Presbyterian as well as Episcopal, was well pleased. The procession and ceremonial of that day might once have caused a riot, but only one old woman was moved to protest: 'There they gang, the whited sepulchres' as the clergy passed in their surplices.

That day was still distant, though doubtless seen in vision, when the new Bishop gave his first charge to his Synod in 1853. He paid tribute to his predecessor, David Low, to his pastoral care of the diocese and his generous endowment of the now separate diocese of Argyll and the Isles: 'The first and only Episcopal see in Scotland which has been endowed since the Revolution was endowed through the munificence of a poor Scottish Bishop.' He spoke of the problems of coming from an established to a disestablished Church, to his efforts on his election to realize the position of the Scottish Bishops and their relation with the laity. The spiritual relation was clear, being 'based upon an imperishable because a Divine principle; a relationship which visibly existed under all the varying and chequered fortunes of the

Church's warfare'. Their Episcopal gifts and powers came to the Scots as to the English Bishops through the Catholic Church. But it was difficult for an Englishman to realize the Episcopal power unsupported by the State and the civil power: the obedience of clergy and laity must depend, to some extent, upon the way the Bishop exercised his authority, the respect and affection in which he was held. Eden realized that the essence of the Episcopate lay in the Apostolic Succession and in consecration, and also that the heart of it, the emotive power, lay in the Father-in-God relationship with the flock. 'Episcopal authority sustained by love no more needs extrinsic aid for its support than does the authority of a loving father over his affectionate children.'

He urged the need for education at every level, lay and clerical; for more priests, solidly grounded in both sacred and secular learning. The value of the classical and philosophical teaching in the Scottish Universities could not make up for lack of theology. The new college at Glenalmond had begun to fill the need but there must be elementary education also, for the poor as well as the rich. There must be well-trained teachers.

Touching the problem of living with other kirks, especially with the Established Church of Scotland, Eden would not have Episcopacy's ancient heritage and endowments restored at the cost of peace. Poverty had not killed the Church. Even the law forbidding more than four persons to meet for worship had failed in effect, for the four might be three Bishops and one priest whom they could consecrate and so maintain the succession. 'Thus was the Episcopate preserved without transgressing the law,' a reflection suitable to a law-abiding Englishman.

He lived at peace with his ecclesiastical neighbours but he would not commend that easy intercourse in which some Episcopalians delighted, whereby those who, in England, would not enter a Presbyterian church did, when they came to Scotland, worship in the parish kirk. The Faithful Remnant must remain faithful and defend the truth:

'Let us demonstrate that Episcopacy is Catholic and Apostolic, and because Apostolic, Divine.'

In government and administration Eden was a pioneer and reformer. He advocated the admission of the laity to Synods. 'Our [the clergy's] present state of isolation would thus be got rid of.'

More than twenty years were to pass before his plan was fulfilled in the Representative Church Council. This, in 1876, replaced the Church Society, created by Dean Ramsay, which was no longer adequate or efficient. The reformed Council, like all reforms, aroused fierce opposition, but Eden, who was by that time Primus, calmed the storm. He was an excellent chairman, alert and business-like with a capacity for sorting out amendments and keeping order. He was courteous and urbane. 'He had a surprising power of quelling fiery spirits by a humorous remark' according to *The Scottish Guardian*; or, in the words of his biographer in the *Dictionary of National Biography*, he 'composed many heated debates by his courtly suavity and excellent knowledge of business' – an excellent assortment of episcopal virtues.

There were other stormy meetings: that of the General Synod of 1862 when the canon was passed which admitted lay electors to the election of a Bishop. It was part-fulfilment of his desire for lay representation in the Courts of the Church, and it was by his tact and patience that it was won. Again in the sorry debates over the Scottish Prayer Book he achieved a compromise: the Book might be deposed from its primacy over the English Liturgy, but it was permitted not only to those congregations who already used it but to new congregations who desired the use.

As Bishop he saw the growth of the Church in his diocese: as Primus he renewed an old friendship – that between Scottish Episcopacy and Eastern Orthodoxy. He visited Russia and in 1866 published his *Impressions of a Recent Visit to Russia*, a pamphlet on 'Intercommunion with the Eastern Orthodox Church', and later wrote a preface to Tolstoi's *Romanism in Russia*. The Eastern Church Association was formed about this time.

The cathedral begun in this wonderful year, 1866, was opened and dedicated three years later: it was consecrated at Michaelmas 1874, when the Bishop of Derry, Dr. Alexander, preached. Forbes of Brechin was present and said that this was not only the consecration of a cathedral but the consecration of the Primus's Episcopate. A Bishop's House, Edencourt, was also built in Inverness.

According to the *Dictionary of National Biography* he was better as Primus than as diocesan Bishop, yet his record of pastoral work and of building and extension was good. The *D.N.B.* also suggests that his considerable gift of humour 'somewhat scared strict spirits'. But *The Scottish Guardian* pronounced, when he died:

'There probably has never been a Bishop in recent days who was personally so popular with all grades and sections of society.'

Besides his accounts of Russia and the Orthodox Church he published many sermons, some on the Prayer Book, some in defence of Scottish Episcopacy and one against teetotalism.

Living beyond his threescore years and ten he saw many hopes fulfilled. The strength of his years became weakness before the end: ill and paralysed he was unable to attend the Seabury Centenary celebrations in 1884. In 1885 a Coadjutor Bishop, James Kelly, was consecrated, who in 1886 was elected Diocesan Bishop. The old Bishop lingered for two years more, dying in 1888.

2. CHARLES WORDSWORTH, Bishop of St. Andrews, Dunkeld and Dunblane. A Warlike Episcopate

Wordsworth, more than either of the Alexanders for whom he prophesied strife, was to spread discord over the not particularly tranquil land, and most of all in his own diocese. His rule began badly; he voted himself into the Episcopate. As Warden of Glenalmond he was one of the clergy and so one of the electors of the diocese of St. Andrews, Dunkeld and Dunblane, when Bishop Torry died. Two names were proposed; his, and that of Bishop Eden whom many of the electors wished to have translated from Moray. The other votes being equally divided between the two, Wordsworth gave the casting vote for himself, of whom he had a high opinion. The proceeding was legal if unseemly. His own account of it naturally places himself in a good light:

'The men who supported me urged that I ought not to allow them to be defeated. Caring little for the issue on my own account, I cared much for theirs. . . . I voted as they urged. The act was not, I confess, agreeable to me. It was scarcely consistent in appearance either with a nice sense of propriety or with Christian humaneness.'

He wrote to his chief supporter, Dean Torry, son of the late Bishop, that he could not support a candidate who was already a Bishop. To translate Eden 'would be iniquitous to the diocese we propose to rob, and discreditable both to ourselves and to the Bishop so translated'.

This was fair enough, and this difficulty was removed by Eden's withdrawal. His supporters then proposed Dr. Suther, the incumbent of St. George's, Edinburgh, first, however, offering to support Wordsworth if he would resign his office of Warden of Glenalmond. This he refused, maintaining that he could hold both offices without neglect of either. Again he voted for himself 'in compliance with the urgent entreaty from the more important moiety of the Presbyters'. His opponents appealed to the College of Bishops, accusing Wordsworth 'of being a party man, of having unscrupulous ambition, of having canvassed the electors, and of an act, the act of self-election, unheard-of in the Catholic Church'; also of 'want of temper, want of judgement, want of tact'. These defects were to be manifest. The Bishops, however, upheld the election and rebuked the opposition. Wordsworth had won but victory was hardly a sweet one. Two years later the General Synod ruled that no elector might vote for himself.

Charles Wordsworth was consecrated on St. Paul's Day, 25th January 1853. In his *Annals of My Life* he quotes freely from letters of congratulation, and explains the hostility as 'Prayer Book revenge' for his having attacked the Prayer Book approved by Bishop Torry and used in the cathedral.

'It cannot be denied,' his nephew and biographer, John Wordsworth, Bishop of Salisbury, wrote years afterwards, 'that he was over-eager and anxious for completeness in all he did.' So his reign began in tension, 'to be expected' as Bishop John puts it, 'in a country where the free expression of opinion on religious subjects, and a critical attitude to the opinions of others, are part of the daily atmosphere of life.'

The cathedral was the storm-centre. The Chapter, Tractarian to the point of spikiness, used the condemned Prayer Book and followed a constitution approved by Bishop Torry but not by the College. It was admittedly peculiar. Power lay with the Provost and Canons Residentiary; the Bishop was to be consulted and have the power of veto, but he had no real or active authority. The Scottish Office alone was to be used. Provost and Canons must remain celibate while members of the Cathedral College and Chapter.

The Provost, Fortescue, was a man of refinement but no great learning, ignorant of Scottish traditions, impractical and 'deficient in some of the stronger qualities of character'. He was donnish and reserved in manner, although 'when it pleased him, and in a select circle, freely to unbend, he was full of mirth'. His churchmanship was less of the old, reserved Tractarian type than of the new Anglo-Catholic way. Startling and paradoxical in talk, he was given to defending extreme views. Provost Fortescue held office until 1871 when he resigned and married: soon afterwards he made his submission to Rome, as a layman, his marriage preventing his new ordination.

His colleague Canon Humble (distinctly misnamed) was the bad boy or Bishop's Pest of the diocese. Strong in will and character, aggressive and combative, he preferred a fight to a compromise. He had been a journalist, editor of *The Durham Advertiser* and had a gift for pungent and provocative writing. John Wordsworth has described him as kind, generous, humorous and friendly – often the qualities of the defects of such a character as his – as one likely to be loved or detested, never regarded with indifference. He has many spiritual kindred and descendants.

The new Bishop naturally wished for more authority in his own cathedral, to have the Chapter subject to him in canonical obedience. The cathedral should not be an *imperium in imperio*. He proposed that the five senior presbyters of the diocese should be made prebendaries, that the Cathedral Prayer Book be given up, and that while the Scottish Office be continued in use the English Rite should also be permitted. The tension continued, complicated by a cross-schism in which some of his former supporters opposed him about these demands, and by criticism of his remaining Warden of Glenalmond. This one vexation was removed by his resignation from the Wardenship in 1854.

In that year he delivered his first charge, mainly on the theme of reunion with the Established Church of Scotland. This was to remain the dream and desire of his life. His was the first attempt, since Archbishop Leighton's in the seventeenth century, to break down the wall between the two Churches. He advocated the recognition of Presbyterian baptism as valid: here he becomes sympathetic, speaking with the voice of today. Believing firmly in Episcopacy as founded on scripture, supported by tradition, universal in Christendom whether Roman, Orthodox or Anglican and as the true centre of unity, he none the less deplored the separation and commended the faith and holiness of many of 'our separated brethren'. Was he the first to use this phrase? 'Separation is a sin' – the guilt shared by all: recognition of guilt and subsequent contrition might be God's way of bringing men to mutual charity. The best defence of Episcopacy was to present it in so fair an image that it would win Scotland.

'If the cause be of God it will prevail. . . . Hitherto they have seen little of God's mark upon it. Our weakness has lain and still lies in our own unfaithfulness.'

That was by no means just to his own side; the older generation of Episcopalians had been very faithful; but his attitude towards Presbyterians had both charity and humility, and he was to go yet further in conciliation. If he had shown his own brethren half that courtesy, tolerance and understanding the story of his episcopate would have been much more edifying. For him the principle of Establishment was almost an article of faith. He might have stated his belief in 'One Holy, Catholic, Apostolic and Established Church'. This did not commend him to those who regarded Episcopacy as the true Church, her disestablishment merely an historical accident.

Within the cathedral the battle raged on; within the diocese another battle between the Scottish and the English Prayer Books. Four congregations, of Alyth, Meigle, Muthill and Forfar petitioned for the use of the English Rite. The Bishop consented though not eagerly: for a time he favoured the Scottish Liturgy and his teaching on the Eucharist, given in his Glenalmond sermon, agrees perfectly with that of Jolly and others of the old tradition:

'We are to see the same Bread and Wine which have been offered as the symbols of the Body and Blood of Christ first consecrated into a most holy mystery by prayer and the laying on of sacred hands, and then returned to us from God by the same representative of Jesus Christ, to be to us all that the mystery portends, and all that we ourselves had signified by the Offering we had made.'

He commended the Epiklesis: of the Real Presence he had no doubt, nor of the source of sacramental grace in the Sacred

Humanity. He saw the Eucharist as the extension of the Incarnation. 'The Manhood of Christ is truly present.'

His admiration for the Scottish Liturgy was so to decrease that he had much to do, in the Synod of 1862, with the decision to depose it from its primacy of honour, and give equal rank if not precedence to the English Prayer Book.

The battle of the cathedral continued and became, in local legend, The Thirty Years War. He became increasingly anti-Tractarian as the Chapter grew in devotion to the Oxford leaders. In the heat of strife he removed his episcopal chair to St. John's Church in Perth.

It was not a tranquil or a tolerant age; party feeling was intense, the spirit of individuals was fiery. These Victorian Bishops are formidable. There was, too, a constant fear of Rome, because of the surge of conversions or submissions, and especially after the restoration of the Roman Hierarchy. There were two forms of Roman fever, a feverish hostility and an excess of admiration. The latter afflicted the cathedral clergy, the Bishop suffered intermittently from the former; and both suffered from bad temper.

John Wordsworth, whose respect for his uncle was not un-tinged by irony, says that the Bishop did not suffer from doubt, did not indulge in abstract speculation, and was little moved by the mystical and mysterious in religion: that while holding his own opinions firmly 'he did not enter very fully or easily into the views and feelings of other thinkers'. This analysis fills one with admiration for the quietly effective dagger-work of the Victorian biographer.

Wordsworth took as his motto: '*Manus ad clavem, oculus ad coelem*' and indeed he kept a firm hand on the tiller, while the eye with a steely glare glanced from heaven to earth, being especially directed at the cathedral. The historian of Episcopacy in Perth, Canon Farquhar, was to reflect: 'It has been so ordered by Providence . . . that whatever trials beset the Dissenting Church of Scotland at large, they should appear in their acutest form in Perth.' Priests were no longer imprisoned, services were not interrupted or chapels burned down; but trials and troubles continued.

The plan of a collegiate cathedral was not fully developed; the

Bishop carried out some of his reforms. He declared, in Synod, his intention of being watchful and active against anything 'which a faithful and well-informed member of the Church would be displeased to see'; a well-gloved phrase covering an iron grasp. The quarrel came to a head in 1858 when the prebendaries elected from the diocesan clergy resigned in sympathy with the Bishop and disagreement with the Provost and Canons. Within this quarrel raged that concerning Bishop Forbes. The cathedral clergy issued a statement in 1859 in his defence, with many signatories: these Wordsworth dismissed as being, many of them, those of women, boys and persons of the poorer class 'receiving alms or support from the Church'. There could be no excuse for 'inducing or allowing women and children' to express their opinions; such persons had, in effect, no right to hold opinions on such high matters.

'There is, indeed, nothing in which the Word of God is more express than in the condemnation of conduct of that kind . . . nothing more unblest, nothing which more surely excites the Divine displeasure than a spirit of bold and presumptuous irreverence on the part of the young, and I feel deeply for those young persons who have been misguided by their own persons to display such a spirit.'

This was magnificent and it was also war. The Bishop withdrew all support from the cathedral party; they must repent and submit before he would look upon them with favour. Already, on Whit Sunday 1857, he had publicly rebuked the celebrant at the early Eucharist for having celebrated with only one communicant. His feelings were acerbated by two secessions to Rome: the one of a lady in the congregation, the other of Canon Campbell. There were moments of uneasy truce, but still the Bishop had his chair at St. John's and came to St. Ninian's only for confirmations and ordinations. He had no official residence, but had taken a long lease of The Feu House in Perth where he found in his garden, some relief from controversy.

So far this has been a record of animosity which, unrelieved by mention of his pastoral zeal, would be an incomplete picture of Wordsworth. Although he favoured St. John's, he disapproved of the prevailing tone of wealth and gentility there. In the days of poverty and difficulty people had been Episcopalians first and essentially, members of a local congregation only by circumstance and convenience: they were now becoming congregational, self-conscious and often exclusive. The poor might not be forbidden to enter, but they were not welcomed. The Bishop, knowing that the church must be a place for God's poor, built the chapel of St. Andrew as a mission and transferred much of his help and favour to that congregation. The chapel was always crowded: a school was also built and it is good to find among the contributors to the funds the Bishop of Brechin. In 1868, fifteen years after his consecration, Wordsworth could report the building of twenty-one churches or chapels: there were now thirty-seven in the diocese, all but two (Blair Atholl and Kirriemur) built in the nineteenth century, and the number of clergy had increased from seventeen to twenty-nine.

Wordsworth's goodwill towards the Established Church was meeting with some response. Among some Presbyterian ministers there was a sympathy with Episcopacy along with a desire for some form of liturgic worship, an admission that to read prayers was not to worship the devil. Men of learning and tolerance, like Dr. Lee, Dr. Bisset, Dr. Norman Macleod, Principal Tulloch of St. Andrews University, looked benignly upon their Episcopal brethren. Dr. Bisset, as Moderator of the General Assembly in 1862, gave a remarkable address deploring the sin of disunity, urging the unity of Christians against contemporary infidelity.

The movement was slow, only a slight thaw in the ice, but the ice-blocks did move. Then an impetuous cleric, Rorison of Peterhead, rushed in: he wrote a letter to *The Scotsman* – then, as now, a receptable for explosive epistles – declaring that nineteen-twentieths of the Episcopal laity, most of the southern and about half of the northern clergy, with five or six of the Bishops, were in favour of reunion. The source of his estimate was not given but what he lacked in proof he made up in emphasis:

'I would never pen a line or stir a step in this matter if I did not believe reunion practicable without the slightest disrespect to the clergy of the Established Church. Their full recognition as ordained Presbyters is a *sine qua non*.'

This went far beyond the views of most Episcopalians: a conference between the two Churches was proposed but both sides took fright and drew back. Disappointment in this added to Wordsworth's bitterness about his diocesan troubles, and he talked of resigning his Bishopric.

Even the departure of Provost Fortescue and the appointment of Provost Burton, one of the diocesan clergy upon whom he looked with hope, did not ease the tension; the new Provost was influenced by Canon Humble more than by the Bishop, who wrote in his *Annals*:

'I made once more the attempt to attend the services, but I soon discovered that they were still conducted in a manner for which I could not make myself responsible without serious damage to my influence throughout the diocese.'

His disapproval was not passive. His charge to the Synod in 1872 was an open, almost violent censure of the Chapter and all its works; he set forth all his grievances, naming some of the offenders. The charge was published and lit a conflagration. Canon Humble took it as an indictment of himself, and in turn indicted the Bishop to the Episcopal Synod or College for having thus publicly censured him without warning or giving him an opportunity for self-defence. The Bishops dismissed this indictment but the episode did not make for peace. The Bishop would not even meet the Chapter for a conference. He had his sympathizers, including the Bishop of Connecticut who wrote to him:

'We have all had, I suppose, our share of trouble from those men, who have, as I told one of them the other day, "taken up everything in Romanism but the principle of obedience, and abandoned everything in Protestantism except its self-will".'

With the decrease of charity there often comes an increase of epigrammatic pungency.

Full of self-pity, Wordsworth accused his opponents of breach of faith. Letters followed and were not kept private; the flames flickered and blazed, fed with drops of unholy oil. Again the Bishop threatened to resign; a flood of remonstrances followed which he probably expected and he withdrew the threat.

'Much as he desired to retire,' wrote his nephew, 'he could not with equanimity think of being succeeded by one who might take a party line in opposition to his own.'

He did, however, preach occasionally in the cathedral and his family sometimes worshipped there. Peace broke out again, though uneasily, but the beginning of the end of the war had come. In 1876 Canon Humble died, sending the Bishop a last message of regret for 'any harsh or unfitting words' he might have uttered. The Bishop's tribute to him lacked generosity: 'A man of adamantine mould ... his range of vision was a narrow one ... Faithful and kind, especially to the poor in the discharge of pastoral duty, his chief interest lay in the maintenance of ritual which not only prevented progress but went far to empty the church in which he ministered.'

There was, however, a little mellowing with age, and even the years of conflict were full of achievement, both pastoral and scholarly. Wordsworth published numerous sermons: his nephew comments on him and on his own father, the Bishop of Lincoln: 'Few churchmen of their age used the printing press more freely.' He published charges, tracts, articles, and, at the height of his ecumenical fervour, a National Catechism which amalgamated the Presbyterian Shorter Catechism with that of the Prayer Book. On the secular side he produced a Greek Grammar and a study of *Shakespeare's Use and Knowledge of the Bible.*

In 1876 he left Perth for St. Andrews, where he took a large house, calling it Bishop's Hall. He was now seventy and the fires were dying out. His last chapter was to be the most peaceful of his long story. Three of his contemporary fellow-Bishops, Terrot, Ewing and Forbes, died in that decade. Wordsworth saw many changes – the move, which he opposed, of the Theological College from Glenalmond to Edinburgh after the fire in 1875, the formation of the Representative Church Council of which he approved, and the more frequent meetings of the General or Provincial Synod. He saw the building and consecration of two other cathedrals, in Inverness and in Edinburgh.

*The Times*, as we have seen, objected, with a singular impertinence, to the presence of the Archbishop of Canterbury at Inverness, while *The Scotsman*, with good sense and friendliness, approved. Wordsworth broke into Latin verse:

Jupiter a coelo fulsit tonuitque sinistro
Anglus, et inde sequens nil nisi fumus erat;
Dextrorsum at Scotus respondit Jupiter, et mox
Inde sequens tot lux erat alma polo.

This was Englished by his nephew:

> Heaven lightened on the left; in thunder spoke
> The English Jupiter, then all was smoke;
> But on the right the Scottish Jove replied,
> And genial light was spread on every side.

His latter years were full of honour which mellowed the old warrior. He was happy in St. Andrews, finding there 'a literary and clerical society nowhere to be surpassed'. The University bestowed on him the Doctorate of Divinity. His friendship with Principal Tulloch and other Presbyterian scholars was deepened. There was a new and younger friend in Professor Milligan of Aberdeen University who shared his hope of reunion and proposed as motto: 'Visible Unity and Mutual Helpfulness'.

The movement towards unity revived and quickened somewhat in the eighties. There was a liturgic renewal in the Established Church, ever since the publication by the Church Service Society of a Book of Common Order or *Eucholgion*, which offered a simple and beautiful liturgy in harmony with Anglican rites. The admission of Episcopal laymen to Church Courts and Councils brought the two ways of government more closely together. That the movement did not gather momentum was due, probably, to indifference rather than hostility among the average members of both Churches. Mutual understanding and desire for reconciliation were still at top level.

The Bishop used to preach in the parish church and in the college chapel. On one occasion he was heard by a student poet, Robert Murray, author of *The Scarlet Gown*:

'He is a most venerable old man . . . one of the last voices of the old school and I wish there were hundreds like him . . . [His sermon] was full of wisdom and the beauty of holiness which even I, poor sceptic and outcast, could recognize and appreciate . . . confound it, how stupid we all are . . . the whole lot of us. We all believe the same things to a great extent, but we must keep wrangling as to the data from which we infer these beliefs. . . . I believe in a great deal that he does, but I certainly don't act up to my belief as he does to his.'

The war was over and the Bishop was at peace with most men. But there were still some vexations; he took it hard that at the celebrations of the Seabury centenary he was not given the precedence he thought due to him: he was however invited to give the toast of the Church at the official banquet, and this was received with enthusiasm and published.

In his charge of 1885 he dealt sympathetically with Presbyterian Orders, not, indeed, granting them full validity but suggesting that they might be valid but irregular where there had been 'no conscious departure from the Catholic faith'. His friendliness was not always commended. The new Bishop of Edinburgh, John Dowden, asked him not to preach, as he had promised, in St. Cuthbert's parish church in Edinburgh, and he deferred with difficulty to this request. When Bishop Eden died he hoped to be elected Primus as he was by far the senior Bishop: his disappointment was bitter and he probably found comfort in believing the reason suggested by *The Glasgow Herald*: that he was 'too friendly to Presbyterians'.

But the peace of those last years was larger than the acerbity. In 1888, when Archbishop Benson summoned the Lambeth Conference, he was elected to the Committee appointed to consider Reunion. Their views were favourable if not decisive: they laid a quadrilateral basis of agreement. Holy Scripture, the Creeds, the Dominical Sacraments, the historic Episcopate, stressed the value of discussion, and expressed their willingness 'to recognize, in spite of what we must conceive as irregularity, the ministerial character of those ordained in non-Episcopal communions, through whom, as ministers, it has pleased God to work for the salvation of souls'.

It was the climax of the old Bishop's efforts, a benediction upon his work for reconciliation. The rest was peace. With the new Provost of the cathedral, Dr. Rorison, he was in sympathy and friendship.

His family of eleven had most of them gone out into the world: one daughter, his only child by his first marriage, was a nun in the Community of The Sisters of the Church: one son was in Holy Orders. A smaller house became desirable and he gave up Bishop's Hall for one, Kilrymont, on The Scores. Six thousand books were transported, only part of the vast library accumulated since young Lord Henry Kerr had helped him to unpack the cases at Glenalmond.

He was able to attend the Jubilee celebrations of the school in 1891 along with Mr. Gladstone whom he surpassed in eloquence. That year saw also the publication of his *Annals Of My Early Life*. At Easter, 1892, he was presented with an episcopal chair and staff, in the fortieth year since his election. Looking back over those years he saw a goodly increase in his flock – from one thousand to over three thousand communicants.

In December of that year he died and was buried in the Cathedral Cemetery in St. Andrews.

A Memorial tablet on the wall is inscribed:

'Remembering the prayer of his Divine Lord and Master for the Unity of His Church on earth, he prayed continually and laboured earnestly that a way may be found in God's good time for the Reunion of the Episcopal and Presbyterian Bodies without the sacrifice of Catholic Principle or Scriptural Truth.'

POSTSCRIPT on a Learned Priest

Bishop Forbes could truly be described as 'a godly and well learned man', but he was equalled, possibly surpassed in liturgical scholarship by his younger brother, George Hay Forbes, who played a part in the episcopal drama of Forbes's antagonist, Wordsworth. George Hay was born in Edinburgh in 1821. An illness in childhood left him paralysed from the knees down; at the age of thirteen he was sent to France, to be under the care of the orthopaedist, Humber, but no cure was effected. If however his body was not healed, his mind was greatly enriched by French culture and he kept up his French reading at home, along with the study of the classics, mathematics and Church history. Alexander wrote to him from Oxford about the teaching and practices of the Tractarians, no new thing for this boy, steeped in the tradition, theology and liturgy of Scots Episcopacy. At eighteen he was already a scholar, mature in mind, and had begun his special study of St. Gregory of Nyssa.

This cripple led no crippled or secluded life. He moved about on crutches, helped his father with the administration of Church affairs, published a pamphlet on 'The Christian Sacrifice in the Eucharist' and in 1846 went to Venice to examine and collate manuscripts of St. Gregory. It was a most difficult journey for one who had to be helped to climb stairs and to be lifted into carriages: how he contrived to get in and out of gondolas is not very comfortably imagined, but then and to the end of his life he forced Brother Body to be obedient to his demands.

That bodily infirmity was given by Bishop Skinner as a reason for refusing to ordain him. An appeal to Bishop Torry was successful and he was appointed deacon in 1848, serving, for a short time, Mr. Lendrum of Muthill as curate. In 1849 he was priested by his own brother, now Bishop of Brechin, and was given by Bishop Torry the charge of Burntisland, Fife. The congregation was small; there was no church and he held services in the Town Hall. He began a weekly celebration of the Eucharist. An uncompromising High Churchman, he met a good deal of hostility in a very Presbyterian town. This was, in time, to be overcome by his sincerity and devotion, and before long an elder of the kirk who came to argue remained to pray, was converted and confirmed. In the Prayer Book controversy Forbes was a strong defender of the Scottish Liturgy, and he had a hand in the preparation of Bishop Torry's Book. Like his brother he taught the Presence and the Sacrifice in the Eucharist, but he refused to speculate, to define, or to use the phrase 'The Real Presence'.

In 1853 he made a happy marriage; his wife, Eleanor Mary Wemyss, devoted herself to him and all his work, including the printing press set up in the basement of the parsonage, the famous Pitsligo Press. The house was large and austere. J. M. Neale's description of it recalls the more famous parsonage at Haworth: the wood was plain deal, there were no papered walls, no curtains, few carpets. Every room overflowed with books. From its lair, the printing press dominated the house. Mrs. Forbes managed her housekeeping with only one servant, an economy unheard-of in those days among gentlefolk of private means. Forbes's study was also the dining-room; a board was set across his knees for table; a speaking-tube communicated with the basement, but he made many journeys up and down the stairs. The house had a wide view, in the physical as well as the figurative sense, over the Forth to Edinburgh and to Berwick Law.

The new parson had great plans for building a church but he began modestly with a baptistery, which would for the time serve as a chapel. The Eucharist was celebrated by the Scottish Rite and was attended only by communicants. Matins with the Litany and Evensong were celebrated in the schoolroom which Forbes also built, and all who cared might attend. In the baptistery there were two fonts, one for babies, one for the baptism by immersion of adults.

Like his brother, George Forbes had many friends among French Catholics: their kinsman the Count de Montalembert, the abbé Bertrand, a fellow bibliophile, librarian of the Abbey of Solesmes, and the patristic scholar the Abbé Migne who invited him to contribute three volumes on St. Gregory of Nyssa to his *Patrologiae Cursus Completus*. This unhappily was unfulfilled, either because of Forbes's inability to work to the abbé's timetable, or because of an order to the latter to withdraw the invitation.

Local animosity was overcome to such a degree, in fact, that in 1869 this Episcopal priest was elected Provost of the town. With his first diocesan, Bishop Torry, he was completely happy, but with Wordsworth he was in divergence, both ecclesiastical and temperamental. Both were party men and both were vigorous and outspoken. Wordsworth saw the Church of England as the ideal to which Scottish Episcopacy should conform, Forbes found the Scottish Church nearer the primitive and Catholic model. There was, besides, a mutual antagonism of temperament. Wordsworth was the schoolmaster Bishop, the first of his kind in Scotland. Dean Perry has well said that he 'ruled his diocese by rubrics and canons much as he had governed Glenalmond by the fifty rules which he had framed for the boys there'.

The antagonism was exacerbated by Forbes's increasing absorption in his Pitsligo Press. In addition to many valuable reprints of liturgies he published a monthly, *The Gospel Messenger*, from 1853–1858; later it became *The Panoply*. Wordsworth accused him of neglecting his pastoral duties for his 'employment as a general publisher', which may not have been altogether unjust and a complaint which Bishop Forbes admitted to have some reason; and in 1856 he wrote to Forbes withdrawing his 'countenance and support' from his periodical because 'it stirs up strife', which may have been true or may simply have meant that it opposed his way. To this Forbes replied with pungency if not diplomacy: 'I was not aware that *The Gospel Messenger* had been enjoying your "countenance and support". As, however, you assure me of that fact, I beg respectfully to tender you my thanks for it.' He proceeded to deplore the Bishop's habit of rebuking him on hearsay. His sarcasm pierced the episcopal skin and the wound festered.

There was a brief reconciliation about 1858. George Forbes did not go all the way with his brother in Eucharistic doctrine and some of his articles gave Wordsworth useful matter. He adhered to the old Scottish teaching that the Eucharist was 'an offering, not of mere bread and wine but of bread and wine as the representatives of and substitutes for Christ's absent Body and Blood. . . . The Sacrifice of the Eucharist is a different Sacrifice from that of the Cross, inasmuch as they differ in the offerers, in the things offered, and in the ends for which they are or were offered'. Both were offered to God, but the Eucharist was not 'the unique Offering of Christ for the perfect redemption, propitiation and satisfaction' which He alone could effect; it was 'another Sacrifice to procure a personal application to ourselves of the Grace of Christ'. In the traditional phrase it was a Presence of Grace and Power. Both Dominical Sacraments conveyed the remission of sins. Baptism was the image of Christ's death, burial and resurrection; the Eucharist the image of His Body and Blood, offered representatively to God:

'The one is no more the reality of His Body and Blood or of His Sacrifice than the other is the reality of separation between soul and body as when He truly died.' In his view the 'intrinsic valuelessness' of the Elements enhanced their spiritual value. The offering was 'transparent'; there was no barrier to 'looking through it and beyond it to what it represents'. This seems to echo Henry Scougal's phrase: 'The outside of this ordinance is very poor and mean.'

This came short of his brother the Bishop's proclamation of the Presence, and George Forbes deprecated the Bishop's emphasis on the Sacred Manhood. It was a difference of emphasis, not of belief, and made no separation of affection between the brothers, but it did bring argument and disagreement.

'Had they not argued they would not have been Forbeses,' comments Dean Perry. Nor would they have been true Scots. They went together most of the way in churchmanship, in culture and in scholarship. Of the two, George was the more Scottish, Alexander the more Latin. George never felt the faintest flush of

Roman fever: he detested not only ultramontane rigidity but sentimental piety, little books of sugared devotions 'all written for young women . . . womanized Christianity is thoroughly contemptible'. The brothers shared some liturgic work, notably their editing of *The Arbuthnot Missal*.

George helped Bishop Wordsworth to draw up that admonition to Bishop Forbes which ended, with such ironic mildness, the bitter Eucharistic controversy. And with that ended the brief truce between this priest and his Bishop, both equally obstinate if not turbulent. A further cause of offence was provided by the deposition of the Scottish Office from its primacy of honour, this largely by Wordsworth's activity. To his argument that this was necessary in order to have the final disability removed, and Scottish priests permitted to take office in England, Forbes retorted that they ought to stay in Scotland and serve the Scottish Church. The English Prayer Book was 'a mixture of ultra-Romanism and ultra-Protestantism', its Prayer of Consecration 'bastard Roman', while other parts were German Protestant. His gift for unfavourable comment was remarkable.

One of the Canons of the Synod of 1863 enjoined that 'No clergyman shall be at liberty to depart from the Book of Common Prayer in the Administration of the Sacraments or in the performance of the other Divine Offices except so far as the circumstances of the Church require'. The Scottish Office was not to be introduced, only to be continued where it was already in use.

Bishop Wordsworth insisted on exact obedience: Forbes ignored this and published an Open Letter to the Bishop on 'The Doctrinal Errors and Practical Scandals of the English Prayer Book' which the Bishop ignored. Forbes took the matter to the College and the dispute culminated miserably in a lawsuit: Forbes versus Eden and Others. On both sides there was 'too much law and too little love'; too much plain Scots devilry. In Forbes's favour it must be said that it was only when the College rejected his plea that he took it to the Court of Session: then, after judgement was given against him, to the House of Lords. There he achieved a feat of advocacy in presenting his case, without books or papers, in an exposition which lasted in all for five hours. He was complimented but he lost the case. Asked at one point whether he believed in The Real Presence he replied: 'No, I might with as much ground say "The Real Absence",' which is comprehensible if one studies his teaching, already quoted, but which is uncommonly like provocative clerical flippancy.

He admitted the legality of the Canon but put his own interpretation upon 'the circumstances of the Church', thus legalizing to himself his disobedience, of which his brother disapproved. At the next diocesan Synod he was threatened with suspension from office. A wise friend, Gilbert Rorison, drew up a modified form of submission which he and Mrs. Forbes persuaded this intransigent priest to sign.

To see him only in revolt is to see the picture of his life out of focus. He was a most faithful priest and pastor, teaching his people, bringing them into the fullness of sacramental life, enriching the Church by his scholarship. The accomplishment of his life of only fifty-four years is impressive, and the more so for his crippled state.

The brothers were closely bound together in affection. Bishop Forbes's death was a fatal blow; George survived him only by a month or so. Mrs. Forbes died three years later.

The Pitsligo Press continued for a time.

'The *fons et origo* of the Press was the love that its founder had for the Scottish Communion Office.' That is the tribute of another scholar, the Reverend J. B. Primrose, who published a treatise on the Press in *The Transactions of the Edinburgh Bibliographical Society*. Forbes's work for the Scottish Liturgy began in his youth when, as secretary of The Scottish Tract Society, he supervised the translation of the Office into Gaelic. Besides editions of the Office and publications directly relating to it (*an Explanation of The Scottish Office*; his *Open Letter On the Doctrinal Errors and Practical Scandals of the English Prayer Book*; his father Lord Medwyn's *Address to Scottish Episcopalians*) he printed and published: *The Drummond Missal*; *Archbishop Bainbridge's Pontifical*; *The Arbuthnot Missal*; the *Pontifical* of David de Bornham; *The Thoughts of Lord Pitsligo*; a book by another of his kinsmen, Sir J. S. Forbes, called *The Cottar's Ingle* on the shocking condition of rural cottages; J. M. Neale's tale *The Farm of Aptonga*; a reprint of Newman's *Arians of the Fourth Century*; part of the Works of

St. Gregory of Nyssa; much of Bishop Rattray's work; and his own periodicals *The Gospel Messenger* and *The Panoply*.

*The Gospel Messenger* was a substantial compilation of essays and reviews, sermons, and an occasional poem. Like many such estimable publications it suffered from under-subscription and deferred payments.

'We have written to several friends lately from whom we should be glad to hear. In particular we should like it if the Rev. G. T. would pay the small sum we have several times written for.'

In his will George Forbes bequeathed money to found a Trust to continue the Pitsligo Press and to complete the chapel he had begun to build, to endow a library and pay the salary of the librarian who must be a priest.

'I wish to use my small fortune to found a position of learned leisure in which a succession of clergy of The Scottish Episcopal Church may devote themselves to theological study.' The priest-librarian was to 'celebrate the Holy Eucharist on every Sunday, Christmas Day, Maundy Thursday and Ascension Day when he is at home and not hindered by grave sickness, and shall, during it, pray audibly for me, and for blessings for my father and mother through whose kindness I am able to make this foundation'.

Among the trustees were Lord Mar and Kellie, Lord Glasgow, William Forbes of Medwyn and other churchmen of distinction and devotion. Bishop Wordsworth was not impressed; he attacked the Trust, refused to have it administered, withdrew his licence from Forbes's curate, and organized a new congregation. He was supported by the Synod. The trustees appointed as librarian the Reverend William Bell who lived in the Parsonage, taught in the school and managed the Pitsligo Press. On the death of Mrs. Forbes the house had to be sold to release funds for the Trust. The school and the baptistery were removed. Bell somehow contrived to carry on the work of the Press until 1882, when he moved to Edinburgh. He died in 1892. Of the Pitsligo Press there is, sadly, 'na more to say', except that the books, with Forbes's own library, found a home in the Theological College which still appoints a Forbes' Librarian. And so this scholar-priest and Miss Kathrein Panton should be remembered together, with devout thanksgiving.

# 9

# The Other Alexander.
# Bishop of Argyll and the Isles

Of all the Scottish Bishops he has the grandest signature: N or M Argyll and the Isles. The hero of this chapter muffled it slightly in his *Alexander, Bishop of Argyll and the Isles*, but he loved the romance and tradition of his diocese.

Alexander Ewing seems at first like a character from one of Charlotte Yonge's novels. He was devout and cultivated, delicate and refined. He came of good Highland stock; two grand-uncles had been out in the Forty-Five and had suffered at Carlisle for their loyalty to the Stuarts. His father died when Alexander, the eldest of three children, was only fourteen, his mother not long afterwards. The three children, Alexander, John and Christian were brought up by a kind uncle.

They were born in Aberdeen, Alexander in 1814. After being tutored at home the boys went for two sessions to Marishcal College, then to London, to a private school in Chelsea. Alexander was deeply influenced by the schoolmaster, an Evangelical, and while there was confirmed. On returning to Scotland he attended classes at Edinburgh University with interludes of country life on Deeside. Their uncle, a doctor, was aware of hereditary delicacy and the brothers and sister enjoyed a good deal of outdoor freedom. Alexander read enormously; he loved poetry, he had a gift for languages, he sketched, and along with these accomplishments he and his brother enjoyed botanizing, walking, riding and shooting.

It was a happy, almost an idyllic boyhood except for the renewed shadow cast by their sister's death. Their uncle, more than ever anxious about the boys, kept them in their country freedom: regular study was forbidden but there were quantities of books. With a young friend they went on a pony tour, each with a knapsack, riding south as far as the Lakes. On their return the brothers took a house for themselves by the sea, at Inverugie, about six miles from Elgin, settling down for another spell of that serene and wholesome life of books and sport, study without weariness, pleasant society, and, for Alexander, first and lasting love.

Katherine Stewart was eighteen, gentle and devout: they were married in 1835 when the bridegroom had just come of age. His inherited delicacy did not appear to deter his bride or his or her family, but all that autumn and winter he was ill. They were still living at Inverugie, looking for their ideal house, and what strikes the modern reader is the utter absence of any worry about money or a career. After the birth of their son they moved to Elgin and there the sense of vocation, at first hardly more than a dream, began to stir. There was an Episcopal congregation in the place but no priest. It was suggested that this devout and cultivated young man might take charge, as a lay reader. Nothing came of that, but his mind turned definitely towards the priesthood. In September 1838 Bishop Low appointed him deacon. His health was still uncertain and almost immediately after this he went with his wife and little son to Pisa for a winter of content.

It was the first of many sojourns in the warm south. Italy was to become his second country, the country of his heart. He assisted the English chaplain, learned Italian, read a great deal, went upon pleasant excursions. They did not return to Scotland until 1841, when he was priested by William Skinner, Bishop of Aberdeen, and given the charge of Forres. The congregation still worshipped in a room but in the second year of his incumbency Ewing had a church built to his own design, modified by a professional architect.

These were happy years, shadowed at times by illness, but full of peace and of cultured pleasures: reading, music, versifying in both English and Italian. It was also a good priestly life: he cared for his people, he learned more about the Church and wrote a pamphlet, widely circulated, on Episcopacy in Scotland. His evangelical fervour deepened. But it is still a world slightly remote, one easily to be set in fiction, one very different from the primitive and learned seclusion of Jolly, the social and theological passion of Forbes. His devotion was noted. In 1847 he was elected Bishop of the diocese of Argyll and the Isles, newly disjoined from Moray and endowed by Bishop Low. And so we come to that consecration of the two Alexanders, and a convergence of forces enough to set not only the heather but the Forth and the Tay on fire. It was a meeting, that day in the church of St. Andrew, Aberdeen, of north and south, Catholic and Evangelical, the old tradition and the new ways. Of the consecrating Bishops, the Primus, Skinner, represented the old Scottish Episcopacy, Terrot and Russell looked south towards England. The two newly consecrated had much in common: both were Scottish, both of the gentry, both godly and well learned men. Their divergence was to become wide, and Wordsworth who preached the sermon was to enlarge the division. All that the Church had been in the past hundred years, all that she would become during the rest of the century, was personified that day.

At this point Ewing passes completely out of that borderland between fiction and reality in which we have seen him. He is no longer a type, the incarnation of a character in a novel: he is a real and complex individual of strong beliefs and prejudices. At the same time he remains very much of his period in his culture, his elegance, his cosmopolitan background, and his evangelical fervour. This was to increase and is to be honoured. His Protestantism was also to increase and in this he antagonizes many of his Church, even today. For most Scots his most attractive quality is his love of the Highlands and the Highland people. It was both romantic and realistic: he was aware of the tragedy of those lovely, deserted places whence the people had been driven out by cruelty and poverty: first after Culloden, then in the clearance, and still into an exile made necessary by poverty.

His own circumstances were comfortable: he had known ease and leisure but he had, and it remains his most amiable quality, a true pastoral love of the poor and love of souls. All these elements and emotions come together in one personality. Regarded objectively, Ewing is the most fascinating of the Scots Victorian Bishops.

Almost at once he was, as his biographer Alexander Ross puts it, 'Initiated into that locomotive, amphibious kind of life which must be led by every Bishop of Argyll who simply does his duty.' The diocese was wide, the charges were few and scattered. At first the new Bishop lived on the most southerly island, Bute; then for a time in Duntroon Castle lent by a friendly laird, Malcolm of Poltalloch; finally, in 1852, in a house of his own, Bishopton at Lochgilphead.

The Faithful Remnant in Argyll held together in their small and scattered congregations. The Scottish Office was used and the people had their Prayer Book in Gaelic, translated by Patrick Stewart in 1794, probably with the help of the last Gaelic-speaking Bishop, Macfarlane. Much of the work was done, as in Bishop Low's first years, by itinerant priests. At Ballachulish that good priest Paul McColl – Mr. Paul – had been succeeded by James Paterson and he, in 1847, by Duncan Mackenzie.

When the latter moved ten years later to Fort William, Bishop Ewing appointed an Englishman, John Ikin, to Ballachulish.

'Having been a missionary in the Bahamas and subsequently curate to Bishop Ewing at Lochgilphead, this clergyman was supposed to possess special fitness for preparing promising Gaelic-speaking young men for admission to Glenalmond or Cumbrae.' So J. B. Craven has described him, adding that Ikin was 'a man of strange fancies and eccentric habits'. He tried to learn Gaelic.

'It was, however, Gaelic with the gutturals left out, and with a pronounced English accent, and his attempts in the language tended neither to edification nor reverence for sacred things.'

The Bishop, ignorant of or ignoring the absence of the arch-diaconate in Scotland, made him Archdeacon of Appin, a title he cherished. He is said to have improved the internal condition of the church and to have introduced instrumental music; his incumbency otherwise was not a happy one, but it was brief.

Except for this interlude Ewing's episcopate was full of pastoral and practical concern for his flock. One of his first acts was the founding of The Highlands and Islands Episcopal Fund to provide for the Highland clergy, schoolmasters and schoolmistresses, to build their houses, and to buy Bibles and Prayer Books.

His first Synod was held in 1848 in Oban which was then little more than a fishing village. The congregation met in a house; then, as they grew, in a hotel and finally in the Masonic Hall where the Synod was held. In summer their numbers were increased by reading parties from Oxford or Cambridge, Jowett sometimes among them. The Bishop's first charge to his clergy was very practical, very pastoral, very evangelical: he bade them teach 'the great and substantial verities' rather than 'that which we have gathered only from the tradition of men'. He advised good salesmanship:

'In the language of commerce, provide a good article, provide the right thing, and you will have demand enough. The Apostles, though persecuted, never wanted hearers.'

The clergy should pay attention to detail, be punctual and punctilious; baptism should be administered publicly: above all, Holy Communion should be celebrated as frequently as possible and at least six times a year. They must be pastors.

'If we feed our flock, my brethren, they will feed us.'

The flock did not always respond as they should, especially the rich. 'The rich are far from the Kingdom of God.' He added, with a bland pungency which may have been learned in Italy, that only the Divine Power could overcome this passive resistance, but to that Power the clergy had a special right of appeal:

'Let it be our constant prayer that He will, my brethren, help us in this respect' – shoving, one might say, the camel through the eye of the needle. Two warnings were given, one against acrimonious controversy and the party spirit, the other against dilettante devotion:

'We cannot treat religion as a matter of elegant amusement or theatrical show, or as an imitation of early Christianity, or as a matter dependent on antiquarian accuracy or architectural design.'

This was characteristic and not untimely: the spiritual heirs of the Oxford Movement were, some of them, unduly preoccupied with forms, ceremonies and imitations. Ewing remained, for a man of his sensibility and Italianate culture, constantly and curiously unaffected by aesthetic religion or religious aesthetics; but then he was also unstirred by the resurgence of Catholic teaching. For all his love of Italy he felt no throb of Roman fever.

What did, above all, quicken his imagination and move his heart was the Celtic heritage of the Church as he saw it: simple, fervent, evangelical. He also upheld the Apostolic Order as well as the Evangelical Truth of the Church, and because of their lack of this Order and Authority could not praise unreservedly the faith and devotion of Presbyterians. He claimed that Episcopacy showed more earnestness in teaching morality 'than perhaps Calvinistic doctrine either enjoins or permits'. This unexpected blow may have been aimed at the Calvinistic doctrine of predestination and the ineffectualness of good works, or at the common sport of fornication. Presbyterianism suffered, moreover, from schism and disruption, whereas Episcopacy provided 'a sanctuary where the soul could shelter from party quarrels and ceaseless strife, in holy doctrine and devout response'. To our hindsight this comes near *hubris*.

The Synod adjourned to Iona, to worship in the ruined abbey. The Bishop wrote his sermon on board a crowded boat. It was an expression of all the Celt and the poet in him. He lamented that here, where the Gospel had first come to the Isles, there was heard 'but the wild bird's cry and the moan of the sullen waves'. He falls easily into the rhythm of verse. 'Coming as we do today on a pilgrimage to the graves of our spiritual fathers we cannot but mourn the silence and solitude of their tombs. . . . We have come to reverence here, at the fountain of Christianity in the west, the Glory of God in His saints.'

The light had been kindled on Iona but it now flickered very low. All his life he was saddened by the dimming of the light, by the ebbing of life from the Isles, as all his life he was captivated by their magic and their memory of holiness. He went about a good deal in those years and came to know the people.

'We always feel so strong, your righteousness, when you're among us,' a Highland roadman told him.

He was realistic about the cause of this dwindling life. In 1852 he preached a sermon in London on behalf of The Highland Emigration Fund. The need for this was itself tragic, but at least it provided means for families to emigrate together, most of them going to Australia.

The Bishop dwelt on the growing distress, the near-famine on the Isles. The potato crop had failed, the kelp manufacture was finished, the herring fishery had declined, and 'illicit distilling of whisky had been put down' – which one hardly expects a Bishop to list among the disasters.

At the same time the population had increased. The present way of life could not continue. Money had been given and spent, the people were beginning to depend on help from outside, the land was uncultivated and poor. Overseas the land was fertile, the inhabitants were few.

'Bring Scotland into connection with food, and Australia into connection with labour. As Australia cannot be brought to them, our destitute people must be brought to Australia.'

But it was a desperate remedy.

'Alas! They go – never to return. Shall we not miss them from our shores, that long-descended race, that loyal, patient people? But they perish if they remain.'

He foresaw what we, in our time, have seen:

'Doubtless a time is coming when the face of the world will be once more changed as it has been changed before; when this great nation will have gone the way of all great nations before it; when the mighty heart which beats in this centre of the civilized world will still vibrate, but not here. These men who go are possibly the patriarchs of an infant world.'

The old tradition would be renewed, for those men took their virtues with them; not the Saxon quality but the Celtic, that of the ash rather than the oak:

'From the highest to the lowest, this long-descended people have by nature what is called "the next best thing to Christian Grace" – the grace of born gentlemen.'

And with that secondary grace they had Christian faith: 'a religious, reverential people, a people of deep piety' who might well prove to be missionaries as well as emigrants, 'the St. Patricks and St. Columbas of a new continent'.

This man has something of the spell-binding gift of the Celtic poet and story-teller. One listener described him as 'a godly warlock', and there is a story of the manager of a London shop finding all the staff gathered about the Bishop, held by his 'affluent talk'.

His spiritual life was visionary rather than sacramental. Outward appearances were of little significance:

'I feel always like a stranger about outward things, but all things relating to the unseen and transcendental seem the only real facts to me.' And he once said to his brother: 'Man has a body but it is scarcely a part of himself. It is merely a temporal vestment. He himself lives in God, and truth, righteousness and love are his only proper aliment.'

But that temporal vestment was once worn by the Divine Man, and from His Incarnation comes the sacramental life of His people. This connection Ewing seems never to have comprehended, and from this defect in his spirituality may have come his antagonism to sacramental Catholicism.

'Perhaps you will think that I am as daft about Protestantism as I am about the Highlands and the Highland scenery. Only remember that in one form of mania I have the companionship of William Wordsworth, and in the other of Martin Luther.'

His churchmanship was nebulous. 'Episcopacy was secondary to him,' his biographer has said, 'compared with the profounder interests of Protestantism itself.' His sympathy with the ideals of the Cathedral and College of Cumbrae was imperfect: far from commending Keble's vision of it as a refuge, he dreaded an influx of Tractarians:

'Sooner or later I suspect there will be a secession of malcontents from the Church of England. And these would appeal to our Scottish Bishops for the consecration of a Bishop for themselves, in order to form a second non-juring Church; but in the event of such a consummation, the loyal, Protestant clergy and laity of our communion would only be drawn more closely to the Church of England.'

Although he loved so much in the Scottish tradition he would gladly have seen the Scottish Liturgy not merely deposed from primacy but altogether banished. The congregation of Holy Trinity, Dunoon, who desired to retain it had a dusty answer from him:

'If you, individually and collectively, are convinced that, unless you were permitted the use of the Scottish Office, your moral sense would become blunted and your loyalty to the Ten Commandments would become treacherous, by all means, as anything is better than sin, use the Office. But can or does the Scottish Office make a profounder demand on the heart and conscience than the Anglican? If you will show me the passages of the Scottish Office which tend to make the users of it more childlike men in love of truth and lifelong devotion to the highest interests of their brethren, I will reconsider my judgement.'

As an argument this looks slightly aslant. He treats the Liturgy as a textbook of morals.

To Wordsworth he wrote:

'The assertions as to "Scottish use and venerable antiquity" are mere stalking-horses or delusions. We shall never do justice to the broad Catholic truth which is contained in our standards, or gain a hearing from the great mass of Scotchmen until we get rid of this sham or insidious poison.'

If he did not, like Wordsworth, make Establishment almost an article of faith, he was equally emphatic about the need for conformity with the Church of England. He deplored any 'romantic feeling of veneration for the non-jurors' and thought that the Scottish Liturgy has 'simply infected our Communion with the virus which caused the death of the Episcopacy of the Stuarts'. Altogether allergic to the old Episcopacy of the north-east, he dreaded the 'intrusion' of Scottish clerics into England, reversing the usual dislike of English intruding into Scotland. Dislike of the Scottish tradition in the Church became an obsession. The attempt to restore the Scottish Office to primacy he described as 'altogether a Tractarian galvanizement' (a fine word!): he even moved away from his once firm belief in Episcopacy, telling the Bishop of London that what had brought him into the Church was 'not Episcopacy, not sacramental instrumentality, but the truth that God the Son hath redeemed us and all mankind'.

At one point his Protestantism went so far as to inspire a dream of a mission to the Waldensians in Italy. He himself, as a Protestant Bishop, would be head and would be acceptable. There can have been few more fantastic visions in Church history. He was surprised and offended by the warning of a friend against 'the Waldensian heresy' and by being told bluntly that he was more needed in Scotland than in Italy. The dream faded.

There was work enough for him in Scotland and he set about it with zeal, visiting his diocese, seeing to the building of churches, parsonages and schools. He was now settled in his permanent home, Bishopton, Lochgilphead, with charge of the church there.

In his private life, in marriage, parenthood and friendships he was happy. Jowett was a valued friend. The Bishop stayed with him when he was given the degree of D.C.L. by Oxford, and was introduced to the famous and venerable Dr. Routh of Magdalen. The latter received him coldly but afterwards apologized, saying he had mistaken him for a mere Colonial. He had many friends in the English Episcopate and was the first Scots Bishop for nearly a century to join in a celebration of the Eucharist in Westminster

Abbey – with the Archbishop of Canterbury and the Bishops of London and Oxford.

A letter of his in 1855 gives some statistics. The Scottish Bishoprics were not of princely opulence. In Argyll the income from Bishop Low's endowment was about £20 and in that particular year it had been swallowed up in legal expenses. The stipend of the Provost of Cumbrae, in which office he had himself installed, hoping no doubt to arrest Tractarian developments, was £70. Bishopton was valued at a rental of £50. Fortunately he had private means.

Mrs. Ewing died in 1856, on the birth of a baby. This was one of the long families of Victorian fact and fiction; the eldest son had already begun his career in India. The Bishop, his biographer says, was burdened not only by natural grief but by remorse, accusing himself of having failed his wife in spiritual guidance and sympathy. She remains a shadowy figure: the clue to her husband's remorse seems to have lain in some marked passages of her devotional books. She had made her own way of faith. Had she spoken, and been unheard or impatiently rebuked, of beliefs and longings he could not understand or share? The family life continued, shadowed but not unhappy. A sister of Mrs. Ewing came to stay for a time, a governess was engaged as a companion for the older girls, and one of those girls, Nina, became her father's confidant. In the sound Victorian fashion the older children looked after the younger, and the new baby was cherished. There is an account in a Christmas letter from the Bishop in 1859 of the family absorbed in new books: the two eldest sisters in Ruskin and a volume of ballads, respectively, the youngest 'contemplating a wretched old man on the cover of a picture-book which he seemed to value as a very happy likeness of his own father'. It was a sober happiness, but gaiety entered with some neighbours and they all danced to the bagpipes until the house seemed to 'rock with the reels'. His own health was uncertain. An illness in 1860 was followed by an agreeable convalescence in the kind house of Sir John Malcolm of Poltalloch.

'If I could always live as I do here, without anxiety, in a large, warm house, I might live for ever.'

Illness kept him from the trial that year of Bishop Forbes, which he had tried to prevent, trying to make peace between the antagonists, though himself opposed to Forbes's teaching. He came very near the Receptionist attitude. Some months later he expounded his views in his Charge to his Synod:

'The first Christians regarded the Eucharist as the symbol of their own lives as well as of the death of their Lord, and partaking of the bread and wine in the light of that conception, they returned from their worship to their lives, refreshed and strengthened.' In the Eucharist they received Christ 'as the life of their lives, in conscious fellowship with Him' and offered themselves to the Father in His Name, remembering His perfect Oblation. They were one with Christ in 'the one life of sonship'.

So far, very good; so good that it leaves us again bewildered by the dispute between men who held so much in common, who loved so devoutly the Lord of the Eucharist. In what follows, however, Ewing sees with different eyes from those of Forbes. He has a dread of sacerdotalism, of any hint of magic and materialism:

'The mere outward expression of the inward self-consecration became, in course of time, the equivalent of, or substitute for the reality itself.'

The fusion between outward and visible sign and inward and spiritual grace is not comprehended.

'The Eucharist lost its divinely symbolic character.' The worshipper's confession of allegiance to Christ and thankful remembrance of His Incarnation 'was transmuted into an apparatus manipulated by a priestly caste, from contact with which alone eternal life was to be secured'.

This is the Protestant rejection of the Sacrifice of the Mass, the Protestant subjectivity of confession and worship.

'The shadow was made the cause of the substance, and as such was worshipped.'

In his dread of materialism, Ewing took a material view of the sacramental change. Christ's miracles had appealed to the senses: men had drunk the good wine, the blind had received sight, the lame had walked, but of the 'material miracle' in the Eucharist there was no proof. This forestalls a notorious declaration of Bishop Barnes, that the sacramental change could not be chemically proved. Finally came a somewhat startling peroration:

'It is with our minds only that we can enter into the mind of

Christ, as it is only with our minds that we can understand the thoughts of a fellow-creature. But according to the materialistic conception of the Sacrament the secret of Hamlet would be mastered by eating a bit of Shakespeare's body.'

This was as far as possible from Forbes's teaching; yet, much to his credit, Ewing added his dissent from the admonition delivered to Forbes. His dislike of definition made him dislike the condemning of another man's definition as wrong. This and his own too Protestant approach brought him into disfavour with his fellow-Bishops when the Charge was published. After a meeting as Glenalmond he wrote to his brother:

'The bishops were not exactly what you could truthfully call pleasant persons in their behaviour to me at Perth, and it seems that I have offended some of them at least in many ways,' including the Waldensian scheme or dream. One of them went so far as to tell him he 'deserved a presentment' or indictment, which would have been the final irony. Ewing took it calmly, quoting Galileo; and like the earth, Scots Episcopacy still moved, and moved at last into comparative calm. The final disabilities were removed in 1864, the Argyll Fund was begun to help this diocese, the Archbishop of Canterbury (Sumner) and Bishop of London among its sponsors; but the Bishop's antipathy to the Scottish Liturgy increased along with his Protestant fervour. It was a bee in his bonnet which never ceased to buzz and which could sting.

'Plain, earnest, honest old England! . . . without identity with England we must give up our future.' He had no idea of unity without uniformity. It is difficult to understand this obsessive antagonism to one rite in a man who made so little of form and ceremonial. And he could mock his own obsession. In a letter to Bishop Wordsworth, describing the unpredictable changes of weather in the West Highlands, he wrote:

'Last week the winds and sleet were dashing everything to pieces. Today it is as quiet and sweet as a saint who has seen for the first time the Scottish Office.'

A tinge of cynicism appears from time to time in his utterances, bringing a certain astringency. Separation between Church and State appeared to him inevitable and sectarianism would increase, not by any means on matters of doctrine or order.

'It is not *religious* separation which is coming. Denominationalism (our future) is among Protestants not a thing of "orders of the ministry" but of social rank and taste. Peers and lairds choose Episcopacy, professional men and farmers choose an established Presbytery, and mechanics and shopocracy a free Presbyterianism. Thus it now is in Scotland, and thus it will be in England. It is a matter of clothes among Protestants, after all.'

He saw the contemporary rush of conversions to Rome as dilettantism on the part of the upper, superstition on the part of the lower ten thousand: the eighty thousand in between were blessed with common sense and formed 'a royal democracy, enthusiastic for the Queen'. A very neat arrangement!

'I have good reason for becoming more distinctively Protestant,' he told Wordsworth, adding that as regards Presbyterians: 'Your views have been that they should come to us, and mine that we should go to them. . . . I am, however, thankful to be where I am. I do not wish to be a Presbyterian. I am thankful not to be a Roman Catholic.' In another letter he was still more definite:

'I cannot but think that one day or other the more liberal Presbyterians and Episcopalians, represented by Macleod and Tulloch and, shall I say, myself and the Bishop of St. Andrews, may find themselves in one Northern Establishment.'

His Protestantism was like that storm of wind and sleet he described, his love of the Highlands and of his people like the day of serene sun.

His private happiness returned in 1862 with his marriage to Lady Alice Douglas, daughter of the Earl of Morton. She was a true helpmate, caring for the welfare of the poor. 'We are getting quite a congregation of the lower orders, which I have long wished to have,' he told his eldest daughter, now married and away from home. Lady Alice had a Sunday School; his second daughter looked after the music in church. The Argyll Fund was of great help. Why, the Bishop demanded, should everything be done 'for the heathen and for publicans' and nothing for the good Highland people?

'To try and raise them has been my work here for the past fifteen years.'

His lack of the Gaelic grieved him.

'I have tried, but I cannot learn it. I hope Bishops will come after me who will know it.'

The want of a common language was felt in places where the

people had little English and had to translate their thoughts from the Gaelic. Once when Bishop Blomfield was staying with him, Bishop Ewing took him to call on an old man who said he was honoured by having 'so ancient a hero' in his house.

Recurring illness sent him abroad for a long spell, from August 1864 until June 1865: most of it he spent with his married daughter who had her home in Sicily. From there he wrote a Charge to be read to the Synod, which is full of nostalgia for the Highlands and the Celtic Church.

In his journey through Switzerland and northern Italy he had come upon many traces of the Celtic missionaries, Columbanus and his followers:

'In Switzerland they still pray for the Scotch and Irish, not knowing why; we know, and it is pleasant to stand at St. Gall and to think that he who first brought Christianity hither was one of ourselves . . . And now the descendants of these men are perishing from our shores; and they who hereafter may know Lochaber shall not know them. It is a noble race, my brethren, even in its decline. It is a people who deserve to be cherished. By and by we shall seek but we shall not find them; and the place which now knows them shall know them no more.'

No Episcopal Charge can ever have come so near a poem and a lament. One can almost hear the echo of the pipes playing a coronach.

'He who sails along the shores of Argyll and lands in any of its mountain caves in the still of an autumn morning, and finds, as he may, in almost every bay the ruins of an ancient chapel, sees that which he will not see elsewhere, and that which it is probable he will never forget. Small and weatherworn and unroofed as it is, it is yet the church of one of those Celtic Fathers, and his cell is close at hand. There, among the grassy knolls, or under the cairn overgrown with ferns and ivy and through which the fox-glove and wild rose lift their heads, sleeps, and for a thousand years has slept, an Apostle and his congregation.' Others are sleeping in the fields of France, 'amidst the snows of Switzerland, the cities of the Rhine, or the far Italian plains . . . They were Apostles of Christ. Their brotherhood was removed, no doubt for some greater good. Let us, however, believe that the removal is but for a time.'

The Celtic Church would revive, perhaps among the High-landers overseas, in a new apostolate. Meanwhile at home there appeared to be only silence and slumber.

'On these sweet lochs and dreamy shores where the islands lie asleep as it were upon the main there is indeed more than one Iona; more than one green bosom is surmounted by that memo-rial and monument of the past – the round-headed cross with its mysterious interlacing and runic knots, emblems of pagan and Christian strangely mixed together, but where all are equally in repose and silence reigns unbroken. It seems useless, nay, a desecration to awake the echoes even to restore the past.'

In some places the sleep had been broken, the past still lived; there were still members of the ancient race who met for a worship not unlike that of Iona long ago. This Faithful Remnant must be honoured and aided.

'Would that some young Cuthbert or Columba would again arise to rekindle the flame on the Celtic altars, to preach the word in the native tongue.'

Much of this was contained in his book on Iona, published in 1866, with a Life of St. Columba and a history of the Celtic Mission. He had also published some pamphlets, and he now had the idea of collecting and publishing a series of *Present Day Papers* by various hands. His own contribution was on The Eucharist, and in this, and in his Charge of 1866, he gives his fullest teaching. The Charge was a warning against 'Materialism in the Church' or 'Gross Conceptions of the Sacrament'. Fear of any approach to a magic cult, to miracles against nature, had become almost an obsession.

'The laws of the kingdom of grace are not contradictory to those of nature . . . The kingdom of grace is on the same plane, and is but an extension of the kingdom of nature.'

Matter and spirit were opposites, each with its own food, its own order:

'The regions of mind and matter are distinct . . . Matter never passes into mind so as to become mind, nor mind into matter,' but matter could be brought into relation with mind or spirit by being given 'a connection of a spiritual kind' through symbol or association, through being 'clothed, invested, as it were, with a spiritual garment'; matter acquired a *character*, not a change of substance. The priest, when he set aside and offered the Elements conferred this character upon them 'by connecting them with the Life and Death of Christ, *investing* them with the narrative of His Passion'. The Eucharist could be seen as a representative Sacrifice, as 'the exhibition of a tremendous fact in the Divine Nature, the Revelation of the Divine Mind as to sin and sinners'. Christ's Body was the vehicle of that Revelation, manifested in Jerusalem, reflected in the Eucharist.

'The Life and Death of Christ are the Light of men; that Light is mirrored in the Eucharist.'

The material conception of religion was due to sluggish thought. 'Spiritual apprehension demands spiritual energy.'

He shrank from mystery: 'It is Light we have to convey, Light or Revelation . . . Christianity is the daughter of knowledge . . . Revelation is not the giving of a law, but the opening of a door, the door of heaven, and the manifestation of God therein.'

It is high and holy doctrine: on the positive side it is the teaching of a mystic, on the negative, when he denies or denounces transubstantiation, it becomes mere polemics. The idea of a localized Presence repelled him.

'The Incarnation is the acme of Revelation, and the Eucharist mirrors its culminating point. Both are vehicles of light. It was to this end, to give light that God became incarnate in Christ . . . God took our nature to give us a revelation of His Own. He clothed Himself with flesh to reveal spirit. . . . He took our nature that we might have His. . . . He brought the distant nigh, He made the far-off near. He took our flesh, not to make it a mystery, but that by so doing, mystery might be explained.'

Ewing was not merely a receptionist, although at times he comes very near that attitude. For him the Sacramental Presence was real, not the creation of our own will or mood. 'Christ as one with God must ever be the same, and therefore ever present.'

He was specially present in the Eucharist, present to our consciousness; present like light filling the landscape, while we receive that light with our own eyes.

But the problem of matter and spirit perplexed Ewing:

'If Christ's material Body cannot be present in the Eucharist, no bodily Presence can be there at all.' He was forgetting the catechism:

'The Body and Blood of Christ are verily and indeed taken and received by the faithful.'

Protestant and Evangelical, Ewing was also on the liberal or modernist side in Church matters. At the first pan-Anglican Conference at Lambeth in 1867 the dispute about Bishop Colenso almost disrupted the assembly. Colenso, Bishop of Natal, had been excommunicated on a charge of heresy by the Bishop of Capetown, Metropolitan of South Africa. This judgement had been reversed by the Privy Council. The Bishop of Capetown now demanded that it be upheld by the Church here assembled. He was supported by the Bishop of Vermont who wished to put a resolution to the Conference that if the judgement were not upheld against the Privy Council, the Church should separate herself from the State.

The Archbishop of Canterbury refused to put this resolution to the meeting and was supported by the Bishops of London, Winchester, Ely, Lincoln and St. David's. This, in Ewing's opinion, saved the Conference from disaster.

When asked in conversation afterwards what his feeling was, he replied:

'Relief, relief, relief.'

'Was there any sense of solemnity at any part of the proceedings?'

'Only the solemnity of being on board a ship that might blow up at any moment.'

To a further question of whether he had felt the Holy Spirit at work, he said:

'That depended on where I sat' – whether beside a sympathetic or an antagonistic fellow Bishop. One stormy session had reminded him of a scene from Kingsley's *Hypatia*.

To the final question:

'What is the worst thing that has been done?' he answered:

'That the meeting has taken place at all.'

His biographer talks of his 'rich and racy conversational powers, which can be believed; one only wishes more of his table talk had been given, although it would probably be startling at times to the more decorous faithful. He could, in our modern jargon, shed his inhibitions. His account of the Conference, written to Dean Stanley, has pungency:

'The Pan-Anglican has sat and seems to have done no harm.

No supreme spiritual council seems to have been erected, no tribunal of heresy or holy office; but the evil is done and established. . . . It not only glorifies the element of sacerdotal judgement, apart from lay co-operation, but it also introduces foreign *sacerdotes*. [Capetown? Vermont?] Many prelates who attended meant no harm, but their very attendance did all that was required.'

The sardonic streak in him comes out in some of his letters. When it was proposed by the Primus and Bishop Wordsworth to revive the Archbishoprics of St. Andrews and of Glasgow (when their separated Roman brethren were about to resume those titles and dignities) he wrote to his brother:

'We should only revive the memory of Beaton in Scotland, and I do not wish to wash my robes in the blood of Sharpe. Most Scotchmen have as much horror of bishops as a bull has of red serge.' It would make the small Episcopal Church look as ridiculous as the clan who prepared to go to battle 'with twenty-four men and five-and-thirty pipers'.

His friendliness with the Church of Scotland, like that of Wordsworth, increased:

'Let us arise from systems, whether of Episcopacy or of Presbytery, above all material apparatus,' he said in his Charge of 1868. He approved warmly of the Archbishop of York's and the Bishop of Winchester's preaching, when on holiday, in a Highland kirk. In 1871 he himself accepted an invitation to preach in Glasgow University, in the hall which served as chapel. This the Bishop of Glasgow (Wilson) forbade. Ewing resented the interference, denied the right of jurisdiction, but for the sake of peace he gave way. His letter of apology to Principal Caird was adroit:

'I am sure the Bishop had no object in view save the preservation of those ecclesiastical barriers which the wisdom and piety of our fathers erected, and which he thinks himself bound to maintain as of primary importance. I have myself formed a very different estimate of their value.' To the sympathetic Wordsworth he wrote about 'the scandal of refusing to join in common worship with fellow Christians. . . . We have shocked the whole Christian sentiment of the country'.

His anti-sacerdotalism deepened:

'These apparently innocent things, Apostolic Succession and high views (as they are called) of the Christian Sacrament are really anti-Christian in their operation,' he told a friendly Presbyterian, Dr. Macleod Campbell; and to another said:

'I certainly do not believe that Apostolic Succession is *needful*, any more than I believe that it is needful for the Queen to be a Stuart to be a queen.' This was a *non sequitur*. What *made* the Queen was her sacring, her anointing and crowning by sacramental rite, not her descent, whether Stuart or Hanoverian. Another minister, Dr. Story of Rosneath, who was to succeed Dr. Caird as Principal of Glasgow University, invited him to preach in his church and he longed to accept:

'I feel more and more that our little Church here in the north, if we do not allow it to enter into relations with the other Christian bodies of the land, will become a mere caste and appanage of the rich, and tend to divide social life in Scotland even more than it has hitherto been divided.'

Again he wrote to Wordsworth:

'The question is being forced upon us, and we must answer it, both to ourselves and to those among whom we live here: "What is the object of our ministry?" If the spirit of which I complain represents the spirit of our Scottish Episcopal Church, it is a grave question whether we should take part in a ministry which has so manifestly departed from the object for which it was instituted.'

Episcopacy had become for him the *bene esse* not the *esse* of the Church: 'Episcopacy, as you well know, while claiming superiority of degree for the *well*-being of the Church, never did, among us, claim to be necessary to its *being*.' But it was the *esse* of Episcopacy, of the Apostolic Succession and threefold order which had held the loyalty and unswerving belief of the Faithful Remnant through all their troubled days.

More and more he disliked dogmatism. The Athanasian Creed was a stumbling-block. Many devout worshippers must 'shrink from describing God, as it were, to Himself, and insisting on the precise relations of the elements of His triune personality, as to which we are in no position to speak with authority'. He would have had it kept 'as a curious heirloom in the charter-chest. It might be looked at occasionally, but it should never be intruded into Divine Worship'.

There were further visits to Sicily: his health, never robust, was declining.

'I am but held together by needle and thread.'

At one time or another he met Continental Catholics of liberal sympathy: Döllinger, Montalembert (who shared his devotion to the Celtic Church), Père Hyacinthe in whom he found both liberal views and devotional fervour; but that was a tragic figure of failure. His contacts however were, in spite of his knowledge of Europe, more with English than with foreign clerics.

Home again he wrote to his brother of the practical, clergy-wifely activity of Lady Alice. She went herself to the slate quarries at Ballachulish to order slates for the church; she organized a bazaar with the help of Lady Glasgow. It becomes very Victorian, rather cosy. His love of the Highlands deepened. There is a lovely description of Evensong in Glencoe, before the church was built, out of doors under the fir trees by the bridge over the Coe, with the mountains for walls and the sky for roof:

'It was a more splendid dome than is that of St. Peter's, and the writing larger than there: "Te Deum Laudamus" rather than "Tu es Petrus". The keys of the kingdom were delivered in Gaelic and the whole service was in the same language.' The murmur of the river and 'the sea-like noise of the light breeze in the pinewood' were clearly heard 'in the silences of the service'. Here was the scene of the massacre; many of the worshippers were descendants of those who had suffered then. They worshipped with the same Liturgy. 'It was a little piece of the past fallen into the present'. [The author may here recall the broadcast, a few years ago, of Evensong in Gaelic from St. Mary's, Glencoe, the church begun that summer of 1872. It was conducted by the Bishop of Moray, in Gaelic. The Psalms were sung in metre. The language was unfamiliar, the Office well known. There was a timeless quality about the act of worship; here too was a 'piece of the past fallen into the present'.]

Reading Ewing's description it is more than ever difficult to understand his antipathy to the Scottish Liturgy, or his weakened sense of Episcopacy. He was so sensitively aware of this local tradition and heritage:

'The only remnant of the past here is the Church. The lairds of Appin are gone; the old holders of the lands and property are no more; but the Church remains. Charles Stuart and his cause are extinct, but the creed of the non-jurors still holds its ground in the Strath of Appin, in Lochaber and Glencoe. Here, under the living vault, are living men using the Prayer Book of King Charles and the sacramental vessels of the Stuart Establishment.' The paten used in Ballachulish was inscribed: '*Parish* of Appine.'

He delivered a much-needed rebuke:

'It is strange and remarkable how little interest is taken by the English Church or by the Episcopalians of Scotland in these still remaining vestiges of their own and the older faith still here.' A further rebuke was given to the Anglo-Catholics; they concerned themselves with 'the revival of antiquarian usages and sentimental practices' rather than with the needs of the living Church in these places.

Then he gave a charming picture of the burial place on Eilan Munn, the island of St. Munn who had preached here, quoting a lovely epitaph inscribed by a man in memory of his wife: 'The delightful Anne.' The Bishop had looked for the grave of one Mary Robertson, a faithful member of the congregation in Ballachulish:

'She tended the church as the holy women in Scripture the temple. It was not only her place of worship, but to some extent the object of her worship also. Gifted with a reverence and awe which are the privilege of few, she was so little awake to the common affairs of life that it seemed as if her mind were at times deficient. Yet she said a thing occasionally which showed great insight into character, and a just appreciation of its merits or defects.'

The heroine of a Highland tale is lost in Mary, and another in the delightful Anne.

About this time Ewing wrote to Lord Glasgow about the collegiate church in Cumbrae, that it might well become 'a working cathedral on the plan of the old abbey on Iona'. There should be more canonries, honorary for old and retired clergy, active for those in service. They would enlarge 'the working clergy' so much needed in Argyll and the Isles.

He was near his end now. There was still some happy voyaging; on a visitation of the Isles by yacht he had among his fellow passengers a Free Kirk minister who afterwards recalled his impressions:

'With regard to the wit, the delicate humour, the playful fancy that existed alongside of so much serious thought, the fun in which he so far outwent us all, it would be as wise to offer the picture of a rainbow by producing in a cup the water of its rain-drops, as to give in a page of sentences the material he made so bright.'

The Bishop saw another winter: he was not yet old, barely sixty, and at the height of his intellectual vitality. In the spring of 1873 he went south, to spend Holy Week and Easter with his brother at Westmill. In the church there he preached his last sermon, on Easter Day. Then the final weakness came upon him: he died on Ascension Day, 1873.

He remains not the most loved, venerated or influential Bishop of the Scottish Church in the past century, but certainly the most enigmatic. In an objective way he is the most fascinating. His duality of mind and personality are almost baffling, the poet in him warring with the Protestant theologian, the mystic with the controversialist.

His abiding passion, that love of Gaeldom and the Celtic tradition which is his most endearing quality could not change his approach to sacramental worship and belief, or overcome a rigidity, a prejudice, almost an obsession about what he judged to be materialism, superstition, magic. The poet and mystic in him were never wholly victorious.

At his best, he was truly fulfilled as a pastoral Bishop.

# 10

# Second Scholastic Interlude.
# Sequel to Glenalmond

1. ALMOND OF LORETTO. An Episcopal Schoolmaster

Glenalmond remained unique among Scottish schools, but Loretto, although not founded with a special purpose like Glenalmond, acquired a special ethos. It was the creation of one man of emphatic impact upon scholastic life. He made Loretto as Arnold made Rugby, and in any Episcopalian portrait gallery he must have a place.

Hely Hutchinson Almond was born in 1832, the son of the incumbent of St. Mary's, Glasgow, a priest with a late but true vocation: he had been in business and had served in the Militia during the Napoleonic War. His son said of him that he had 'no great learning except of the practical parts of his Bible, no higher qualification for the ministry than the average apostle'. Young Hely inherited his intellectual power from his mother's family, the Hely Hutchinsons, one of whom, John, was Provost of Trinity College, Dublin, and Secretary of State for Ireland. The boy began learning his letters at sixteen months, arithmetic at three years, and Greek at seven. Early steeped in learning he was also steeped in evangelical piety. Heaven was about him and he knew its ways. There were no tears there, but there must, he thought, have been a good deal of crying on Good Friday. When he fell out of bed it was the fault of a naughty angel, his own guardian being asleep. A kindly child, he hoped to meet Goliath in heaven.

At thirteen he matriculated at Glasgow University which was not an exceptionally precocious age for that generation. With his scarlet gown he wore a Glengarry bonnet and looked even younger than his years. He had William Ramsay as Professor of Humanity, Lushington in Greek (Tennyson's brother-in-law who wore his learning lightly like a flower) and Robert Buchanan, 'Logic Bob', in metaphysics. They were great scholars, great teachers, great personalities, and this student had the wit to know it; but he worked too hard, with too little play and no real, companionable college life. He won prizes in Logic, in Greek, and in Latin the Cowan Gold Medal which is a feather in the classical cap of Glasgow: in 1850 he went up to Balliol on a Snell Exhibition. The Scottish Church was thus enriched, as her pious benefactor had intended, if not by a priest then by a good scholar and teacher. Almond was to serve her well in his own vocation.

'I went from Glasgow a pale-faced student, having had nothing to do with my afternoons but roam aimlessly about. . . . But for the boats at Oxford, I could have had no hold as a schoolmaster, and but insufficient vigour for the work of life.'

At eighteen he hardly knew how to play or how to mix with other men. Oxford taught him these lessons, yet he was by no means in love with Oxford.

'I hated Oxford,' he said towards the end of his life. 'There was an absence of, a dislike of enthusiasm which always rubbed me up the wrong way.'

Yet a generation earlier, Alexander Forbes had loved the place for its enthusiasm, finding there a new spring of spiritual life, and in Almond's own time two young men came up to begin a lifelong friendship and to fall together under the spell of Oxford: Edward Burne-Jones and William Morris.

Almond continued to work hard though fitfully. He was unlucky in his tutors. When he asked Jowell, his classical tutor, to tell him his weakest points, that worthy gave the edged reply:

'It is difficult to say what are your weakest points.'

His biographer, Robert Mackenzie, an old Lorettan, records that Almond 'got a first to spite him'. It was in fact a double First in Classical and Mathematical Moderations. In Greats he was less fortunate, taking only a Second; this partly because of ill-health. Even so, his record was excellent. What was sadly lacking was any awareness of the fun and friendships of Oxford. His despondency was deepened by the cooling, almost to evaporation, of his religious fervour.

The river saved him. His biographer has written:

'It opened his mind to a new set of virtues. His love of the open air, his passion for health, his appreciation of manly endurance, his reverence for loyalty and public spirit were to him the gifts of the river.'

On those virtues he built Loretto: those were the treasures he brought back to Scotland, as Forbes had brought riches of devotion, Catholic teaching and missionary zeal.

Oxford, through her river if not through her Colleges, gave him the spirit of the English public school which his strength of personality could adapt for his own Scottish creation. He himself said that he 'drifted into schoolmastering', but it was for him as truly a vocation as the priesthood was for his father. He drifted into Loretto itself in 1857, when it was a private school owned by an Oxford friend, Langhorne, and his brothers: after a year, during which he made an impact by his whirlwind way of teaching and his vigour at golf and football, he went to Merchiston. Here he found a headmaster of like mind with himself, and something of the new discipline of games. At this time came a crisis in his spiritual life. The apathy was passing. His dearly loved father was dying, and Almond vowed to himself that if, at the last, any sign were given that the hope of glory was to be fulfilled, then he would believe. The sign was given. Almond's sister wrote to him that at the moment of death their father's face was lit with ineffable joy.

There was a crisis also in his career. He bought Loretto from the Langhornes.

'I give him two years to ruin himself and the school,' said one critic. Almond was to admit that he nearly did it in one year. The school was small, with a few private pupils known as 'pewters' among the boys. Andrew Lang was one of them for a short time. His impression of the new headmaster was strong and favourable. When Robert Mackenzie came in 1866 the number of boys had risen from thirty to sixty; the pewters had departed. Loretto continued to grow in character as in numbers. Almond brought it from a preparatory to a public school, and made it *his* school. The atmosphere was physically and mentally bracing. He taught, he talked, discussing all kinds of subjects with his boys; he played games and compelled them to be played. When necessary he punished and he kept sound discipline, but high spirits and high jinks were not accounted sin.

The boys slept with open windows, wore tweed suits and flannel shirts, and went walking, golfing and running without top-coat or cap; this in a period when everyone, men and women, girls and boys wore layers of underclothing with heavy wraps on top.

'Pit on yer bonnet, my lamb, ye'll catch an awfu' cauld', the fishwives of Musselburgh, sailing along in their heavy petticoats, used to advise. Some people talked fretfully of 'that man Almond and his fykes' – or fads or fancies; but the boys throve.

The school was well run on the domestic side by the matron, Mrs. Weaver, who had been Almond's nurse. She was fat, comfortable, forthright and endlessly kind, inclined to be overcredulous about boyish ailments. The poor little boys had colds and must not go out. Almond, who knew the species, drove the young malingerers out for a bracing walk.

Mrs. Weaver had married a fascinating but roving character who had been apprenticed to many trades, had served in both army and navy, and now settled down to versatile work in the school. One of his trades had been that of baker and his bread and rolls were excellent. Mackenzie recalls the breakfasts of porridge with lashings of cream, rolls or baps 'enfolding a swathe of butter' (a heartsome word 'swathe'!), with herring or Finnan haddies or bacon. There were home-baked scones and oatcake for tea; all the meals were ample.

Weaver kept the accounts, was in charge of supplies, looked after repairs and in his leisure time played the flute and the harmonium which he taught some of the boys. He read a good deal of poetry, especially Byron in whom he delighted. With the smaller boys he was somewhat impatient; the masters he despised; Almond he respected, and with reason. Almond was endlessly patient with him even when Weaver returned from a day out, roaring drunk, in a brougham and four with postilions, charged to the school. The headmaster knew that the man was fighting a devil in himself.

Games were played strenuously: fives, rounders and shinty as well as the usual football and cricket. Golf was played at Musselburgh and on special occasions at Gullane. There were two special Loretto ball games, 'Goosie' and 'Dax'; and there was no off-season for play.

'If I were a gentleman,' said one caddie, 'ye'd no' find me playin' gowf on sic a day. I'd be sittin' a' the aifternoon at the fireside, drinkin' sherry an' blawin' clouds.'

In winter the boys went skating, and Mackenzie recalls with

delight many an afternoon on Duddingston Loch, with the curlers out as well as the skaters, and a following host of apple-wives and coffee-men with little tripods on which they heated the coffee.

Work and games followed more or less the conventional pattern, but there was room for hobbies, for music, for reading; and there was room for religion which was not too strictly cut to pattern. The boys attended Morning Prayer in St. Peter's Episcopal Church, Musselburgh. It was one of the oldest congregations in Scotland but antiquity had little appeal; the services were long and dull. For Evensong they walked over to Dalkeith, to the Duke of Buccleuch's private chapel, St. Mary's, built in the mid-century surge of activity in the Church. Here the full beauty of the Office was brought out, in prayers and canticles, psalms and anthems. The organist, one Hewlett, was a fine musician, although one worshipper declared him to be 'a godless little devil' caring little for the prayers and taking refuge from the sermon in a novel bound like a Prayer Book.

The sermon was however by no means tedious and did not always occur. The chaplain, Mr. Bushby, sometimes thought it enough if he preached in the morning. He prepared the boys, faithfully if unexactingly, for Confirmation; beneath his genial ease lay true religion. The Duke always attended service when in residence at Dalkeith Palace, usually accompanied by Lord Lothian who came over from Newbattle Abbey, and old Lord Melville who looked like a Raeburn portrait. Almond himself was a faithful worshipper and a frequent communicant.

These Sundays left a happy memory with one boy and his description makes a picture of attractive, unforced devotion. Sunday was a pleasant holiday and holy day. The evening was free and ended with a practice of psalms, hymns and anthems and then prayers. Almond used to hold Bible readings during the week: in Holy Week he took the boys through the story of the Passion. On Good Friday they all wore black ties. Almond taught many good things but above all loving-kindness, 'that pity for the helpless which lucky boyhood is so slow to learn'. There was something more than muscular Christianity here.

The school grew beyond the capacity of St. Mary's and held services in a hall in Musselburgh; and when Almond married in 1876 the school's gift to him was a chapel. It was an iron building lined with wood and placed on a piece of waste ground close to the pigsties and the stable-midden. 'The approaches lacked the seemliness to which worshippers are used' – as Mackenzie temperately puts it – but the chapel was bright and cheerful within. The services were robustly musical. They sang Anglican chants interspersed by the metrical psalms to the grand, old tunes, and by hymns 'of the robust type. . . . No Loretto schoolboy ever admitted that he was "weary of earth" or that he "craved for rest".'

The Head preached. In one sermon he spoke of the Eucharist as any of the old Bishops might have done:

'We commemorate a death; we adore a Person who is our present Saviour . . . We cannot define, we dare not localize. Let others dispute while we believe and do.' They might, some of them, have deprecated his going beyond the authority and tradition of the Church: 'We may also believe that our Saviour, according to His Word, is present in this Sacrament – present not only by virtue of any power of Pope, Bishop, priest or minister, but by His own still existing Power exercised as He has promised . . . present amid the incense and the lights and the vestments and the prostrate forms of the Roman ritual; present when the minister, with uplifted hands, blesses the bread and wine on the bare hillside; present alike for those for whom reverence has darkened into superstition, and for those who, while they still obey His bidding, know not that the Lord of the feast is personally there.'

On the death of Dr. Hannah, Almond was invited to succeed him at Glenalmond but would not leave the place he had made his own, and so missed a well-sounding title, Almond of Glenalmond.

'My idea of a school is that it should be the harmonious embodiment of the thought of one person who is not necessarily the headmaster.' It would have been difficult for any other man's thought to be embodied in Loretto while Almond lived. His biographer, himself a schoolmaster, admits that he could be difficult with his staff, having more sympathy with the boys than with the masters. The latter were expected to live for the school, giving up, if it were necessary and it often was, their leisure and social life. Some of them found Almond's system too flexible, and he for his part said:

'There is hardly any class of men so bigoted, so like popish priests at the time of the Reformation, as the ordinary public school and 'Varsity man.' To one applicant he wrote warningly: 'The life is rather humdrum, with little variety. . . . The hours of work are suited rather to my ideas of the good of the boys than the convenience of the masters.'

With boys he was sympathetic but never slack. He would not condone vice: 'I have a great belief that the best chance for a boy being cured of evil propensities is his suffering for them,' he told parents, adding that he had found in one case that a flogging induced contrition and stopped stealing and forgery.

Parents were kept in their place in a way that has rarely been equalled. They came lower than the masters.

A great Victorian, Almond lived into the new reign, dying in 1902. He left instructions that there was to be no mourning, no cancellation of matches, no interruption of the school routine.

Health and cleanliness of body, mind and soul were his ideal. He taught his boys to play, remembering his own austere boyhood. Schoolroom, playing-field, chapel made a trinity. Were they equal? The shouts of players may seem to predominate. Yet above that clamour there does arise, from time to time, the sound of chant and psalm, the murmur of prayer; and sometimes a silence falls. Loretto, once a shrine of Our Lady, a memorial of the Holy House at Loretto in Italy, perhaps received and kept a blessing, a devout remembrance of the Holy Manhood, the abiding Presence in the Eucharist.

2. Professor of All Things. JOHN DOWDEN: A Scholar Bishop. From Glenalmond to Edinburgh.

Scholars can be bridge-builders over the great river of time between past and present. John Dowden, Bishop of Edinburgh from 1886 to 1910, joins the Church of Bishop Jolly with that of his own day, for he came to Scotland as Pantonian Professor at Glenalmond, under Miss Kathrein Panton's bequest: his scholarship did much to restore the Scottish Liturgy to use and honour and it surveyed the whole background of Church history in Scotland, Celtic and medieval.

He was born in 1840, in Cork, of an Anglo-Irish family. His

father was Presbyterian, his mother Church of Ireland; the boy knew both Churches and both Catechisms. He was clever and bookish, sharing the tastes of his brother Edward, the future Shakespearian scholar. At sixteen he went with a scholarship to Queen's College, Cork, and two years later to Trinity, Dublin, where he took a First in Logic and Ethics, and also in Divinity. Ordained Deacon in 1864 he was appointed to a curacy in Sligo, and married in the same year: priested in 1865 he became, in 1867, Perpetual Curate of Calry, with a stipend of £70. His daughter Alice was to recall a happy childhood there with a father who, 'though in a sense awe-inspiring was much sought after by his children' and who, while he forbade noise and crying, welcomed his children to his study and allowed them to build forts and castles with his books.

The scholar in him developed at this period: he absorbed some of the antiquarian knowledge which was to inform so richly his *Celtic Church in Scotland*, he contributed to *The Contemporary Review*, and he began the liturgical studies which were to be the intellectual, perhaps also the spiritual, passion of his life. This was the time of the disestablishment of the Church of Ireland with subsequent controversy about revision of the Prayer Book. Dowden made suggestions which do not appear to have been used, but the labour was not lost. It was an apprenticeship for the master-work of his later years.

In 1870 he was made chaplain to the Lord Lieutenant, Lord Spencer, which took him occasionally to Dublin, and two years later he moved there on being appointed to the staff of St. Stephen's Church. These were not peaceful years; controversy bubbled and boiled over Prayer Book revision, ritualism and such heating matters. Dowden published a sermon on 'The Saints in the Calendar and the Irish Synod', in which he castigated the latter for their attempt to remove the names and days of black-letter saints. 'Thoroughly and vulgarly provincial,' he called them, which did not make him popular. As his biographer and fellow Bishop of later days, Anthony Mitchell, temperately put it:

'It is unlikely that his further contributions to the difficult ecclesiastical situation would have been of a soothing character.'

The call to Scotland was timely. It came through an old friend, the Reverend Percy Robertson, now Warden of Glenalmond, who invited him to go there as Pantonian Professor of Theology and Bell Lecturer in Education. The school was flourishing, but not the Theological College. When Dowden arrived he found one student – 'My one ewe lamb.' Undeterred, he began preparing and delivering lectures.

'My style and dignity is that of Pantonian Professor, so called from the Greek *Panton* because I am Professor of All Things.' Other students came, although not in overwhelming numbers, so he had leisure for study, concentrating more and more upon liturgic learning. He seems to have taken a part in the discipline of the school. There is a legend which ought to be true that when boys were sent to him for chastisement, Mrs. Dowden used to meet them when they came out of the study, with the solace of an apple or an orange.

He was interrupted in the library one day by an apologetic sixth-former who with true public school diffidence announced:

'I thought you might like to know, sir, that the College is on fire.'

No lives and only a few books were lost but the seminary part of the College was so badly damaged that the students moved to Edinburgh, to live, first in lodgings, then in Old Coates House, Manor Place, and attend lectures in Dowden's own house. For him the change was a good one: a university and capital city was a better place for his young men than a remote glen in Perthshire.

'The College may return to Glenalmond but the Pantonian Professor stays here.'

There was a good deal of discussion, long continuing and not untinged by acrimony, but the Professor won. The College stayed in Edinburgh, coming in due time to its present home, Coates Hall, Rosebery Crescent. In 1874 the Cathedral of St. Mary was begun, largely on the endowment left by the Misses Mary and Barbara Walker; it was consecrated in 1879, the fourth in the Scottish Church, having been preceded by St. Ninian's, Perth, St. Andrew's, Inverness, and the Cathedral of the Holy Spirit, Millport.

And now the College flourished. Dowden was Principal as well as Pantonian Professor; a Vice-Principal was elected, the staff increased. His own College, Trinity, Dublin, made him a Doctor of Divinity. In 1884 he published his *Annotated Scottish Communion Office*, with a treatise on The American Prayer Book, dedicated to the American Bishops. Two years later, on the death of Henry Cotterill, he was elected Bishop of Edinburgh, after a storm rivalling that of the election of Wordsworth.

Henry Cotterill, like his predecessor Terrot was an Englishman, born at Blakeney in Norfolk, a Cambridge scholar and again, like Terrot, a brilliant mathematician. He served as chaplain to the East India Company in Madras, came home for nine years, then went to Africa as Bishop of Grahamstown, in 1856. All his life he had a deep interest in missions. In 1871 he came to Edinburgh as Coadjutor to Bishop Terrot, and in 1872 succeeded him as Diocesan. It was a period of growth. He saw the building of his cathedral and of other churches in the diocese: St James, Inverleith Row; Christ Church, Morningside; Christ Church, Trinity; St. Anne's, Dunbar. The growth was not only diocesan or even provincial. In 1871 the Scottish Church undertook the care of Chanda in India, and in 1872, at Cotterill's suggestion, the Scottish Bishops consecrated Dr. Callaway for the diocese of St. John's, South Africa. The Churchwomen's Association for Foreign Missions was formed. It was an episcopate of progress and of going out.

(Irrelevent but interesting is the fact that the Bishop's niece, Ruth Cotterill, married a young master at Fettes, W. P. Brooke, and became the mother of Rupert Brooke. The Bishop married them in his new cathedral.)

An Englishman had followed an Englishman and there was some criticism of the apparent neglect of good Scots priests who had served the Church faithfully. This was renewed and intensified in the dissension over Cotterill's successor.

The first name to be proposed was that of Dean Liddon, who was elected after some opposition by the nationalists. Liddon then declined the Bishopric. The electors met again and three names were put forward: Dowden, Hugh Jermyn (already Bishop of Brechin) and the Reverend Robert Dundas, a Scot by birth, who held an English living. He, poor fellow, though recommended by his proposer for being of old and good Scots family, won only three votes from the clergy and none from the laity. Dowden and Jermyn were equally favoured, the former for his scholarship.

One of his supporters, Canon Murdoch of All Saints, said that 'he seemed to have an answer to every question at his finger's end'. It had been objected that his voice was almost inaudible in the great cathedral; Canon Murdoch did not find it so. He did not think it mattered over much if the multitude found him difficult to hear. 'When he did preach a sermon it was worth their trouble to listen to it.' Another cleric agreed, adding that the cathedral was not after all the only church in the diocese: there were many others, smaller and easier in acoustics, in which he would be heard clearly and be welcomed as Bishop.

On the other side, Mr. Grant of Roslin, while admitting Dowden's rich scholarship – 'It was even put forward as a recommendation that he was a critic of the drama' – thought it untimely to take him from his principalship. It was important for the Church that her young ordinands should be taught by a man of such wide culture, vast learning and infectious enthusiasm. Canon Dowden was comparatively young and might, if he were spared, become a Bishop at 'the age at which Bishops were usually made' and even hope to be translated from some lesser Bishopric to the more exalted atmosphere of the diocese of Edinburgh. Meanwhile, Mr. Grant argued, it would be unjust to exalt him and deprive others whose service in the Church had been longer, notably Hugh Jermyn, Bishop of Brechin, who deserved translation 'to what he might call the metropolitan diocese of the country'.

Votes were equally divided between Dowden and Jermyn; on a second voting Dowden had a majority. He was consecrated by the other six Bishops and the Bishop of Durham. Although no longer 'Professor of All Things' he continued to lecture in the College where one of his students was a future Principal and future Bishop, Anthony Mitchell.

Dowden was much criticized for ecclesiastical strictness. He would not allow his clergy to preach in Presbyterian pulpits, and this ban was extended to a fellow Bishop (Wordsworth); he began the use of the Latinized signature, J. Edenburgen, a mark of Prelacy unpopular with Presbyterians. The Bishop held calmly on his way and in time won great respect in the city and in Scotland generally for his scholarship. His *Celtic Church in Scotland*, which remains a classic, appeared in 1894; his study of *The Workmanship of the Prayer Book* in 1899, followed a year later by *Further*

*Studies in the Prayer Book*. His *Mediaeval Church in Scotland* was published after his death in 1910.

'He was, in his day, the Church's Scholar-Bishop' is the tribute of his former student and fellow Bishop, Anthony Mitchell. In retrospect the emphasis may seem to lie on the scholar rather than on the Bishop. He was perhaps of the same type as Gleig. But neither he nor Gleig failed to be chief pastor, builder, defender and expounder of the faith.

Living through all but three years of Victoria's reign and the brief rule of her son, through two ages in history, almost to the end of the old world which finished in 1914, he saw many changes and much growth in the Church. He came to a new cathedral, he saw another church, St. Paul's, Dundee, raised to the status of cathedral, and under his rule began and continued the growth of the Theological College. He was truly a bridge-builder, although neither in his inheritance nor in his youth was there any bond with the Scottish Church of the past, but scholarship made the bond and built the bridge. When he was a boy in Cork the Scottish Church was still ruled by Bishops who had known poverty and seen the last shadows of the penal days; when he came to Scotland their memory was alive. The Church in his episcopate was prosperous, well-favoured and esteemed, if not always for the right reasons. Snobbery and worldliness were slipping in. There was a good deal of complacency and in Edinburgh especially a strong tendency towards England, so that outsiders were not unjustified in talking of the English Church.

This tendency was emphasized by the neglect of the Scottish Prayer Book and it is largely due to Dowden's liturgical scholarship and sense of the past that our Liturgy was restored to use and honour. That was his greatest bridge. The edition of 1912 and that of 1929 both owe much to his work.

In his defence of the book, the introduction to his *Historical Account of the Scottish Communion Office* (1884) he wrote:

'Its true reflection of the spirit of primitive devotion and the unquestionable merits which it possesses as a formulary of worship, have won the admiration of theologians and liturgiologists of high eminence . . . It is a worthy monument of the learning and piety of the Scottish Church.'

The Scottish Liturgy has not been formed by one man or one

age, not in haste but gradually, with 'perhaps a greater variety of sources than any known liturgy' and yet it was no patchwork but a living thing:

'conceived in no mere antiquarian spirit . . . no product of a dilettante affectation of the antique. Like everything that lives, it came into being from a living impulse; but also, like everything that lives, it was sensitive to its actual environment, and exhibited the living power of adapting itself to that environment without permanent detriment to its life.'

Primitive but adaptable, its appeal was not only to scholars. It had expressed the worship and supplications of thousands of the faithful through many generations. 'The most precious gifts of God have come to them through that channel.'

There was a rebuke, in passing, for English complacency for 'our incomparable Liturgy'; but there was a beginning of comparison, in England, between the two Rites. Should corporate recognition and intercommunion come between Orthodox and Anglican, the Scottish (and the American) Liturgy could be accepted by both as having the essential elements, the true shape, placing the Invocation equal with the Words of Institution.

He did not, for all that, altogether commend the 1764 book prepared by Bishops Forbes and Falconar. He found that there the Invocation 'occurred with startling abruptness . . . introduced abruptly . . . passed from abruptly; it stands in nakedness and baldness which has no parallel'. They should have followed the guidance of Bishop Rattray.

Dowden's book reprinted the Scottish Office of 1637, the Office of the non-jurors in 1718, with its singularly beautiful Invocation; and that of the Episcopal Church of America which so closely follows the Scottish Rite. He quoted also the Invocation from various Eastern Orthodox Liturgies. The Scottish Church was reminded of this portion of her rich inheritance.

This volume is invaluable at once as an historical survey, a commentary, and a compendium of liturgies. In modern idiom, he puts us in the picture and the picture is a rich one.

His comment on the book of 1764 was that here 'expression is given to a great truth but not to the whole truth as we find it in the corresponding parts of the liturgies of the ancient Church. And for many a year our Communion has been suffering from the inevitable nemesis that sooner or later overtakes every departure, made in the Church's formularies of devotion, from the even balance of the primitive faith'.

Forbes of Brechin had made the same criticism – 'A great truth but not the whole truth,' and had been punished by his fellow Bishops. All the ancient liturgies brought out the purport, and the consequence to the faithful of the invoked Descent of the Holy Spirit upon the oblation of bread and wine.

Dowden praised Bishop Rattray's Office, published after his death; a Rite which came close to the primitive Liturgy of St. James. He spoke of the Eucharistic doctrine of the non-jurors with its emphasis on the Sacrifice as well as the Sacrament:

'A solemn Memorial or Representation of Christ's great Sacrifice offered to God the Father. The Bread and Cup are made authoritative Representations or Symbols of Christ's crucified Body and of His Blood shed; and in consequence they are in a capacity of being offered to God as the great Christian Sacrifice.'

He was quoting from the Catechism of Bishop Deacon (1734) which had been followed by Bishop Jolly. Bishop Rattray had expounded the same high doctrine; and Robert Forbes had believed and taught it, yet somehow, in their revision of the Liturgy, he and Bishop Falconar had omitted something precious and valid.

Dowden did not quote the other Forbes, of Brechin, but his book may be read as a vindication of that great Bishop and his teaching. And many today agree with his conclusion:

'Of late years there has been (happily, I think) a greater disposition among us to be content with the language of Scripture and the primitive Church, and to avoid speculation upon the mystery of the Eucharist.'

If in this or the next generation The Scottish Liturgy be again revised, we shall realize our debt to this scholar-Bishop. We must go back to him for instruction, and from him further and further back: to Alexander Forbes, to Jolly, to Rattray; but always remembering 'the language of Scripture and the primitive Church'.

# 11

# The Church Extending. A Kaleidoscope. Schools; Congregations; Religious Communities

I

Glenalmond had led the way followed by the young and independent Loretto; the public school pattern was extended by Fettes which was not, however, particularly Episcopalian. Other schools were Church foundations. One was at Lenzie, begun in the 1870's under the headmastership of the incumbent of the church, St. Cyprian's. Another was the Northern Collegiate School, Inverness, founded in 1873 under the direction of the Primus (Eden) and a group of Highland gentry, 'for the purpose of providing for the sons of gentlemen resident in the northern counties a thoroughly good and liberal education at a moderate cost.' Pupils were nominated by shareholders. It was both a boarding and a day school, with a classical and a modern side, preparing boys for the universities, the services, 'and also for the mercantile and professional life.' Music and drawing were extras, drill 'a compulsory extra', and the school had a gymnasium, cricket ground and playing fields. It was not exclusively Episcopal; Presbyterian boys went to the church of their parents' choice, young Episcopalians to the cathedral.

For girls there was St. Mary's opened in Edinburgh in 1878 by the Society of Reparation of St. Mary and St. John, of whom more will be told in a later section. Founded in 1870 by Elizabeth Ann White, widow of an incumbent of St. James's, Leith, the Society had its mother house in Aberdeen, with day and night schools for poor children.

St. Mary's was planned as 'a school which shall afford a liberal education to girls belonging to the Scottish Episcopal Church', especially the daughters of clergy. Fees were £45 a year for juniors, £50 for seniors, which could be reduced by scholarships. Music, dancing, laundry and medical attention were extras.

The Society was, by its rule, devoted to the work of Christian education. The curriculum was wide and varied. The idea of higher education for girls was still new and exciting but not shocking, and these Religious were sympathetic. Their aim was 'the formation of highly cultivated gentlewomen fitted for any state of life to which God's providence might call them', which might be a career through one of the new colleges for women, perhaps Lady Margaret Hall, Oxford, whose Principal, Elizabeth Wordsworth, was daughter to the Bishop of Lincoln, niece to the Bishop of St. Andrews. Pupils were prepared for the Oxford and Cambridge Local Examinations. They played games; hockey had not yet occurred but it was admitted that, without being unlady-like, a girl might run, might throw and hit a ball, and generally enjoy more physical training than was given by dancing, deport-ment, and the right way of getting in and out of a carriage. The Sisters did not hope for profit: 'The prime object of the promoter will have been gained if the great cause of Christian education be advanced by this effort, and the clergy assisted in giving to their daughters an upbringing suitable to their station in life.' Thus it was stated in the *Church Year Book* of 1878. The school moved to Aberdeen in the 1890's.

About the same time began Lansdowne House School which still happily flourishes. A small beginning has had a steady growth. The founders, Miss Charlotte Fenton and Miss Annie Emerson, came to Edinburgh in 1879. Miss Fenton had suddenly found it necessary to earn her living after her father's loss of fortune; she had had a good deal to do with children in her own family and liked teaching them. On holiday in the Isle of Man she met Miss Emerson who had a small school there, attended by Miss Fenton's two young half-sisters. The two women found much in common, especially a love of teaching and a love of youth. They decided to open a school in Edinburgh. It was a modest beginning, with four pupils in a house in Lennox Street, moving as the numbers grew to a larger one in Coates Gardens, then to Lansdowne Crescent. Those first pupils went out to classes and lectures, including Professor Calderwood's on Moral Philosophy and Sir Archibald Geikie's on geology. Later, all classes were held in school, including dancing and deportment. They were taught to enter a room gracefully: 'My dear, don't try to come through the key-hole' was Miss Fenton's crisp advice. There were riding lessons too, and a good deal of outdoor life such as Miss Fenton had enjoyed in her own girlhood in Yorkshire; and there was solid instruction. This was no Miss Pinkerton's Academy.

A healthy school, it grew rapidly. The final move was to the present school, Lansdowne House, in its own grounds. The atmosphere was very much that of a cultivated home. Both mistresses were well liked; Miss Fenton, the stronger personality of the two, stamped her impress on the school. The cathedral clergy gave religious instruction and the girls attended morning prayer on Sunday in the cathedral, Evensong in the new and neighbouring Church of the Good Shepherd. The founders' primary aim was 'the upbringing of girls on Christian principles, and the religious teaching given shall be in accordance with the standards of the Episcopal Church in Scotland'.

Both ladies saw the new century, Miss Emerson dying in 1902. Miss Fenton was joined by Miss Ellen Hale as Vice-Principal, and on Miss Fenton's death in 1924 Miss Hale carried on the tradition, adapting it to the new age with a wider scope and achievement. If Miss Fenton made the Victorian school, Miss Hale made that which lives so healthily today. From her brief but vivid account of her predecessors this story of her school is derived.

There were by this time many Church schools for what the Victorians plainly called the lower classes. St. Columba's, Edinburgh, had, from its foundation, a school for poor children under the care of the Order of Holy Charity. All Saints followed this good example both in having a Sisterhood and in opening a school. These are only two examples of the many congregations having a school, in most cases under a secular staff but within the jurisdiction of the Church, and teaching Church doctrine. *The Scottish Guardian* in 1886 published the Report of the Inspector of Schools in the diocese of Brechin, which may be taken as illustration. In Cove, the schoolmistress 'has produced very fair results among somewhat dull children. She gives proof both of energetic and painstaking teaching. Whatever can be done by memory is well done, but I would like to see more intelligence displayed.'

This desire was satisfied in Dundee. St. Paul's, in spite of having too many classes in one room, showed 'a vigour, earnestness and readiness which is very pleasing'; the head-mistress had 'impressed her own spirit not merely on the staff but also on her pupils from the lowest to the highest'. The infant mistress 'maintains the necessary discipline without harshness or noise' and the whole atmosphere was bright and cheerful. In the boys' school at St. Salvador's 'there is life, energy and spirit everywhere, and the general accuracy is noticeable. The quietness, order and discipline were very pleasing'. The girls' school gave the inspector equal pleasure: 'The neatness, attention, readiness and general accuracy of the children are very enjoyable.' The infants were also praised: 'Miss Hinsley manages her numerous young charges in a very pleasing manner.'

Brechin had its orphanage, Baldovan, Bishop Forbes's foundation, and this won the highest number of honours in the inspector's list: there was 'an amount of thoughtful answering in the upper section which I have not often met with'.

These schools were a worthy memorial to the great Bishop who loved the poor and loved scholarship. There were other orphanages: St. Mary's was founded in 1873 for girls by Miss Fraser Tytler, a member of All Saints. After her death it was moved to Culross.

'The object is to train girls for domestic service by giving them such an upbringing as may help them, with God's assistance, to fulfil religiously and usefully the duties of that state of life to which He has been pleased to call them.'

Aberlour was founded in 1875 and by 1895 had over two hundred and seventy children. 'This institution is for the reception of orphans and fatherless children of poor Episcopalians and others in Scotland.' Both these houses depended chiefly on contributions, but St. Mary's expected the friends of each child to help by giving £9 a year.

Most of the teachers in these Church schools were women, trained at The Scottish Episcopal Training Institution for Schoolmistresses, Dalry House, Edinburgh. It had begun as a training college for men but so few had come and so many girls had wanted training that it had become entirely feminine. Schoolmasters were presumably trained either in one of the secular or

St Ninian's Cathedral, Perth:
the nave looking east

The Cathedral Church of St Mary, Edinburgh

St John's Church, Pittenweem, Fife

The Carmelite Priory Church, South Queensferry, West Lothian

undenominational centres, or in England. Dalry House had room for sixty students: it provided tuition, board, laundry and medical attention for an admission fee of £12, with an additional £2 for books. French and music were included in the tuition.

Between the seventies and the nineties these schools increased from forty-six to seventy-four. A report was given in 1894 to the Representative Church Council by the Reverend J. M. Danson, who warned his hearers against undue complacency: 'The Roman Catholics have multiplied the number of their schools by eight, we have not succeeded in doubling ours. The Roman Catholic hierarchy, priesthood and laity are of one heart and mind as to the duty and wisdom of maintaining their denominational schools.' Our seventy-four schools had over eleven thousand pupils; the young Romans numbered more than forty-two thousand. Church Schools had received in 1893 a Government Grant of over £11,000. Teachers' salaries ranged from the maximum of £146 16s. 8d., with a free house for men, if principals (headmistresses had about £80, with a house) to just under £50 for a female assistant. Passing rich with ten pounds more than Goldsmith's schoolmaster!

The increase in schools was one of the signs of growth and vitality in the Church. Another sign, or perhaps more truly a cause of this life, was the presence of religious communities. The first, that of St. Andrew of Scotland, began in 1858 with the opening, by Mrs. Mackenzie, wife of an Edinburgh lawyer, of a penitentiary or House of Mercy for prostitutes, in Gilmore Place: this moved to a house in Lauriston Lane and it was in the chapel here that Bishop Forbes and his friends made their Communion on the morning of his trial. In 1862 there was another move, to Greenside House, off the London Road. The women did laundry work. In 1865 mission work was begun, and a Mission Chapel of St. Andrew opened in the old High School Yards. The head of the house was Miss Grant, and in 1867 she and her companions were formed and consecrated as the Community of St. Andrew of Scotland, with Miss Grant as Superior, taking the name of Mother Regina. It was the first Sisterhood native to Scotland and she was the first Scots Episcopalian to be professed a nun. Their motto was: 'Crux Christi, Clavis Mundi' – The Cross of Christ, the Key of the World. In 1884 the Community opened a house at Joppa, near Edinburgh, for difficult or delinquent girls who were trained in laundry work. This continued until 1919 when it was taken over by The Sisters of St. Peter. It has given up within the past few years.

The Mission Chapel became an incumbency and in 1888 moved to Hill Square, taking over a disused Free Kirk building and dedicating it to St. Michael. The incumbent was the Reverend Thomas Ball who had begun his priestly work at St. Salvador's, Dundee, continued it at Cove, at All Saints and at St. Columba's, Edinburgh, and who now began at St. Michael's, the high Anglo-Catholic, almost ultramontane tradition of St. Michael's with its intense, sacramental devotion. [As this book is being written St. Michael's has given up its separate existence to unite with All Saints, with the name and dedication of St. Michael's and All Saints.]

The Sisterhood of St. Margaret of Scotland was founded in 1864 from St. Margaret's, East Grinstead, and had, and still have their house in Aberdeen, with their parish work, nursing and embroidery. They had, besides, a small convalescent home and a hostel 'to provide a bright, happy home for mill girls who have no homes of their own'.

The Scottish Church was not the pioneer in restoring the religious communities within the Anglican fold, but it did lead the way in one restoration. 'The Episcopalians have the credit of founding the first Community of Reparation in Scotland': so Peter Anson writes in his *Call of the Cloister*. This was the Society who, as we have seen, opened St. Mary's School for Girls. It really began in 1865 when Elizabeth White opened an orphanage in Perth under the pastoral care of the Provost of St. Ninian's Cathedral; it was her memorial to her husband. She was joined by two other ladies and they went, after a time, to that nursing mother of the new Anglican Religious, All Saints, Margaret Street, London, as novices under Mother Harriet Byron. In 1870 they came back to Scotland to found The Society of Reparation, with Mrs. White as Mother Superior. Their purpose was 'the offering of Reparative Adoration to Our Lord in the Blessed Sacrament on the Altar', their activity the helping of the clergy through teaching and any other work asked of them in the parish, in the sacristy, in any service that might glorify God and aid His poor. At the heart of all their work lay contemplative adoration and prayer.

In 1873 Bishop Suther asked them to come to Aberdeen. At first there was no suitable house for them but they found one at Cove in the bordering diocese of Brechin. Here they began a mission for the fisherfolk, with Thomas Ball as their chaplain and director; he compiled for them their Book of Hours, or Day Office, the first in the Anglican Church to include the Feast of the Sacred Heart and of the Assumption, and a form of Communion of the Sick from the Reserved Sacrament. After two or three years in Cove they moved to Aberdeen, to their House of Bethany, from which radiated all their work. They had a Mission House with day and evening classes for both children and adults; an orphanage for girls; and they visited the sick and poor. Then, as we have seen, they opened St. Mary's in Edinburgh. They were the Episcopal Church's first and nearest approach to the Ursulines, to the Society of the Sacred Heart, and to the Sisters of Marie Reparatrice. [That Roman Community came to Scotland fourteen years later, in 1884, to Dumfries, invited by Lady Herries.] The Society of Reparation, rooted in prayer, flowered in works of mercy.

Almost contemporary was the Sisterhood of St. Mary and St. Modwenna in Dundee, formally founded and consecrated by Bishop Forbes in 1871, though it might claim to have begun sixteen years earlier. Peter Anson links it with the Sisterhood of the Holy Cross, one of the earliest Anglican Communities. A member of that Sisterhood had worked in Dundee under the Bishop in 1855, as Superior of his Institution for Schoolmistresses. He quotes also a reference to Forbes from a book on Sisterhoods, by a Miss Goodman, published in 1863:

'I could name a Scottish Bishop who as a scholar and gentleman is second to few men, whose Bishopric is worth less than £400 per annum, and who cannot spend less than £500 annually in expenses connected with his diocese.' For every need the chief call was upon him. 'Added to which he works harder than the meanest curate.'

The ground was prepared when, in 1870, two ladies, Frances Holland and Margaret Neish, offered to establish a Sisterhood. A house was procured in King Street and a chapel built, the first to be *built* in Scotland for a Community. These ladies, with one or two others, made their novitiate with the Sisters of All Saints in London, returning to Dundee in 1871 to make their vows, with Mrs. Holland as Superior, and to have their chapel consecrated by the Bishop. Their first name, The Sisters of the Poor of St. Mary the Virgin, was presently changed to that of St. Mary and St. Modwenna; they were affiliated to All Saints. In their chapel the Sacrament was reserved in an aumbry or Sacrament House, for the sick and dying. They visited the poor and sick, laid out the dead, performed countless works of mercy. After the death of their foundress in 1890 the Sisterhood was taken over by that of St. Margaret, East Grinstead.

The Order of Holy Charity – *Societas Sanctae Caritatis* – was only a little junior, founded in 1872 by the Reverend Edward Bowden, incumbent of St. Columba's, Edinburgh, and by a devout lady of the congregation, Isabella Leaf. She became Superior of their house in Johnston Terrace. Their object was that of true charity, to express the spirit of love 'in ever-increasing devotion to God and in a perpetual stream of loving-kindness towards man'. This active love was shown in visiting and nursing the poor, of whom Edinburgh had God's plenty, in maintaining a home for old people and one for children, in teaching and in sacristy work. In 1880 the Sisters opened a small Convalescent home at Port Seton. Their work was extended over the border and in 1889 they left Scotland. One of the Sisters, Jessie Moncrieff, founded the Community of Benedictines at West Malling.

Besides the religious communities there were an increasing number of lay societies and guilds. A good deal of the picture may be seen in successive *Directories* or *Year Books*. By 1890 the congregational pattern has become much as it is to-day; entries in the *Year Book* give details of services, usages, organizations. The Society of Reparation had its Tertiaries: 'men and women clerics and laics, living in the world yet desirous of sharing in the devotions and works of mercy of the Society, and furthering its aims by all the means in their power.' The Confraternity of The Blessed Sacrament and The Scottish Church Union both took root and flourished. For the clergy in particular there was The Society of the Holy Spirit, with a rule enjoining the frequent celebration of the Eucharist, weekly if possible, the daily recital of the *Veni Creator*, the Lord's Prayer and the Collects of the Society, the regular study of the Bible and an annual Retreat of at least one day.

For women there was the Churchwomen's Association in Aid of Foreign Missions (which became, more succinctly, The Churchwomen's Missionary Association) founded in 1875 'to consolidate the desultory and partial efforts of local or isolated workers by introducing a system of harmony method and mutual aid into women's work for missions'.

In Edinburgh there was the Earl Grey Street Flower Mission, opened in 1874 by some ladies. Flowers were received, arranged in nosegays, and taken, each with a text-card, to the sick and poor. Some were sold in aid of the Mission at the railway stations. In Edinburgh also there was a Guild of Aid Free Registry under the presidency of Lady Kinnaird: 'a means of communication between employers and servants of the Scotch Episcopal Church'. The former paid a fee of 1s. 6d., the latter nothing, unless they chose, after finding a post, to contribute sixpence or a shilling to help less fortunate girls. There was every hope of employment: 'Superior servants are always greatly in request; all must bear good characters and be thoroughly efficient.'

For men there was the Brotherhood of St. Andrew whose object was 'the spread of Christ's Kingdom among young men'. It had a rule of prayer and of service, and asked for quality of membership rather than numbers. Candidates must fulfil a probation or postulancy of three months. Each congregational chapter had the incumbent as chaplain, but a lay leader and lay secretary, and leaders and secretaries made up the Council. Besides this there was a Working Man's Society for 'the spreading of the principles of the Episcopal Church of Scotland among the working classes, and the removal of mistaken ideas about the said Church'; which was very sound and necessary, but the need was by no means confined to the working classes. The Victorians had no notion of ignoring class distinctions: their snobbery, however comic or deplorable, was direct and not inverted, and their social language plain spoken. This Society worked through lectures and classes, the distribution of tracts and the general assisting of the clergy 'in such mission work as meets with their approval'. The Young Men's Friendly Society relaxed a little by providing some amusements and recreation, but it had a high and serious purpose. The inner ring of working associates were expected to 'make the acquaintance of the members, gain their confidence, get into touch with them, be their friends, guides and counsellors, and so lead them to appreciate the higher aims the Society has in view'.

The Home Mission Association was for both men and women. Missionary work both at home and overseas was increasing but was becoming more and more needed. There was need for missionaries in Chanda and in St. John's and equal need for them in our own cities. The Church in her new growth must care both for the scattered members in the Highlands and Islands, and for the new influx of English and Irish in the industrial towns. The convener of the Home Mission Board in 1895 said: 'In the city of Glasgow alone there are districts in which we know there are thousands of Episcopalians as yet almost untouched by our Church.'

The St. Andrew's Waterside Church Mission looked after sailors, fishermen and emigrants, its special object being 'to encourage the worship of God at sea, and to care for those travelling by sea'. A brother society, The Missions to Seamen, did similar work, providing chaplains, lay readers and other helpers at ports, furnishing a church ship in dock and establishing mission rooms.

The Scottish Episcopal Friendly Society begun in 1792 by Bishop Skinner to raise funds for the repeal of the Penal Acts, still existed; the balance of money left after the repeal was set aside for clergy widows and orphans. The West Highlands Mission Fund was devoted to the poor and scattered charges in the north and west. With some charges and variations it is much as we know the economic or working life of the Church today. The centre of all practical activity and management was the Representative Church Council, formed in 1875, largely by the efforts and influence of Bishop Eden, to include lay representatives, one from each congregation, and to co-ordinate all efforts and organizations. It was sub-divided into various Boards. Women were not yet elected but that would come in time, for their work in their own guilds and associations was increasing, and increasingly recognized.

2

The Church of the latter part of the century may be seen, as it were, through two kaleidoscopes: the *Directory* or *Year Book* and *The Scottish Guardian*, the weekly newspaper which began in 1864. A lively history may lie behind some of the discreet entries in the *Year Book*, notably in the case of All Saints, Edinburgh. Its Catholic standard is evident in the factual account of a daily Eucharist, and two Celebrations on Sundays and holy days, and the use at early Celebrations of the Scottish Office. Beneath and behind this lies a small but intense dispute between this young congregation and its unloving parent, St. John the Evangelist. All Saints began as a Mission in Earl Grey Street, under the care of the Reverend Alexander Murdoch; he so fostered it that in 1867 it petitioned the Bishop to be raised to an independent charge. This was granted by the Coadjutor Bishop, Thomas Baker (Terrot being ill and inactive), as was the further petition for the use of the Scottish Liturgy. Writing of this to Dean Ramsay – who was also incumbent of St. John's, and therefore at this moment his superior – Mr. Murdoch gave his reasons for desiring the Scottish Rite – chiefly that it was of great help in giving Holy Communion to the sick – and stated that it was desired also by the Committee representing the congregation. Unfortunately the Dean was ill and was not dealing with his correspondence. He appears to have known nothing of the matter until the Bishop, good, innocent man, mentioned it almost by chance to his chaplain, Daniel Fox Sandford, grandson of an earlier Bishop and curate at St. John's. A contemporary account says that they were walking together and Sandford was so astounded that he stood rooted to the pavement while the Bishop placidly walked on. Sandford knew Dean Ramsay's dislike of the Scottish Office, and his equally strong dislike of opposition. He foresaw squalls and his foresight was clear and accurate. The Dean in a long and intemperate letter accused Mr. Murdoch and his congregation of deceitful and base dealings. He had not been informed of the petition. (His convalescence, during which he was protected from letters, had apparently been a long one.) Protesting himself free from personal animosity he declared he must, on principle, oppose their request. The letter had barely a top dressing of courtesy;

the rising temper is very evident; the fox is shrugging off the sheepskin. Vindictive rage and incensed vanity burst out through the formal phrases:

'Although I am quite willing to extend to others the due consideration which I hope for in regard to my own conduct, still I must decidedly tell you that I decline to enter upon any discussions with you upon the question. . . . In your letter to me you put the question not merely as expressing the wishes of others, but as a partisan pleading for the continuance of an Office among us which I think should be confined to those congregations where it has been hereditary . . . On this question I will enter no more', which is one way of ending an argument. He refused to admit that the congregation could know anything about the Scottish Prayer Book. 'I can only look upon the movement as got up on party principles by a few who have influenced the many. . . . My personal feelings in this matter form quite a minor consideration compared with the interests of the Church at large. . . . I had not the remotest idea of any intention to introduce the S.C.O. into the new church. I have therefore by your silence been led on to make unusual exertions in my own person, and to become an earnest applicant to others for establishing an incumbency where an arrangement of services was to be adopted of which I entirely disapprove – an arrangement against which I had at least consistently argued as always producing evil consequences to the Church generally.'

His contemptuous reference to the members of All Saints was taken up by one of them, a member of the vestry who wrote to Mr. Murdoch expounding his own thorough knowledge of different Liturgies, and his devotion to the Scottish Rite as part of the heritage of a Church that was free to order her own affairs. 'The day may come when we may be the only Church in this realm that has not unchurched herself by casting longing eyes upon the State.'

All Saints won its freedom and Mr. Murdoch was elected and instituted as incumbent. There was a comparatively civil interchange of letters with the Dean; but later in the year he declined an invitation to attend the service of dedication of the organ in All Saints. It was a sad and silly quarrel, and we shall hear an echo of it in another chapter.

The Catholic tradition, renewed by the Oxford Movement, was

strong in the north-east. St. Peter's, Fraserburgh, Bishop Jolly's church, had the Eucharist every Sunday and on Saints' days. The church itself, reconstructed in 1840, is described as 'peculiar in shape and is not in any style of architecture'. That is the entry in the *Year Book* of 1880; five years later it is described in a gem of a phrase: 'architecture intended – Norman.'

One church in this diocese, St. Margaret's, Aberdeen, happily escaped any mere intention or imitation, whether Norman or Victorian-Gothic. The incumbent was John Comper who combined the old steadfastness with the new ardour and love of beauty, and whose brother, Ninian Comper, was the architect. John Comper had a double link with Bishop Forbes: he had been priested by him and had served in his first church of Stonehaven.

The Bishop of Aberdeen was Thomas Suther: he had come to Scotland from Nova Scotia, been ordained by Bishop Walker of Edinburgh, served in St. Paul's, York Place, and St. James's, Leith. In 1855 he came to Aberdeen, to St. Andrew's Church, and two years later was consecrated Bishop. In 1864 Orkney and Shetland were brought into his diocese.

And behind that event lay a history which is an epitome of the whole story of Episcopacy in Scotland. It was written by James Craven, incumbent of the church of St. Olaf in Kirkwall, which Bishop Suther consecrated in 1878. (There was a church on Shetland, too, St. Magnus at Lerwick, with James Walker as priest.) The history of *The Episcopal Church in Orkney* was published in 1883. It does not lack grimness.

The Bishop of Orkney before the Revolution, Andrew Honeyman, had been a friend of the murdered Archbishop Sharp of St. Andrews. 'He died in 1676, his health having been destroyed by the shot of a poisoned bullet he received, when stepping into the Archbishop's carriage, for whom the shot was intended.' A poisoned bullet would seem to be a refinement of malignancy. His successor, Murdoch Mackenzie, 'much beloved, a man of moderate views and strict life' died in 1688 aged a hundred. There were at that time eighteen Episcopal clergy in Orkney, of whom most remained faithful under great trials. One, Alexander Mair, fell away after being 'sharplie rebuked for his many irregular steps, and particularly for his receiving of ordination from the pretended Bishop of Murray' by the Presbytery Court in

1698. He was then asked if he were 'truly sensible of his gross, sinful and scandalous error, and intreated to beware of what he did, for albeit he might deceive men, yet the all-seeing eye and heartsearching God will not be mocked' but would pursue him with vengeance and judgement, 'and if signal repentance prevent it not, with everlasting torments amongst the damned reprobates and hypocrites hereafter'.

What this lacks in charity it superbly makes up in style. Mr. Mair acknowledged his guilt, conformed to Presbyterianism and was appointed to a parish. When asked some years later why he had deserted the Church of his ordination in her time of trouble he did not plead fear of damnation but gave 'the elegant yet significant reply: "What will a man not do for his bannock?"'

The Bishop who had ordained him, Hay of Moray, was indicted to the General Assembly of the now Established Presbyterian Church for 'the licensing many profane youths' to Episcopal orders. These profane young men must appear, to other eyes, to be of a most gallant loyalty and devotion; they went from all over the north-east to Inverness to receive Holy Orders 'by the imposition of the palsied hands' of this old Bishop.

At a purging of the clergy roll in Kirkwall in 1698 Thomas Fullerton of Westray and Papa was summoned both for being 'a bitter enemy against the government both of Church and State' and for making 'reproachful ryms [rhymes] against the present ministry'. Mr. Fullerton prudently demitted his charge.

Lampoons were a favourite weapon with the Episcopal clergy. One unhappy Presbyterian minister, Thomas Baikie of Kirkwall begged to be translated elsewhere, having suffered much from 'some wicked and atheistical verses which are going abroad in this place to my great discouragement'. The people in general were 'mocking, slandering and cursing him'.

Another Episcopal cleric, Alexander Pitcairn, Dean of Orkney, was charged with neglect of duty, seldom celebrating Holy Communion, and miscalling his congregation 'rogues, rascals, villains, knaves and perjured men'. To this he replied that he visited his people as often as he could and never ignored a sick call; that he celebrated the Sacrament 'as often as any in this country'; and that 'he never called any villains or knaves but such as he knew to be so, and that not very often, and certainly never in the pulpit'. He was, however, deprived of his charge.

Of the eighteen clergy in 1688, five were ejected, five forced to demit office, four died, and four conformed to Presbyterianism. The people as a whole were like their neighbours on the north-eastern mainland; they adhered to Episcopacy and despised the conformers. And so the Church endured, though with a shaken vitality. One stalwart priest, James Lyon, continued to use the Prayer Book and to pray for King James. He was denounced by Mr. Baikie aforesaid, who told his own congregation that the Litany was 'derived from the worshippers of Baal', and, much to their amazement and even terror, began to repeat: 'O Baal, save us.'

Laymen were also denounced; one, John Dunbar, an excise officer, was said to have threatened a man with eviction from his house if he did not attend Episcopal services; another had called the ministers a pack of knaves; a third, a lawyer, had been heard to say 'God damn the government', though he denied the charge. It would seem that the Piskies, although harassed, were by no means like the conies, a feeble folk.

Between 1688 and 1864, then, the waters in the north had been turbulent. In the neighbouring diocese of Brechin the Church prospered under Bishop Jermyn. In Dundee there were three churches, St. Paul's, St. Salvador's, St. Mary Magdalene's, all with a steady record of work and worship. At Inchture, in Perthshire, there was still a reminder of the penal days when people worshipped in an upper room. The Knapp chapel was simply 'the second floor of two cottages carefully fitted up'. It was served by the chaplain of the Kinnaird family at Rossie Priory.

There were a few private chapels in some of the great houses, the most notable being that of St. Michael's and All Angels at Glamis, in the diocese of St. Andrews, Dunblane and Dunkeld. One of the oldest in the Church, it had been consecrated in 1688. It was adorned with pictures by De Witt, the Dutchman who painted the 'portraits' of the Stuart Kings at Holyrood. This chapel, after having been closed for many years, was re-consecrated in 1865 by Bishop Forbes, not by the Diocesan Bishop Wordsworth. Daily services were held, the Eucharist was celebrated at least three times a week, and Episcopalians in the neighbourhood were welcomed. At Blair Atholl there was the tiny and ancient chapel of Kilmaveonaig, which had been 'in the uninterrupted possession of the Episcopal Church' since the Revolution and disestablishment. Inserted in one wall was the foundation stone of an older church dated 1591.

The *Year Book* could be outspoken. The church at Portnacrois in Argyll, the poorest diocese of all, was 'a miserable structure, plastered and whitewashed without and within', with the altar against the south wall and, facing it, a great three-decker pulpit of painted deal. This was in 1880; in 1885 it becomes merely 'a plain structure' and by 1890 'has been recently repaired and much improved'. Portnacrois could hardly be blamed; it was a tiny place. But further south Rothesay was flourishing, a popular holiday resort, and St. Paul's was 'much too small for the congregation that crowd to it in summer, and utterly unfit to represent our Church in such a rising place'.

Argyll was in much need of help:

'There are numbers of Episcopalians among the islands on the west coast, but with one or two exceptions little work has been done among them.' One of the exceptions was the incumbent of Kinloch Rannoch who had charge also of Rum, Muck and Eigg, and who was hoping to have a steam launch in order to visit his islanders more frequently.

The style of 'incumbent' was still in use during the eighties, after a motion to replace it by 'Rector' was defeated at the Representative Church Council. The latter title was in use by the nineties.

The *Year Book* of 1880 spread itself over the new Cathedral of St. Mary, Edinburgh:

'Undoubtedly the finest church erected in Great Britain since the Reformation, it is essentially a cathedral, for although there are many of our ancient ones which it does not rival in size, yet in the scheme of its design and especially in its monumental character it is in full accord with them, while it is probably as large, or very nearly as large, as it will ever be desirable to build a modern cathedral.' (Some critics of this masterpiece of Victorian Gothic might take a naughty pleasure in the ambiguous word 'monumental'.) 'Unquestionably it is this cathedral character which is most striking and abiding, and it is not too much to say that what the designer had most prominently in mind was to bestow this essential character upon his building. The remarkable success which he has achieved in this respect is in a high degree indicative of his great skill and genius; for it must be remembered that although Sir Gilbert Scott restored many cathedrals, he never built one until it was his privilege to be engaged on St. Mary's.'

The cost of the cathedral came to nearly a hundred and twelve thousand pounds.

3

The kaleidoscope of *The Scottish Guardian* is fairly colourful. It made a timely appearance upon the ecclesiastical scene in 1864, being thus able to report the parliamentary debates on the removal of the last disability of the Scottish Church: that which prevented clergy ordained by a Scottish Bishop from holding a benefice in England. The Bill had no easy passage; antagonism flared up in high quarters and was often directed against the Scottish Liturgy. Conform or be damned – or at least kept out of England – was the cry of more than one prelate. In the House of Lords the Bill was moved by the Duke of Buccleuch, supported by the Archbishop of Canterbury, vehemently opposed by the Bishop of Durham who asserted that the Church of England was utterly different from the Episcopal church in Scotland in both doctrine and government, and that it was wrong that 'the living body, the Church of England, should be united to the dead body, the clergy of the Scottish Episcopal Church'. (From what has already been told the latter might seem to be a lively set of corpses or ghosts.) The English clergy should be protected against this intrusion. The matter of the English intrusion into Scotland during the penal days was overlooked. Nationality and establishment were, apparently, to this Bishop, essential to validity of Orders. The Scottish Liturgy was found to be antagonistic to that of the English Book, and to be even more Roman than that of Rome. The Scottish clergy would spread their popish opinions and practices in England, once allowed over the Border. They were, besides, ignorant, intolerant and under-educated; in fact, they were not gentlemen. If the Scottish Church were in need of money, let her laity provide it as they did in the Free Kirk; but 'while the Free

Kirk of Scotland has the full affection of its members, the clergy of the Episcopal Church has not the confidence of the laity'. As a mixture of impertinence, ignorance and spite this comment would be hard to equal, while his lordship's conclusion would rank high in any anthology of snobbery: 'I strongly object to a measure which would call upon me to open my diocese to an invasion of a number of men worse educated than my own, who would deteriorate the position and influence of the Church in that diocese.'

The Bishop of Carlisle agreed, adding that the Scottish Church was divided between ritualistic clergy and anti-ritualistic laity. About the contemporary divisions and antagonisms in the Church of England he said not a word.

The Archbishop of York also showed antipathy towards the Scottish Liturgy, and resentment of the Scots who hoped to share in the higher emoluments of the English clergy. The word 'reivers' was not spoken but it hung in the air.

The Archbishop of Canterbury was, on the other hand, sympathetic, generous and brotherly, maintaining that the Scottish Church held her doctrines in common with the English and defending the learning of her clergy. Ordinands who were not graduates must attend Trinity College, Glenalmond, in preparation for their Orders. With a touch of agreeably sardonic relish he quoted a Scottish friend who had told him that during his time at Glenalmond three Englishmen had been refused matriculation as insufficiently qualified; these three had 'found a refuge either in the diocese of Durham or that of Carlisle'. (It was this friendly Archbishop who came to Inverness for the consecration of the cathedral.)

He was supported by the Bishop of Oxford who praised the Scottish Office: 'Far from tending towards Rome, any theologian whatever, knowing theology and studying the question, would say that it is more remote from the Roman view than our own English Office.'

Lord Kinnaird spoke for the Bill, but it was opposed by another Kinnaird in the House of Commons who 'believed that the Bill was part of a great scheme to establish at any cost Episcopal claims foreign to their Protestant Church of England'; the Scottish Church 'claimed to rule all Scotland in Spiritual matters, its pretensions were akin to those of Rome'. The 'concoctors and promoters' of the Bill 'know well that it will serve for ulterior ends of far greater importance' – an assertion which may well have astonished the promoters. But popery kept rearing its enticing head. Mr. Kinnaird then referred to Scots Episcopalians as a particular sect of dissenters.

The popish head showed briefly in the discussion of the General Assembly of the Church of Scotland. Some of the fathers and brethren feared Romish tendencies and developments in the Episcopal Church; but the majority saw this Bill as mere justice and were altogether sympathetic with their Episcopal kinsfolk. The Church of Scotland, in fact, behaved like a gentleman which cannot be said of certain English prelates.

The Bill was passed but had to be remitted to a Committee for discussion and amendment. Certain conditions were attached: no Scottish cleric was to be admitted to an English benefice without the consent and approval of the Diocesan Bishop who might refuse to institute, without giving reason; any cleric so accepted must subscribe any declaration he would have been asked to subscribe at ordination by an English or Irish Bishop.

The Archbishop of York came north in the autumn of that year to attend the consecration of St. Andrew's Cathedral, Aberdeen. At the luncheon which followed he replied to the toast of the Church of England with bland complacency. The Bishop of Aberdeen had made kind reference to him: 'But to a particular passage in my public duties you were kind enough not to allude. I have not at all repented of the few remarks I made' – in that speech in the House. He had not really opposed the Bill, only asked for its further discussion and amendment: he still deprecated the use of the Scottish Liturgy. It was a smooth act of self-extrication.

*The Scottish Guardian* dealt with figures in one of its first leaders, asserting that 'The poverty of the Scottish Church is greater than the poverty of any religious community in Scotland'. The present aim was a minimum stipend of £100 for incumbents, £500 for Bishops. This was an increase: only thirty years earlier some priests had a stipend of only £20, some even of £10, while Bishops had about £180.

Thirty years later the desired minimum had been reached and

passed, but there was to be little further increase for many years. To take some figures at random from the *Year Book* of 1895: Kirkwall had a stipend of £169; Lerwick £173; Melrose had £210; St. James's, Leith, £674 but with £179 deducted for the salary of the curate; St. Paul's, York Place was also wealthy with £659; St. Michael's poor with only £173; All Saints had £359; St. Columba's £210; St. John's £610. The Bishop's income was £910. Most of the clergy had a parsonage; the Bishop was allowed £150 for a house. Edinburgh was wealthy among the dioceses, contributing nearly £4,000 to the clergy fund, over £900 to Home Missions.

Argyll could give its Bishop only £543. Most of the livings were meagre and most of them under £200. In St. Andrews, Dunblane and Dunkeld, the Bishop had £800, the Provost £400; other stipends ranged from £141 in Dollar to £409 in Crieff, most of them between £200 and £300. The Bishop of Moray was the richest of the Bishops with £1,084; Aberdeen had £611; Brechin £739, of which £130 came to the Bishop, Hugh Jermyn, as Primus; Glasgow had £691.

*The Scottish Guardian* from the first provided varied and often pungent matter: leaders, reviews, reports, lively correspondence. Trollope's Barsetshire novels were reviewed in an early number. Apart from this, his impact upon Scots Episcopal readers does not appear to be known; contemporary opinion of the novels given in letters or diaries would be fascinating. The background was so different from that of the provincial England in which Barchester was placed. *The Guardian* was cordial: 'When the box of books comes from Mudie's, so eagerly looked for in country houses or quiet country towns' few volumes were so welcome as Trollope's. He was praised for his easy narrative and acute observation, for the reality of his characters and their society. No one could fail to love Mr. Harding: 'and at the same time we hope that the pictures of Bishop Proudie and Archdeacon Grantly represent a state of things which has now no existence in the Church, though we honour the Archdeacon for his devotion to his order, and pity the Bishop for being a married man.'

Church news, however, naturally predominated in the contents. There was much sympathy with the needs of the Highlands. More Gaelic-speaking clergy were wanted and the Theological College

The interior of Roslin Chapel

The nave, St Andrew's Cathedral, Aberdeen

Inverness Cathedral

The interior of St Paul's Cathedral, Dundee

should see to that. News was given of other Provinces – especially of America, and other Communions, the Orthodox and the Lutheran. *The Guardian* favoured a closer relation, even inter-communion with those separated brethren. And it urged more zeal for missions:

'Why is it that the Scottish Church will never properly bestir herself in this matter? Are we always to be told that charity begins at home?'

This was in 1865; six years later *The Guardian* consistently and warmly supported the election of a missionary Bishop, Henry Cotterill, to be Coadjutor Bishop in Edinburgh; he, in his episcopate, had much to do in beginning the Scottish Missions in Chanda and in South Africa. *The Guardian* continued to criticize 'congregationalism rampant' in the distribution of money; too little was given to the central funds of the Church, far too little to missions. The complacency of the prosperous was frequently deflated. So too was excess of zeal of the wrong kind. A lively leader in July 1880 attacked the figure of 'Meddlesome Matty in the Mission Field'.

This referred to our intrusion upon other Churches' missions, and to a certain impertinence in moral welfare work. A bazaar had been held in Edinburgh in aid of a Mission in Paris – 'at once impertinent, intrusive and incomprehensible. To see Edinburgh ladies and gentlemen eager to send the blessings of Christianity to the aborigines of Paris, as though it were the chief city of Zululand or of some wild Asian territory, the inhabitants of which were in heathen darkness, is to us a ridiculous spectacle suggesting many curious thoughts.' Among those thoughts was the query whether those ladies and gentlemen were aware of conditions in the Cowgate, Canongate, Grassmarket and other parts of Edinburgh. There were also the slums of Glasgow and Dundee. The opinion of a Parisian workman transported to one of those areas on a Saturday night or on New Year's Day would be interesting; and it would be as reasonable for a committee of Parisian ladies and gentlemen to start a mission to induce temper-ance in Edinburgh as it was for those earnest Scots 'to take the morals of the Parisian work-people under their care'. Paris no doubt needed care and cleansing, but 'so long as brutal and dis-gusting drunkenness is one of the normal public exhibitions of our great cities, we might be so modest as to let the morals and religion of other professedly Christian cities alone'. France was said to lack religion; so this 'holy and godly Scotland was to stretch out her beneficent hand and to present her poor, erring neighbour with her own religion'. It would be better to look to things at home than to attempt 'pietistic missions among foreign Christian populations'.

One of the liveliest contributions to this periodical which rarely lacked that quality was a letter in 1870 by a correspondent, unnamed, on the Theological College at Glenalmond. It could be heart-rending. The condition of the young theologicals was set forth with realism:

'De Hannah [the Warden] is a scholar and a gentleman; but he has been so long a schoolmaster that he treats the students as big schoolboys, sometimes as small ones . . . The masters of the school treat the students as the Jews of old treated the Samaritans – that is, they have no dealings with them. The boys are boys and behave as such . . . Treated by all around them with coldness, dislike and open hostility, the students have no society but their own, and they lead the most wretched life conceivable, quarrelling about everything, from the proofs of the existence of God down to the questions of who shall get the armchairs in the common-room.'

In the playground and playing fields they were in peril from flying balls. When they went walking the roads were usually thick with mud or snow or, in summer, with blinding dust. They made for some hidden spot where they might smoke – which was forbidden in college – but it was no pipe of peace. 'Perched like crows on some wooden rail, they wage the furious faction-fight between High Church and Low Church.' And if, exhausted and thirsty, they came to an inn and asked for beer they were told that 'the Warden has given orders that the students should get nothing stronger than gingerbeer or lemonade'.

Cheerless and beerless they must endure their preparation.

'No wonder Bishop Wordsworth failed in converting to the Church the people round the College, if such an order was in force in his time, for the prudent, canny Scotch will never entrust the care and guidance of their souls to those who cannot themselves be entrusted with a pint of beer.'

The chief cause of the afflictions of the students was 'that they are generally of lower rank in life than the other members of the College, and that these latter know it'; also that they were imperfectly educated, few of them graduates, some admitted by mistaken indulgence on the part of one of the Bishops. With few exceptions they were 'neglected, despised, derided, at variance among themselves, for the most part poor, incapable of receiving high instruction'. There was only one remedy, the removal of the Theological College from Glenalmond, preferably to Edinburgh. The letter is a curious mixture of compassion, sarcasm and snobbery, but the proposal that the students should be attached to the new cathedral and given training in pastoral work is sound. It is not surprising that Dowden found only one student when he came to Glenalmond.

In 1880 Professor John Stuart Blackie started a small strife. He might have claimed, like Dowden, to be Professor of All Things for his interests ranged widely, 'including' (it was said) 'a little Greek of which he was Professor'. He published a sonnet in praise of both Kirks, professing allegiance to both, rather in the spirit of Marjorie Fleming who was an Episcopalian in Edinburgh and a Presbyterian in Kirkcaldy. He liked the Episcopalian prayers, he liked also the fervent sermons of the Presbyterian:

> 'I claim them both – my left hand and my right:
> Bound to one body's use – why should they fight?'

From poetry he proceeded to suggest liturgical reforms, with a glimmering of the modern idea of unity without uniformity. Morning Prayer should be reshaped from 'the inorganic jumble of three services of which it consists', the Athanasian Creed should be ejected 'as an offence which stinks in the nostrils of all reasonable men', and preaching should be improved. On the Presbyterian side there should be fewer sermons, and more prayer and music, above all psalmody. 'The somewhat hard and angular Scot requires, above all things, musical culture.'

He was answered by a Mr. Lewis:

'All have not the strength of mind of Professor Blackie, and although we all admire his independent spirit which can allow him to join in the noble psalms in St. Giles' in the morning, to croon sonnets by the Water of Leith in the afternoon, and then, perhaps, to unite heart and soul in the responses at evening service in St. Mary's Cathedral – such a course I should be sorry to see attempted by the majority of Christians.' He thought the Professor was something of a trimmer in religion as in other matters. His criticisms were not unjust but might have been conveyed with more friendliness.

Mr. Lewis did not attempt to defend the Athanasian Creed but he found Morning Prayer admirable, especially when it culminated in Holy Communion. He agreed about the poor quality of Episcopalian preaching. For this the laity were partly to blame, being apathetic, but the clergy were not absolved:

'It is not too much to say that there is not a Presbyterian minister in however remote a country parish in Scotland who would dare to offer his congregation such a sermon as many Episcopalians are treated to, even in our large town congregations.' The clerical fault lay in under-education and lack of training and preparation. Again the laity were to blame for failure to support their Church financially.

Both contributors agreed in attacking 'genteel' conversions; Episcopacy had become fashionable and there was unhappily some reason for calling it the Church of the gentry and not of the people everywhere.

For the last view in the kaleidoscope we may take that of Canon Murdoch (as he now was) of All Saints, Edinburgh. In April 1890 he contributed two articles deprecating the undue number of guilds, societies and other organizations in the Church: they were a complication rather than an enlargement. Most of them were imported from England where they were in proportion to the size of the Church, but here in Scotland:

'The gifts of mind and heart, of time, talent, means and strength given to these organizations would be well given if the ship were bigger; but as it is, it seems to me that we are whirling round and round, without making progress at all adequate to the energy expended.' He saw the remedy in a concentration upon parish rather than congregational work. Each church should reach out beyond its congregation:

'Your parish priest and his church must be the property of the people of the district. . . . It is because our churches are congregational and not parochial that religious aspirations are sought to be met by these endless societies. I have myself gone upon this line, and in it I have found the value of these societies in meeting certain wants; but I have never considered them potential in themselves, but only as parts of a parochial machinery.' All Saints was, he could claim, working for the good of the neighbourhood; what one church was doing all could do. Then indeed 'we should have a craft that would both answer to the helm and give a good account in her rate of speed for the work of her engines'. The priest belonged to the people, 'as a messenger of the people's Head, Jesus Christ'; and the people must be drawn in to help the priest.

The Church must treasure her heritage, and relate it in a living way to present and future.

'We have gifts to give to Scotland for all time. Let us keep them pure or they are worthless.'

The reader today may wonder whether this was written in the eighteen-nineties or the nineteen-sixties, so aware is Canon Murdoch of the needs and strains of the modern world. We are becoming conscious of our undue congregationalism. That uncomfortable but wholesome awareness was felt by some more than seventy years ago.

# 12

## Victorian Glasgow

'We have frequently pointed out that Glasgow is the only town in Scotland where the Church has not made any palpable advance – that while the sects have made rapid strides, the Church has in great measure stood still.' So *The Scottish Guardian* commented in one of its early issues, adding however that: 'Glasgow is ever slow to move, but when she does so, she does it in right earnest.'

How far and how rapidly Glasgow did move may be seen from the *Year Books*. In 1880 the city had eight incumbencies and two missions; the surrounding counties, including the borders, had thirty-four churches, not counting private chapels and missions. In 1888 the border charges of Melrose, Galashiels, Kelso, Selkirk, Hawick, Jedburgh and Peebles returned to the diocese of Edinburgh but there were more than thirty incumbencies remaining in Glasgow and Galloway, and an increased number of missions and private chapels of great houses. During the nineties the Church grew and expanded through missions dependent on incumbencies, and these in time became full charges: it was very much a period of growth and this missionary vigour was due largely to the two Victorian Bishops, William Scott Wilson and William Thomas Harrison.

The pattern is different here from that of the Highlands or the north-east where Episcopacy was old and indigenous, whether it were of fruitful or of sparse growth; it was different also from that of Edinburgh which also has an inheritance of native Episcopacy, sometimes blended with Jacobite tradition, and which had in mid-century somewhat turned towards England. Glasgow itself had grown large and wealthy through trade, commerce and industrialism; the nearest counties of Lanark and Renfrew were part of Scotland's new black country of coal-pits and iron and steel works and factories. Dumfries and Galloway were rural and the country house, even the great mansion was found in every county, their families in many cases being Episcopalian and maintaining a chapel which served the neighbourhood. Opposed to this was the very strong Covenanting history, the almost ineradicable memory of the dourest form of Presbyterianism. There were, no doubt, conversions, but the mission work was done chiefly among the incoming English and Irish workers in Glasgow itself, and in Lanark and Renfrewshire. The Irish perhaps were less numerous. Most of them were Roman Catholics. For the English congregations churches were built by the Scottish Church which, as a result, was often called English because of this new membership.

Michael Russell, the first Bishop of the restored and united diocese of Glasgow and Galloway, was followed by Walter Trower and he, in 1859, by William Wilson, who lived until 1888 and may be called the last of the old line of Scottish Bishops, entirely Scottish by birth, education and service, separated only by a generation from those of the penal days, knowing them through living memory. When he, born in 1817, was a boy, Jolly, Gleig, William Skinner and Torry were alive and active; and his own best counsellor in youth was David Low, incumbent of Wilson's native Pittenweem. Like those men, the boy went to Aberdeen; like them he was ordained young, at twenty-one, by Bishop Low. For a time he acted as tutor in the family of Mackenzie of Avoch near Fortrose and served the local congregation.

In 1832 he was appointed to the charge in Ayr, which is now Holy Trinity, and there he stayed until nearly the end of his life and Bishopric. Glasgow was not yet a separate diocese and in the city and the west country there were only six congregations. When Wilson died more than fifty years later there were over sixty, representing almost a third of the Episcopal Church in Scotland. His congregation was new, it made the seventh, and it had no church, meeting in a room above a carpenter's shop on the riverbank. His stipend was £28 a year. A church was begun in 1835 and finished in 1839, and a school was also built. He was Dean of the diocese from 1845 till 1859, when, on the resignation of Walter Trower, he was elected Bishop. Consecrated in St. Paul's Church, Edinburgh, by Terrot (then Primus), Trower and the Bishop of New York, he continued to live in Ayr as incumbent, the last of the Scots Bishops to hold such a plurality of office.

'South of the Tay the Church had, since the Revolution and the Jacobite risings, been almost obliterated.' So *The Scottish Guardian* was to state in its obituary of Bishop Wilson nearly thirty years later; but already the Church was playing the part of phoenix. In this episcopate the number of clergy was doubled, that of confirmands trebled; he confirmed two hundred and thirty in his first year, seven hundred and seventy in his last. In one of his synodal charges he said:

'With us the office of a Bishop is purely spiritual with no worldly honour . . . If for the purposes of order it confers on him a certain authority over his brethren, this authority must necessarily be exercised with discretion and humility, and cannot be used for any personal advantage or distinction to himself. His claims are the claims of an office necessary, as we esteem it, in the Church of Christ, and the reverence paid by one order to another must be suitable to the paternal character of the office to which it is paid, as that office is described in the language of the Church, and must therefore be filial or it is nothing.'

In brief, the Bishop must be a Father-in-God. The authority he could maintain: when Bishop Ewing was invited by the University of Glasgow to preach in their Hall which served as chapel, using the Prayer Book, Bishop Wilson refused permission. He was aware of what the Church had lost. When an English cleric begged for a canonry in Glasgow Cathedral, the Bishop answered that he would consider the matter when it pleased Her Majesty to restore, with consent of Parliament, the ancient Cathedral of St. Mungo and its endowments to his jurisdiction.

Scot of the Scots he was yet opposed to the Scottish Liturgy, seeing it as a barrier to progress and full unity with the Church of England.

He died in 1888: 'the last example of a type of Bishop which did noble service in days gone by, when everyone who had dedicated his life to the service of God in the disestablished Church of Scotland, did so with the certain knowledge that he would have to "endure hardness as a good soldier of Jesus Christ".' This was the tribute of *The Scottish Guardian*. Another, a very revealing one, was that he was kind and charitable, above all to the poor, 'who found out that he was like a nut – had all the hardness on the outside'.

So we may hear the end of an auld sang, that heroic song of the Faithful Remnant in the days of penalty, poverty, austere and steadfast loyalty in that part of Scotland that had the least memory of the old days, and the greatest antagonism to the old faith. The Church continued greatly to increase, but a new tradition and ethos had begun.

Wilson was succeeded by William Thomas Harrison, who was elected by the laity as well as by the clergy, eighteen laymen with forty-two priests. The Dean was the Very Reverend John Moir of Jedburgh which a few months later, at the end of the year, would pass into the diocese of Edinburgh.

Dean Moir proposed Canon Harrison, Vicar of St James's, Bury St. Edmunds, and honorary Canon of Ely; a Norfolk man by birth, Cambridge by education, his priestly life lived in East Anglia. He was seconded by Mr. Creighton of Kilmarnock, who regretted that a Scot had not been nominated; but this English-man seemed 'one of the best men whom the sister Church of England can possibly send us', knowing something of the Scottish Church, not a party man and above all a priest of deep spiritual life. 'I believe that he is, next to a Scotchman, well qualified for the high and responsible position of Bishop of Glasgow and Galloway.'

They were opposed by Mr. Low of St. Columba's, Largs, for nationalist reasons; Canon Harrison had no tie with Scotland. He proposed Daniel Fox Sandford, Bishop of Tasmania, grandson of old Bishop Sandford of Edinburgh, born in Glasgow, son of a professor in the University; in short, almost as good as a Scot by heredity. This was seconded and a vote taken; Canon Harrison had a majority of eighteen clerical and three lay votes. The Dean begged Mr. Low to withdraw his opposition and make the election unanimous: Mr. Low stated that he could not change his opinion but he could promise obedience and a welcome to the new Bishop. So Canon Harrison was elected.

There was considerable press comment, not always favourable. Correspondence in *The Scottish Guardian* was lively. One writer protested strongly against this, the third election in five years to the Scots Episcopate of 'a stranger brought in from England. How can a Church be expected to flourish under such treatment?' Glasgow had chosen 'to inflict a stigma upon our whole body', and Glasgow was 'perhaps the most important of all our dioceses'. The new Bishop could know nothing of the Scottish Church.

How could the College approve this choice? This was answered by one of wider view: ignorance of the Scottish Church could be remedied. 'Scotch birth and Scotch orders are not essential for a Scotch Bishopric, and we trust they never will be. In all things let us be churchmen first, Scotchmen afterwards.' Mr. Creighton stated that Bishop Sandford had no more Scottish qualifications than the new Bishop-elect. He was not now living in Scotland nor had he given his life's work to the Scottish Church. There were other objections to his being appointed Bishop of Glasgow: these were not stated, but if the controversy continued they would be: and on this slightly sinister note the letter ends.

The issue lay between those who put nationalism first, and those who emphasized the catholicity of the Church. The last word may be left to Dean Farquhar of St. Andrews, who said it in a sonnet:

> Wherefore is this, my countryman, that each
> High, vacant cure of souls in all our land
> In falling from a native Scottish hand
> Is seized by those who o'er the border reach?
>
> Wherefore is this, that when we wish to preach
> Against the modern, innovating band,
> And in the native paths to take our stand,
> We talk to Scotland in a foreign speech?
>
> Ah! give us homely Scotchmen, who have skill
> To fire the silent, fervid, northern heart,
> Restoring us the Church's rule at length!
>
> Yet faint not, brothers, for God works His will
> Not by astuteness of poor human art,
> But by our weakness loves to show His strength.

It is a consoling thought that Divine Providence is unlikely to be thwarted by any mere Englishmen.

The new Bishop was consecrated at Michaelmas 1888 in the Church of St. Mary, by Jermyn of Brechin (Primus), Douglas of Aberdeen, Chinnery-Haldane of Argyll, Kelly of Moray, Dowden of Edinburgh, the Bishop of Ely and the Bishop of Iowa, who preached the sermon. (Wordsworth of St. Andrews was too old and feeble now to attend.) They all repeated the words of consecration, laying their hands upon their new brother; co-consecrators, not witnesses only.

It proved an episcopate of evangelism. He came to a great city, of much wealth and unspeakable poverty. In the west end the fine, solid houses of the merchant princes were being built in terraces and crescents of classical dignity; new churches followed the movement of the population. The University had some seventeen or eighteen years before it left its medieval home in the High Street, near the cathedral, for Gilmorehill. The south side of the river developed into a prosperous area of houses and gardens. The slums remained and grew in quantity and quality.

The peaceful invasion of English workmen from over the border continued, and for them there must be churches with their own way of worship. Bishop Harrison was a missionary and in the fifteen years of his episcopate the diocese expanded on every side. He resigned in 1903, going to parish and episcopal work under the Bishop of Ely. At his last Synod, tribute was paid to him as 'a Bishop who had been above all an inspiring spiritual influence'. An address from his clergy praised his scholarship, his administrative powers, his sympathy, kindness and hospitality. 'It seemed to me that I might look upon the invitation as a call from God, and thank God that persuasion has never for an instant left me.' He spoke of a great priest and a great Bishop alike in their zeal for social justice: Father Dolling in Landport, and Bishop Westcott, the latter among the greatest of scholars, but without his evangelical passion he would not have been so great. Such zeal was essential in any Bishop of this diocese: 'Glasgow is for Scotland the beating heart of its industrial life' and there was need for missions, settlements, all kinds of Home Mission work.

A letter to *The Scottish Guardian* emphasized this, adding that Glasgow's Bishop should be what Forbes had been for Dundee, while another urged the need for concentrating and strengthening the work that Bishop Harrison had done. *The Scottish Guardian*'s own tribute to him was one that must have moved him:

'Men felt that their Bishop was one of the "holy and humble men of heart" produced by the Spirit of the Saviour; felt in him the pastoral spirit which called to remembrance the Spirit of the Good Shepherd. They had found in him a Father-in-God whose humility had made his intercourse with them like that of a brother.'

He was succeeded by a Scot and a Highlander, Archibald Ean Campbell, Provost of St. Ninian's, Perth, who still lives in many memories. Consecrated in St. Mary's Church, he saw that church become the cathedral of the diocese. His episcopate bridged two worlds – over the gulf of the 1914–18 war – and is beyond the limit of this history.

In 1903 the Primus, Bishop Jermyn, died: he had followed Forbes as Bishop and Eden of Moray as Primus. Following the tradition of Forbes he urged devotion to the Sacrament of the altar, with frequent Communions, at least every Sunday. He wrote no books, gave no charges, but saw much of his clergy. One of them wrote of him:

'Believing with his whole heart that he was a true successor of the Apostles, he would not consent, in order to please friend or foe, to bate one inch of an apostolic bearing in matters of faith and practice; but he drew a line, trenchant and deep, between the spiritual essence and the temporal and social accidents of his office.'

This places him among the Bishops of the old days of poverty.

The Church at the beginning of the new century and the new reign had her two new Bishops: Archibald Campbell in Glasgow, Walter John Forbes Robberds in Brechin. By 1910 there would be a death and change in the other five sees. Two of the late Victorians at least, Wilkinson of St. Andrews, Chinnery-Haldane of Argyll, rank among the great Fathers-in-God as pastors and lovers of souls. One priest serving in Glasgow, Anthony Mitchell, was to be equally great and beloved in his native diocese of Aberdeen.

# 13

# After the Schoolmaster, the Saint. Wordsworth's Successor: George Howard Wilkinson

It is a large claim, but in Wordsworth's successor there is truly the note of holiness; a quiet voice speaks after the boom of controversy and is heard most often in prayer. To classify him in churchmanship would be foolish; he is great among Bishops, not in scholarship, in organizing ability, in force of personality but simply as a lover of souls.

George Howard Wilkinson came of north country stock, born in Durham in 1833. One shadow lay across a happy childhood, the death of his mother. Her memory and influence endured in his own spiritual life.

From Durham Grammar School he went to Oxford, to Oriel, where he was both a reading and a rowing man, and a riding one too; he won the College grind or steeple-chase on a hired hack. At Oxford he began a lifelong friendship with a Highland Scot and future minister of the Kirk, Donald Macleod, brother of the great Dr. Norman, and himself of no mean stature of character. Together the two young men made a tour of Italy in 1855, enjoying the carnival and the Roman spring. There Wilkinson met his future wife, Caroline Des Voeux. From Italy he went to the Holy Land, to Turkey and Greece, then homewards by Italy again and France: 'The happiest twelve months which I have ever spent.'

Next year, in 1857, he married his Caroline or 'Carsie' and was ordained deacon. In 1858 he was priested and after a brief curacy at St. Mary Abbott's, Kensington, was appointed to the charge of Seaham Harbour, County Durham, whose patronage lay in the firm hands of that formidable Victorian, Frances Lady Londonderry. She used to shut her Prayer Book with a clang of the clasp as a signal for the sermon to end. To the young vicar she was benevolent enough, and he was sufficiently conformable though never subservient. If there was more than a touch of Lady Catherine De Burgh in her, there was nothing of Mr. Collins in him. The tradition of the church was moderate, with only two Celebrations of the Eucharist in the month and little Eucharistic teaching, but with much emphasis on baptism and baptismal regeneration. After four years young Wilkinson moved to St. Andrew's Church with St. Anne's Chapel, Bishop's Auckland.

His growth in priestliness had begun; his passion for souls was evident in preaching, in parish work, in a Lenten Mission with a daily Eucharist. From this northern parish he went to London, to St. Peter's, Great Windmill Street, in the centre of the theatrical world, a fairly raffish district with the Argyll Rooms next door to his church. His work here was a continuous mission: he visited, he gave a week-night Evensong in shortened form with an informal talk, sometimes he preached at a street corner. Gladstone used to come to his church and was a warm friend.

This was a brief charge; from here he went to another, St. Peter's in Eaton Square, with which his name is as closely joined as it is with his Bishopric. Here the outlook was bleak, not from poverty or raffishness, but from a chill, Georgian atmosphere of wealth, gentility and respectability and no enthusiasm. The church was ugly, with great square pews, a gallery and no chancel; the pulpit was enclosed in the vicarage pew. Except for some free seats at the back, which were always full, the pews were rented to the best families and entry to them was guarded by female pew-openers and by beadles armed with staves. Some ardent young priests would have exploded in wrath, some lost heart: this man, still in his thirties, did neither, but took his own quiet way of reformation. His goodness and sincerity disarmed opposition. Gradually he introduced the surplice, altar-hangings and other furnishings, and in 1872 began the reconstruction of the church, with a chancel. This structural change was accompanied by an organic growth: parish and mission work increased, school and parish rooms were built and used, a parish kitchen served good cheap dinners and sent them out to invalids. Wilkinson could be claimed as a pioneer of meals on wheels. And at the heart of all this activity lay prayer and the preaching of the Word. He did not adapt his preaching; the same Word was valid for his wealthy hearers as for the fishermen and miners in the north.

That eminent Victorian churchman, diarist and *raconteur*, G. W. E. Russell, has recalled those years of renewal:

'A flame of religious zeal was suddenly kindled in the West End of London. The Church in the Belgravia district was as dry as tinder; it caught fire from Mr. Wilkinson's fervour, and became a conflagration . . . The smartest carriages in London blocked the approach to his church. The great dames of Grosvenor Square and Carlton House Terrace rubbed shoulders with the opulent inhabitants of Tyburnia and South Kensington. Cabinet Ministers fought for places in the gallery, and M.P.s were no more accounted of than silver in the days of Solomon.'

The attraction did not lie in ritual, ceremonial or furnishing, still less in soothing words from the pulpit:

'If Jeremiah had prophesied in a surplice he would have been like the prophet of Belgravia. Even Savonarola, as in *Romola*, could have been heard in St. Peter's.'

It was now a generation and more since the revival of the Oxford Movement. Tractarianism had become tolerated up to a point, and in some fashionable churches had degenerated into 'a sort of easy-going ceremonialism, partly antiquarian, partly worldly' and almost wholly ineffective. 'Into this dead sea of lethargy and formalism, Mr. Wilkinson burst like a gun-boat . . . He rebuked the sins of all and sundry, from Duchesses to scullery-maids, premiers to page-boys, octogenarian rakes to damsels in their teens . . . Society loved to be scolded' – flocked to be denounced and queued to take its medicine.

'Don't stay till three at a ball, and then say you are too delicate for early service'; 'Eat one dinner a day and try to earn that one'; 'Sell that diamond cross which you carry with you into the sin-polluted atmosphere of the Opera, give the proceeds to feed the poor, and wear the only real cross – the cross of self-discipline and self-denial.' These were among his shots at complacency.

Society listened and paid for its castigation in generous alms-giving. One Sunday the Vicar announced: 'I want £1,000'; next Sunday: 'I've got £1,000.'

His preaching was attractive in the true sense of drawing people to God. Belonging to no Church party he combined evangelical fervour with an increasing intensity of sacramental belief and teaching. In our modern phrase, he was both outward-looking in missionary zeal and inward-looking in devotion. Himself a member of the committee of the Society of the Propagation of the Gospel, he founded a Ladies' Missionary Association in St. Peter's, and held the first Day of Intercession for Missions.

In 1874 he organized a Parish Mission. Some of the clergy were accused of urging sacramental Confession and the usual anti-sacramental, anti-Catholic storm blew up. It was calmed by Wilkinson's reasoning, his quiet insistence on Prayer Book teaching about Confession. Sacramental Confession was always to be permitted, sometimes urged, never enforced; priestly absolution could ease the penitent of an intolerable burden.

He was heard in high quarters. Summoned to preach at Windsor he proclaimed the need for Drawing Room District Visitors. Rich as well as poor houses needed 'earnest Christian men and women using their knowledge of Society for Christ and His Church, who will live in the world and yet be above the world' in something like a Third Order. The Queen said: 'What has all that to do with me?' but she invited him again and he preached from the text: 'Be sure your sins will find you out,' thinking this an opportunity to set before the Queen 'the evangelical way of sin and salvation'. Bidden to Sandringham, he preached comfort to a sorrowful family after the death of the baby son of the Prince and Princess of Wales.

'The Princess was much pleased,' one of her ladies reported, 'and only regretted the sermon being too short.'

The 1870's saw a renewal both of life and of strife within the Church. The anti-ritualists scored with the Public Worship Act of 1874 and subsequent prosecutions and persecutions. Wilkinson was a peacemaker; he saw the spiritual reality behind forms and ceremonies.

His private life was saddened by the death of his wife in 1877; she had been a true helpmate, protecting him against intrusion, against the mechanics of daily life which could have drained his strength, and being one with him in spiritual things. Lacking her, he worked himself into a serious collapse, by no means the last in his life of labour.

In 1883 he was consecrated Bishop of Truro, in succession to the first Bishop of that new see, Edward White Benson, now Archbishop of Canterbury. Benson had founded and begun the cathedral of Truro, Wilkinson carried it to its consecration and opening. The choir and transepts were finished in 1887. And like Bishop Forbes whom in pastoral zeal he greatly resembled, he brought the Religious into his diocese. They had begun in St. Peter's, as they began in Dundee, very quietly, very helpfully. A group of ladies under Miss Warrender dedicated themselves to work among the poor. Wilkinson, as Vicar, welcomed them; he gave them a Rule, a name: 'The Sisterhood of the Epiphany', and a habit; not a black one which he disliked, as he disliked the usual close-bound wimple and veil; they recalled to his mind the trappings of death and mourning. Now this young Community followed him to Truro.

The Sisters took life vows, but the Bishop had power of dispensation. Miss Warrender became Mother Julian. Her own sister, Lady Haddington, wrote to the Bishop:

'May my sister be to you what Madame de Chantal was to St. Francis de Sales.' This Community did indeed fulfil the function which St. Jane Chantal and St. Francis planned for their Order of the Visitation: they worked among the poor, visiting the sick in their own homes: they opened a home for penitents, a training house for servants, and one for training parish workers. Their special object was 'the development and deepening of women's work in the diocese'.

The Bishop had always recognized the capacity and the need of women for something far beyond sentimental piety and a talent for arranging flowers. The Sisters had a long novitiate of from three to seven years; final vows were not made before the age of thirty. He prepared their Book of Hours, with brief Offices, each with a special Meditation or Intention. This Book was, however, used only for a short time as it was found better to replace it with *The Day Hours of the Church of England*.

The importance of this Sisterhood in this episcopate is beyond estimate. The Bishop and the Sisters gave mutual help and prayers. He cared for every detail of their communal life, and to individuals he gave wise counsel: in return he had their unstinted service. Though himself a natural ascetic, he enjoined on them a prudent balance and relaxation. They must have periods of rest, a break of four or five days every quarter, weekly periods of rest. He used to inspect the time-table to make sure that everyone, including the

Reverend Mother, had these. His spiritual counsel was good, unfussy, unemotional. He told Mother Julian:

'Remember, for one look at self to take ten at Christ.'

Writing to another nun of the value of spiritual direction he added:

'But we turn the things which should have been for our health into a snare, if we allow any human being, however holy, to free us of our responsibility as individuals standing in the Presence of God. It is better even to make mistakes than to abrogate our freedom.'

Indirectly he helped to found another Community overseas. One of his Missionary Guild at St. Peter's, Cecile Isherwood, offered herself for service, heard the call to the religious life, and at the age of twenty-one sailed for South Africa. There she became Superior of the Sisterhood founded by Bishop Webb of Grahamstown, and as Mother Cecile was one of the most beloved people in the Church in South Africa. Her Community had, as its special work, the training of schoolmistresses for African schools. Besides Mother Cecile, that Missionary Guild sent forth eight other sisters, twelve priests and six Missionary Bishops.

As Bishop of Truro, Wilkinson continued to drive himself to the point – and beyond it – of exhaustion. He loved Cornwall but the climate did not suit him. He suffered recurring bouts of illness: his vitality was intense but his reserves of strength were poor. He collapsed and brooded over the collapse:

'Was it illness which made me so dead and spiritless, or was it spiritual death?'

It was not death but the dark night of the soul, a prelude to dawn and resurrection; having lived for years at high mental and spiritual pressure he was now enduring 'a kind of suffering which only the saints can experience'. He knew the agony of dereliction. A long holiday at Cannes in 1888 and at Bordighera, where he found a good friend in George MacDonald, brought relief but not recovery, and he felt compelled to resign his Bishopric.

In 1892 he went to South Africa, staying with the Bishop of Grahamstown, being welcomed by Mother Cecile, her five nuns and nine novices and the children of their orphanage who wore white frocks and red caps. South Africa brought healing.

'I never knew the Bishop in full possession of his powers until after his visit to South Africa,' one friend wrote of him, adding that his collapse had been a shattering, an apparently final wreck of every mental faculty.

A year after his return, in 1893, he was offered the Bishopric of St. Andrews, Dunkeld and Dunblane. He was still unwell and undecided, though the invitation was not sudden. At the time of his resigning Truro, a Scots friend, R. T. N. Spiers, had written to him that the old Bishop, Wordsworth, was now very feeble and anxious to have a Coadjutor.

'The work of one of our northern dioceses is very light, and Scotch air is very different from Cornish.'

Wilkinson had replied that if God would restore his health he might accept this invitation. The seed took root. When, after Bishop Wordsworth's death, the diocesan electors met to consider their election, only two names were proposed: that of James Kelly, Bishop of Moray, who might be translated, and that of George Wilkinson. The latter was preferred. There were murmured hopes of choosing a Scot rather than an Englishman, but these were 'drowned in the general desire' for this particular Englishman. The vote of both clerical and lay electors was almost unanimous, the atmosphere in singular contrast with that nearly forty years earlier when the redoubtable Wordsworth was elected.

Mr. Spiers wrote:

'Among Presbyterians it is a reproach against our Church that we are wooden and formal, wanting in spirituality and unction. I don't think this is a true accusation, though I wish we could point to the standard among Church people as an evident proof of its unfairness. I believe your coming among us would be a great help to our diocese, especially to our clergy who have had no shepherding for many years.'

And that, perhaps, is the hardest and saddest reproach which could be made against Bishop Wordsworth.

Still Wilkinson hesitated. Then he consulted Archbishop Benson, who told him:

'I shall never believe in a call again if you refuse this offer.'

The call was heard. The new Bishop was enthroned in April 1893. One of his new clergy, Canon Farquhar, described the ceremony, wondering what Wordsworth would have thought of it: the procession of clergy, headed by three Bishops, Jermyn of

Brechin the Primus, Kelly of Moray, Douglas of Aberdeen, walking along Methven Street and Atholl Street to the cathedral, the Primus in cope and mitre; 'with his long white beard he looked like a veritable Patriarch'. In the cathedral the altar-candles were lit, and the Eucharist was celebrated by the Scottish Rite. The Bishop, enthroned, preached his first sermon to his new flock:

'Begin with personal religion or you will never conquer the world. Begin with penitence and with faith and with surrender, and then go out and take this branch of the one Catholic and Apostolic Church to which you belong, this branch which has all the marks of God's election – poverty, small in the eyes of man, martyrs, saints – the Church which can lift up her hands and show the marks of the nails – go out and help her.'

At luncheon afterwards he spoke of Episcopacy and Unity:

'We believe in one great Catholic and Apostolic line – one Church. . . . And it is because we thank God with all our hearts that we have been made part and parcel of that great Society that we cannot, through very gratitude to our God, do anything but love all as He has bidden us love them, and pray God with all our hearts that every wall of division may be broken down in His own good time and His own good way. . . . Now, I am well assured, as I felt that strange, electric sympathy coming out in our cathedral this morning, that you will help me to do nothing that will sever, but to do all that will unite those whom God does not wish to live separated from each other.'

On the following Sunday the Bishop was prayed for in the Free Kirk.

Canon Farquhar wrote: 'The Bishop gives us all the impression of goodness. There is a something about him – a touch of holiness.'

His health and vitality returned; his character as a Bishop became clear.

'He combines "High" Church doctrine and ritual and spirituality with an evangelical and Wesleyan manner of expression.' This was the impression of Canon Farquhar after Wilkinson had been for a year in the Bishopric. 'He has simply imported the devotion of the dissenting prayer-meeting into the Church, but solidified by a substratum of Catholicism.'

Truly he could not be classified; he was quite simply a Christian.

'It is certain that he lives and moves in an atmosphere of spirituality to which most good clergy only occasionally attain.'

Spirituality and gentleness were his most obvious qualities, and with them reserve, a capacity for silence. As Father-in-God he was accessible, responsive, sympathetic, but he avoided intimacies and 'anything like an "undress" conversation'. One priest found in him a will as strong as that of Wordsworth, but not shown in any domineering or overbearing attitude, in obstinacy or rigidity; he was gentle but resolute in following the way he thought right.

The cathedral, once the centre of storm, had been growing, and in 1890 Wordsworth had consecrated the nave. The new Bishop had his own ideas: to open arches between nave and choir, to add a south aisle and a cloister leading from there to the chapter house. The work was done and in July 1901 these additions were dedicated in the presence of Archbishop Frederick Temple.

More urgent and beneficent than any enlargement or embellishment of the structure was the renewal of life in this mother church of the diocese. The Bishop revised the constitution, merging the congregational committee in a diocesan one, repealing Wordsworth's statute which made the five senior clergy of the diocese Canons *ex officio*, giving the Provost ample power and freedom but making the Bishop the ultimate authority, the effective head. He arranged retreats, quiet days, missionary meetings for the diocese with the cathedral as meeting-place. The strife had ended before Wordsworth's death, but there had remained a sense of isolation or separation. Wilkinson overcame this; the see was a living unity; he was Father-in-God to a family.

In regard to the larger unity he moved in charity but in caution and enjoined caution upon others. He would neither preach himself in Presbyterian pulpits nor allow his clergy to do so. It seemed a retrogression from Wordsworth's approach, and there was some rancour in the press, but he went quietly on his way:

'How shall these miserable walls of separation be broken down? . . . We cannot separate ourselves from the thousands now within the veil, who in bygone ages, at the cost of their life-blood, have kept undefiled the faith once delivered to the saints. We must not, in our yearning for unity, raise new barriers between the Scottish Church and the world-wide Anglican Communion. We dare not, as in the sight of God, through our love for our brethren who differ from us at home, do anything which may for ever quench the hope of reunion with other branches of the Catholic Church. . . . And yet we long in our inmost heart to have a more living place in the national life of Scotland.' Controversy was harsh, even discussion might be futile: 'Instead of speaking, it is well that we should rather pray.'

The way of approach was difficult but disunity grieved him. He could not bear the assumption, common in Scotland, that this was natural, even healthy, that the Church was like 'an aggregate of trading establishments' which flourished on rivalry. A deep hurt was done to Christendom by the separation of Anglicans from Presbyterians as well as from Orthodox and from Roman Catholics. The hurt became personal and poignant when he thought of his own Presbyterian friends: the beloved Donald Macleod and Professor Milligan, 'that great and holy theologian who had now passed out of this life into the more immediate Presence of the Divine Redeemer, without having been able to kneel at our side when we received the Holy Communion, and offered the great Memorial of the One Redeemer.'

He made a formal statement on Episcopacy:

'The Episcopal Church attaches great importance to the gift which is conveyed to the baptized and believing Christian by the laying on of hands. It attaches great importance to the Godward aspect of Holy Communion, to that view which describes it as a Memorial Service. It believes that in the Ideal of Our Lord for His Kingdom, the Episcopate has a real and important place.'

There was a new and warm friendship with the Reverend James Cooper, a parish minister in Aberdeenshire and future Professor of Glasgow University. He, in 1896, proposed a conference between the Scottish Bishops and some Presbyterian leaders, suggesting the acceptance by Episcopalians of the Presbyterian system of Church Courts retained under a Bishop, the granting of a wide liberty of forms of worship 'provided there were forms of unquestionable validity for the administrations of the Sacraments'. This was, in fact, that unity without uniformity which is appearing possible and acceptable today. Dr. Cooper went far ahead of his generation, ahead of many successors in ecumenical debate. He went ahead of Bishop Wilkinson who was none the less impressed, and who took the matter to the Lambeth Conference of 1897. There he was appointed to the Committee on Unity. He was given a memorandum by his Presbyterian allies on 'The Catholic Movement in the Presbyterian Establishment represented by The Scottish Church Society'. This was largely a movement towards a deeper sacramental life and expression, and some of its leaders, notably Dr. Cooper, were prepared to accept the Episcopal succession and administration. They were met by Anglican sympathizers, Cosmo Gordon Lang, the future Archbishop, son of a minister of the Kirk, among them. There was an attempt to form a scheme 'which may supply the episcopal succession and administration but at the same time avoid insistence upon episcopal government'. These 'High Church' Presbyterians would, in effect, accept the Bishop in his sacramental office and function if not in his jurisdiction. The distinction was clear to them, though not to the majority of members of the Kirk.

Such a scheme could include the Presbyterian Church Courts and the use of lay elders working with the ministers. The Scottish Episcopal Church indeed came very near that system, having now her lay electors and lay representatives as well as her vestries. The conditions proposed by Dr. Cooper were as easy and modest as have ever been put forth.

'If it could be made plain to us that, in a reunion, our hierarchy of courts might go on as before, with canonical Bishops presiding at all ordinations, moderating at all Synods, and acting as superintendents, one of their number being annually chosen as Moderator of the General Assembly . . . and that our form of worship would not be interfered with in any sudden or violent way, I believe a great wave of enthusiasm would rise which would carry reunion in an incredibly short time. If the Prayer Book were made lawful in our Church, it would come in in virtue of its own excellence, as organs have done in the space of a few years.'

It was true that 'the kist o' whistles' was now accepted, but a Prayer Book was another matter: popular prejudice against 'prayers out of a book' was strong and deep, and still deeper was that against Bishops. The Prayer Book has now in our day begun to come into favour 'in virtue of its own excellence' and would no longer be a stumbling-block, especially as uniformity of worship is not held essential in unity; but Bishops are still suspect, dreaded, and rejected. Dr. Cooper was not only ahead of his own generation, he would be in the vanguard today of the march towards unity.

There was not yet any general sense, on either side, of 'the scandal of our unhappy divisions'. For a great many people the ideal was to have Presbyterianism in Scotland, Episcopacy in England, each knowing its place and having no ill feeling. And on both sides there was still a good deal of rigidity.

Scottish Episcopacy was moving away from the old simplicity, becoming more expressively sacramental, more ceremonial and ritualistic. This aroused suspicion and accusations of near-popery. Memories of past strife and persecution were vivid in both Churches. The historical memory is strong in most Scots, and needs purging.

Both sides moved cautiously, but they did reach a talking-point. They met in Edinburgh in 1899 under the presidency of Bishop Wilkinson. This was a preparation for a larger Conference, in January 1900, which drew together four Bishops, many Episcopal clergy and many ministers from the three main Presbyterian Churches: the Established, the Free and the United Presbyterian (these two soon to be joined in the United Free).

This Conference was a union of prayer. The immediate outcome was a statement of awareness of the scandal of disunity, the pressure of the forces of materialism and ungodliness, and of the inner and spiritual unity of those who shared one faith, one Lord: 'the essential unity in Christ which exists among true believers'.

The signatories to this document included Bishops Dowden, Wilkinson and Chinnery-Haldane, he perhaps the most remarkable for he was the highest and most uncompromising of High Churchmen. An interchange of visits followed, that of a Presbyterian deputation to the Episcopal Synod, that of Episcopalians, led by Wilkinson, to the General Assembly. Yet still he held, with gentle inflexibility, his rule of not preaching in Presbyterian pulpits or allowing his clergy to do so.

He did, however, join the Committee of the Christian Unity Association of Scotland, along with Rowland Ellis, Bishop of Aberdeen. Within the limits of his principles he worked for unity; but his influence was above all through his personal holiness, his activity as Father-in-God, his spiritual force. One minister declared:

'I am never five minutes in the company of your Bishop without feeling I am lifted up into a different atmosphere.'

He succeeded Bishop Kelly as Primus. In the latter years of his episcopate he had welcomed some of the Sisters of the Epiphany to Perth. His daughter Carina had, with some other ladies, begun mission work among poor girls, 'girls who had lost their character', who were homeless and rootless. A house was taken for them in Perth. The work grew so greatly that Miss Wilkinson begged her father to invite the Sisters. They came and began a great and beneficent work.

In 1906 the Bishop saw the departure of his beloved friend and brother in the episcopate, Alexander Chinnery-Haldane of Argyll and the Isles. His own time came two years later. His memory and influence endure.

# 14

# Highland Pastor.
## Alexander Chinnery-Haldane

The second Alexander of Argyll and the Isles was spiritually akin to Alexander of Brechin; had time so arranged it as to bring them together in the episcopate they would have been true brothers. In pastoral zeal and in love of the Highlands he resembled his predecessor at one remove, Alexander Ewing, but was very far distant from him in churchmanship.

He was the son of Alexander Haldane of London, grandson of James Haldane of Gleneagles, who, with his brother Robert, had in the early years of the nineteenth century broken away from the Established Church of Scotland to preach a fervent evangelical and Calvinistic doctrine. The fervour was inherited by this grandson, James Robert Alexander, who was born in 1842 at Hatcham, near London, and was baptized into the Church of England. He was educated first at home, then at a school in Bury St. Edmunds where he was not over-happy. Going up to Cambridge, to Trinity College, he found a congenial atmosphere, much happiness and stuff for memory: one of his remembered pictures was of Charles Kingsley standing on the river-bank 'deeply engrossed in an earnest but stammering discourse on the distress in the North. . . . He was saying something about the wages of the mill workmen. A minute after, he cleared at a bound the ditch which separated the river's bank from a green meadow, and so ended his discourse'; a vignette of muscular and social Christianity embodied in one man.

In 1864 young Haldane married the sole daughter and heiress of a wealthy Irish baronet, Sir Nicholas Chinnery, and assumed her surname with his own: at first they were known as Haldane-Chinnery, then as Chinnery-Haldane, which, as the more familiar, we shall use. According to a cousin of Haldane, Lady Monkswell – the 'Victorian Diarist' of two delightful volumes of journals – the marriage was opposed by Sir Nicholas, who was 'a violent

'Evangelical", what Papa called a "black Calvinist".' Whether he suspected the young man of falling away from the teaching of his forebears, or looked with disfavour upon any suitor as a possible fortune-hunter is not known; he may have been a possessive father. Lady Monkswell describes the girl, Anna, as very pretty and as never having known happiness until she met her lover.

'There is a delightful legend in the family, which I write down with all reverence, that when they were virtually engaged – in spite of the opposition of Sir Nicholas – the first time that Alick kissed Anna was under the shadow of the Marble Arch.'

Sir Nicholas probably did disapprove of the young man's theology, for with a compelling vocation to Holy Orders came also a conversion from evangelical Protestantism to Anglo-Catholicism. Ordained by the Bishop of Salisbury to the diaconate in 1866, the priesthood in 1867, he served a brief curacy in Wiltshire. Here his first child, a daughter, was born to a few brief months of life, and another grief fell upon Anna when her parents were killed in a railway accident.

In 1868 the young Chinnery-Haldanes came to Edinburgh, Alexander to work as curate of All Saints under Alexander Murdoch. All Saints, so recently made an incumbency, was at the nadir of its fortunes. The building itself was unfinished and there was no parsonage. The site was in 'a half-built, semi-genteel neighbourhood' and there was 'a squalid, forlorn look about the whole thing which was very depressing'. So Chinnery-Haldane's biographer, Thomas Ball, has written, and he has probably understated the condition.

All Saints was going on its own Scottish and Catholic way, far beyond the standards of the parental St. John's, and under heavy parental disapproval, shown in the withdrawal of help. Catholic ritual and practices were not unknown in Edinburgh; St. Columba's had introduced them twenty years earlier, but for some reason or for no reason what was tolerated in St. Columba's was reprobated in All Saints. Episcopacy in Edinburgh was, by Father Ball's account, 'an alarmingly respectable form of religion, eminently unprogressive and unexpressive; not without liberal and kindly, of somewhat condescending care for "the poor", but quite content to live and let live without attracting too much notice. The even tenor of Edinburgh Episcopalianism had been somewhat disturbed by the High Church "goings-on at St. Columba's", but there were reasons why St. Columba's was only benevolently disapproved of' – perhaps because after twenty years, Edinburgh had grown accustomed to it: but All Saints was very new and was 'looked on as a kind of by-church attended only by eccentrics'.

The new curate, with his rich, devoted and generous wife, changed all that. The fortune inherited from her father was spent largely in the service of the Church. It helped to complete All Saints and built the parsonage, the school and a convent for the Sisters. There was other, unintended help; this becomes a snob-story. The young Chinnery-Haldanes cared little for social life but they were of the best society, they could mix with the elect. They kept a dignified establishment at Greenhill House and a fine carriage, that infallible status symbol of the Victorians. It was observed by an elderly clubman in Princes Street, who thought he knew every equipage in Edinburgh. Whose was this new one? When told it belonged to the curate of All Saints he exclaimed: 'The curate of All Saints keeps a carriage! By Jove, I'll go and hear him.' History, less edifying than fiction, does not relate his conversion.

A first-class curate who kept his carriage, Chinnery-Haldane was first-class in every way. He and his wife lived very quietly, and he gave himself to the service of the people as ardently as did his superior, Father Murdoch. Together they brought All Saints to full life. There was a daily Eucharist, and the day thereafter was spent in visiting the congregation in general, the sick and poor in particular, the hospitals, the workhouses. A natural ascetic, Chinnery-Haldane rarely allowed himself lunch or tea; he used to carry raisins in his pocket for sustenance, coming home only in time for seven o'clock dinner. In the evening he went back to the church for Evensong, often for a class; sometime or other he fitted in study and the preparation of sermons.

His preaching was unremarkable, but one hearer recalled listening with edification because he spoke 'with intention'. Like Father Murdoch he heard confessions. In his pastoral work he was a true priest and a true gentleman, never gossiping about his people, patient with the impatient, courteous with the grumblers.

His wife and he were hospitable, and their house, which had a private chapel, was more than once used for a Retreat, one being conducted by Bishop Forbes.

In the summer of 1874 the Chinnery-Haldanes were on holiday at Ballachulish; a busman's holiday for this priest who could not remain inactive. They fell in love with the district, and they were warmly welcomed by Bishop Mackarness, Ewing's successor. For the next few years they spent summer and winter in Argyll, returning to Edinburgh for the winter and spring, Chinnery-Haldane still serving All Saints as curate. It was not the best of plans, for it meant a divided heart and energy and in 1878 they left Edinburgh altogether for Ballachulish. Already he held the charge of St. Bride's, Nether Lochaber, the little church which owed its building to Lady Alice Ewing: now he was appointed to St. John's, Ballachulish, and a little later to St. Mary's, Glencoe, which was built by his and his wife's generosity. He was a pluralist of the best, and at this time of a necessary kind; indeed he was performing the work of a Bishop in all but the sacramental functions. He and his wife built a house, Alltshellach, at Ballachulish which remained their home. In 1883 he was chosen to be Bishop of Argyll and the Isles on the death of Bishop Mackarness.

This Bishopric demands an athlete. Chinnery-Haldane could and did walk for miles; he could climb and row. He had his adventures. Returning late one night, from some remote visits, he found the inn where he was to sleep closed and silent; every one was asleep and could not be wakened by knocks on the door or pebbles flung at a window. One window was left unfastened and the wandering priest entered, stirred up the embers on the kitchen hearth, made a supper of oatcakes and milk and went to sleep on a bed of chairs. There he was found in the morning by a startled maid-servant whom he civilly wished a good morning. On another occasion a boatman refused to ferry him across a stormy water, declaring that he would not take the Queen herself if she came. He was right but surly, and Chinnery-Haldane was obstinate; taking a boat he began to row himself across but soon got into difficulties. The boat began to drift in the cross currents, and drifted at last to an islet where he found another stranded voyager. They spent a night of chill discomfort, resolving not to be foolhardy again.

His election to the see was unanimous, indeed his was the only name; already he was known and loved and since 1882 he had been Dean. There was a momentary check. The Primus, Eden of Moray, wrote him that it might be desirable for him, as a Bishop elect, to give up his membership of 'party' (that is, of Anglo-Catholic 'party') societies like the Society of the Holy Cross and the Confraternity of the Blessed Sacrament. Courteously but firmly he refused; with equal courtesy the Primus withdrew his suggestion and on the 24th of August, 1883, this other Alexander of Argyll and the Isles was consecrated in St. Andrew's Church, Fort William, by the Primus (Eden), with Wilson of Glasgow, Cotterill of Edinburgh, Jermyn of Brechin, Lightfoot of Durham, and Kelly of Newfoundland who was himself to come to Scotland as Bishop of Moray, succeeding Eden. Among the guests was Father Mackonochie, once of St. Alban's, Holborn, now of St. Peter's, London Docks, one of the most devoted priests in London, a leader of the Anglo-Catholic party. The sermon was preached in Gaelic by the Reverend Hugh McColl.

The new Bishop found full scope and joy in his office. As organizer, and the day of organizations, councils and committees had come, he was ill at ease and not over-efficient; he was essentially a Father-in-God and pastor. He loved and wanted to know his people. On Confirmation tours he liked to stay at the parsonage or at the inn rather than at the laird's mansion; he wanted to be free and accessible. Confirmations were a joy to him, ordinations almost a dread: his ideal of the priesthood was so high that he feared to lay hands on an unworthy candidate. His ordinands were strictly examined and he always gave them a retreat, preparing them for the sacred duties, truly making them priests.

Given to hospitality, he had everything in his house beautifully and generously ordered, and at the heart of it was the chapel. On Sunday his guests gathered there for the Eucharist, except those who preferred to walk to St. Bride's; they all went to St. Bride's for a sung Eucharist or for Matins and the Litany, and for Evensong to St. John's, for that Office was said in Gaelic at St. Bride's. The day ended with Compline in chapel.

The Monkswells went there in 1884 by sea:

'The *Iona* left us on the pier . . . and we were carried off to a nice, large boat . . . a most romantic beginning.' After being rowed about a mile and a half they came to a rocky island, joined to the mainland by a dyke and made a landing-place.

'I saw that very smart, spruce person, Anna, advancing from a grey house about two hundred yards up the hill, and attended by a great, splendid greyhound. She received us most kindly, and Alec, my Lord Bishop, presently appeared. This household is further removed from commonplace than any into which I have yet been received.

'First there is Alec in a long, black coat, Bishop's apron and stockings, and, when he walks abroad, a very broad-brimmed hat with a little rosette.' There were the two boys, Brodrick and Vernon; and, instead of curates, 'two men, Mr. Lawrence and Mr. Wedderburn, to attend to his concerns and to shore him up': the former made the coffee at breakfast, looked after the estate, stable and boats, and acted secretary. Mr. Wedderburn, known as 'the Bard', 'puts flowers in the chapel, paints chapels and altars and visits the sick. In his evening kilt and lace necktie he looks a tremendous swell. The next most important members of the family are the deerhound, Re, the collie, Pate, and the Scotch terrier, Sperach, with a face like an old seal. There is also the Manx cat and her kitten, also tail-less, who looks just like a sole. This house looks right up the loch and on to the pass of Glencoe. I have never lived, except in Switzerland, so entirely in the heart of the mountains.'

It was a happy visit in spite of copious rain. Another in 1885 was equally enchanting; and again the Monkswells visited Alltshellach in 1903. 'The prize day of our holiday' that year began with chapel and went on to a garden party, seventeen miles away. 'The simple, familiar term "garden party" conveys really no idea at all of all we saw, did and suffered,' going by yacht to Loch Eil in torrents of rain and squalls of wind. When they arrived they were welcomed by their hosts with almost incredulous joy. The party proved worth the voyage, and afterwards they came home by moonlight.

They left Alltshellach with regret; this was to prove their last visit. Lady Monkswell reports her husband as being 'immensely taken with the dear Bishop, his kindness, benevolence and goodness. Among the circle of his friends the Bishop is quite a new variety.'

She had left a lovely picture of this pastoral Bishop:

'. . . that beautiful way he has of consoling the sick, of looking in at midnight on a poor sufferer. I can think what it must have meant in the despair and misery of a miserable night to have heard his voice at the door and to have seen his serene and kind face, and to be strengthened by him with the thought of the power of the Holy Sacrament and the suffering of Christ. No wonder they loved him.'

In 1887 there occurred a tragedy which moved the whole Church in England as in Scotland: the death of Father Mackonochie: long harrying by the anti-ritualists and by his own Bishop had brought him to the point of mental collapse. In December of that year he was staying in Edinburgh with Thomas Ball. He was to go on to the Chinnery-Haldanes at Ballachulish, confused the dates, and arrived in the Bishop's absence. Next morning he insisted on setting out upon one of the long walks he loved, accompanied only by two of the dogs, a deerhound and a Skye terrier. They were seen at Kinlochleven about two o'clock, and again shortly after, going up towards the Forest of Mamore. It was, as the Bishop wrote afterwards, a strange choice of way into the snow, one explicable only by some confusion of mind, a loss of all sense of direction. Darkness was falling.

'After this, he was never seen again.'

In the meantime the Bishop had returned home, and as evening drew on with no sign of his guest's return he grew anxious and sent two men out in search of him, himself following in his carriage. There was no sign of him beyond Kinloch. The searchers returned and next morning, as soon as it was light, three parties went out; again they found no trace. That night two parties went out, the Bishop in one of them. It was a night of storm, the wind blowing out their lanterns while they stumbled over rocks and ice and snow. The Bishop's party went by The Devil's Staircase, the pass between Glencoe and the Kinloch hills.

'It seemed like some other terrible world that we had got into.' Again the search was vain. The next morning a crowd of men and dogs went out towards Mamore, finding no trace until, late in the afternoon, they saw, far off, the two dogs. Some one said:

'No doubt we shall find it there.'

Afterwards the Bishop recalled:

'The word "it" was horrible to hear', for it meant a corpse and no living man.

And so they found him, dead, guarded by the faithful dogs, his body frozen, his head half buried in the snow which had been his last pillow.

'But on his face there was his own look of peace and joy, and not a trace of suffering.'

The Bishop said the prayers for the departed over him, cleared the snow from his head, and he was carried on a bier of sticks to the carriage waiting at Kinloch, and so home to the Bishop's chapel:

'Just at the moment we discovered the body, and while we were moving it, the clouds in the west, over the Glencoe mountains, divided, and such a glorious evening light came out over the whole landscape, that I can hardly think the circumstance was a mere accident.'

He lay in the chapel, vested as a priest, his crucifix on his breast, his Priest's Prayer Book, still wet with snow, beside him. In the morning the Bishop offered Mass for his soul.

For this Bishop the little Cathedral of the Isles at Cumbrae was both a joy and a care. As a seminary for ordinands it had been diminished by the growth of the Theological College in Edinburgh, but it flourished as 'a sort of long vacation resort' for University men reading for Holy Orders and a centre for Retreats; it was still, as it had been planned, a place of study, prayer and worship. Unhappily, in 1885, the generous founder, Lord Glasgow, crashed in financial ruin: his lands in Cumbrae had to be sold and were bought by the laird of the neighbouring island, Lord Bute, a Roman Catholic. The cathedral and college buildings were kept by the Episcopal Church largely through the efforts of the Bishop, but there was a break in the collegiate life and activity. The Provost left for another charge, the choir school was given up, the clergy departed. For about seven years there was silence: then the Bishop invited Father Ball to come to the island as Provost and also as incumbent of the little church of St. Andrew in the village. The college was opened again for Retreats; the *opus Dei* was resumed in the cathedral, with a daily Eucharist and the Offices. The clergy of Argyll and the Isles used to make an annual Retreat as guests of the Bishop: other retreatants were charged fifteen shillings for generous hospitality, 'wine and beer being supplied *ad libitum*' so that there was inevitably 'a serious discrepancy between the cost of entertainment and the sum paid by retreatants' – the discrepancy being made up by the Bishop. Cumbrae and its cathedral were the Bishop's legacy to generations of church-people, both lay and cleric, treasured long after his day. His other legacy was Iona, the holiest of isles, now made available for Retreat, holiday and holy days of worship by this Bishop of the Isles.

It was the realization of that dream of Bishop Ewing that Iona should see the flame, lit long ago by St. Columba, rekindled and burning clear. In 1893 Bishop Chinnery-Haldane was granted a feu on the island by its owner, the Duke of Argyll, who was persuaded to that step by his good Anglican Duchess. The parish minister presented a petition against what appeared to him a scandal, declaring that no one on Iona would lift a finger 'to help in the evil work' of building an Episcopal chapel. The Duke dismissed the petition, pointing out the fact that the signatories outnumbered the inhabitants of the island. The work began; the good men of Iona helped willingly in the building and Bishop's House with its chapel was completed. In 1894 it was dedicated to St. Columba, whose statue stands in a niche in the east wall, looking over to the mainland. Three years later the Cowley Fathers came to live there, maintaining the *opus Dei* and going out as missionaries. They stayed until 1910 and one of them, Father Trenholme, wrote one of the best histories we have of Iona.

Today there are no longer Religious on the island, but the Bishop's House with its chapel is still a place of blessed rest and peace for Retreats and holidays. In the chapel another Bishop of Argyll and the Isles, third in succession from Chinnery-Haldane, offered, in June 1963, the Eucharist, after the Scottish Rite, in celebration of the fourteenth centenary of St. Columba's landing.

Bishop Chinnery-Haldane was uncompromisingly Catholic, even at times to the point of rigidity. One of his decisions involved him in controversy, the announcement in his charge of 1888 that he would not confirm anyone who had not been baptized by a lawfully ordained priest. This, in effect, demanded the conditional baptism of converts from Presbyterian and other non-Episcopal churches. There followed an acrimonious correspondence in the press. The Bishop was unshaken, maintaining that firmness won more than it alienated, that converts who truly desired to be received always ended by accepting the conditions laid down.

This year which brought strife, though not of long duration, brought also a very pleasant honour. Cambridge conferred on him the Doctorate of Divinity. At the graduation the Public Orator spoke of this Highland diocese with its long, and often tragic history, in particular that of Glencoe, 'once infamous as the scene of cruel slaughter, but where now the mysteries of the gentlest of religions are celebrated in the presence of reverent throngs, in their own tongue'.

He was Catholic and he was Scottish, loving the ancient Liturgy, desiring its restoration to equality of use and honour. In this he was at one with his fellow Bishops: Jermyn of Brechin, now Primus, Wordsworth, mellowed by age and near the end of his long episcopate, Kelly of Moray, Douglas of Aberdeen, Harrison, newly consecrated Bishop of Glasgow, Dowden the great scholar, Bishop of Edinburgh. They met in private conclave to prepare a revision of the Scottish Office which would be submitted to the Provincial Synod of 1890. They were working under difficulties, for there was no authorized version of the Scottish Prayer Book as there was of the English. The text of the Communion Office must be decided before it was given final authority and about this there was considerable debate. It was held by some liturgiologists that the Epiklesis was not an exact equivalent of the Epiklesis in the Orthodox Rite which the Scottish had always claimed to follow. The Orthodox form prays for the Descent of the Holy Spirit upon the worshippers as well as upon the 'gifts and creatures of Bread and Wine', praying that these Gifts may be hallowed for the faithful receivers. The word 'become' was an inexact translation of the Orthodox term. In the Scottish Book of 1637 the prayer was that the Bread and Wine 'may be unto us the Body and Blood'; but the text in general use, that of Forbes and Falconar, had 'become' and omitted the words 'unto us'. The Bishops in council proposed this revision:

'We most humbly beseech Thee, O most merciful Father, to hear us, and of Thy Almighty Goodness vouchsafe to bless and sanctify with Thy Holy Spirit this Bread and this Cup that they may be the Body and Blood of Thy most dearly beloved Son, so that whosoever shall partake of the same, being filled with Thy Grace and heavenly Benediction, may be sanctified both in soul and body, and preserved unto everlasting life.'

A draft of this was circulated among the clergy in 1889 with the intention that it should be studied before its formal submission to the Synod in 1890. Somehow it became public and there was an explosion. The Bishops' meeting in private conclave was distorted into a conspiracy (as Father Ball puts it) 'to water down the doctrine of the Scotch Office in the interests of Protestant unbelief' – an interpretation which seems rather forced, indeed distorted. Another draft was submitted to the Diocesan Synods, but the storm raged on; and rather than have this most sacred matter become a centre of strife, the Bishops ended the whole discussion. It was not until 1912 that the Scottish Prayer Book was revised and brought into wider use.

Chinnery-Haldane was Scottish but not insular. As a young man he had made a tour of France and Switzerland, and foreign holidays became a pleasant habit, although never on the ample scale enjoyed by Bishop Ewing. In a visit to Russia and one to Constantinople he learned something of the Orthodox way of worship and renewed the old bond of sympathy with the Orthodox Church: in Constantinople he had an audience with the Patriarch to whom he presented a copy of Bishop Forbes's translation of the Scottish Liturgy into Greek. This was a courteous and fraternal meeting, the Scots guest being saluted as a Bishop by the attendant clergy. It was decidedly happier than an earlier encounter, in Palestine, with an Italian priest, the guardian of the Latin Hospice at one of the holy places. Chinnery-Haldane (not yet a Bishop) found him sympathetic. This priest offered him the use of the altar in order to celebrate the Eucharist for himself and his companion; from Chinnery-Haldane's letter of introduction it was plain that he was in Anglican Orders, not Roman, and he celebrated by the Scottish Rite. It seemed a most courteous gesture on the part of the Roman priest, an unusually generous act of brotherliness. But afterwards a rumour was circulated by an English convert to Rome that there had been a misunderstanding, that the priest had believed Chinnery-Haldane to be in Roman Orders and that Chinnery-Haldane had encouraged this belief. This rumour was at once denied, but it was repeated.

Its maker later seceded from Rome and became a Unitarian. Discredited the story might be, but it did some harm and gave deep hurt.

He was never in any likelihood of Romanizing; his belief in the validity of Anglican Orders and Sacraments was firm. While admitting imperfections in his own Church, he saw no ideal or perfection in Rome, and thought poorly of the logic of those who argued: 'The Church of England is wrong, therefore the Church of Rome must be right.' He deplored conversions to Rome, but did not welcome those from the Roman to the Anglican Communion. His own predilection, outside his own Church, was for Orthodoxy. He abhorred the violence of the extreme Reformers, banning their works from his library. With individual Presbyterians he found much in common through his own evangelical fervour, but he saw little chance of reunion.

In one matter he approved the Roman discipline – that of celibacy, although himself married, so happily, and owing so much to his wife. He had married before being priested. It might be more accurate to say that he approved the Orthodox discipline – that priests must marry before ordination. This he enjoined upon his ordinands, going so far as to refuse to celebrate clerical marriages; but had the Orthodox rule been applied to himself he would have remained a parish priest and never become a Bishop.

He died in February 1906. Lady Monkswell related that in the previous autumn his doctors had diagnosed in him cancer of the lungs and given him only two weeks to live; but he lived for four months 'without severe pain': it was 'in answer to the prayers of his people'.

He was buried in St. Bride's churchyard: the memory of his devotion, his love of his people, endured.

# 15

# Anthony Mitchell.
# A Bishop of the North-East

Of the Episcopal trio whose lives conclude this history, only one was made and nurtured by Scottish Episcopacy, rooted in the north-east, touching a living chain of hands of the priests and Bishops of the heroic, austere past.

Anthony Mitchell was born in 1868 in Aberdeen, in a house near the harbour, which was a delight in childhood. His biographer, Dean Perry, has said that while in other parts of Scotland Episcopacy has had to make itself a home, in Aberdeenshire 'a home has been made for it by men and women whose forebears go back to Jacobite times and beyond'. It is in their bones. Young Anthony was a cradle-Pisky. He was to build a bridge between past and present, partly by his scholarship in one small but precious book, *A Short History of the Church in Scotland*, and even more by his life and ministry. In him the native tradition lived and was renewed in service of the world of his day. Neither sentimentalist nor antiquarian, he had the story of the Church as part of his spiritual heritage, of his own being.

His parents were members of St. John's Church where he was baptized by the Reverend John Comper; he had two godmothers, both of whom became Sisters in the Community of St. Margaret of Scotland. When John Comper accepted the charge of St. Margaret's in the Gallowgate, the Mitchells followed him. The small Anthony took very kindly to the ritual and ceremonial: he liked the vested priest and choir, loved to dress up himself, and one Sunday, when the children were suspiciously quiet, his mother found him arrayed in a white apron, preaching to his sister and brother. Once, when asked what he wanted to be when he grew up, he replied: 'A Bushop'.

When he was seven the family moved to Port Elphinstone near Inverurie, on the other side of the Don. There he attended the Church school. No blameless infant saint, he was told by the mistress: 'You are more trouble to me than all the school put together.' There was plenty of sound mischief in him, but no lethargy: all his life he was a lover of books and learning, one of those who find it easier to read than not to read. The little school could hardly have fed his quick mind, but at least half his education came from the Rector of Inverurie, Canon Harper: 'Popery Harper' to the neighbourhood because of his ritualism which was, by modern standards, very discreet; but he was, in Dean Perry's words, 'one of the first in the north of Scotland to express the old-fashioned, non-juring point of view in terms of the Oxford Movement'. Steadfast in churchmanship, he dealt firmly with Anthony when the latter chose to go walking in a Salvation Army procession. In church, in school and in private talk this good priest taught the boy sound doctrine and tradition, prepared him for his Confirmation (by Bishop Suther), nurtured his soul as well as his mind. Mrs. Harper gave him piano lessons. The Rectory was the entrance to a larger world than that of home or school. And all the time he read voraciously, especially poetry and novels.

His family were poor; he is in the brave tradition of those poor scholars who are part of the glory of Scotland. His parents had intelligence, pride and that generosity which have been the gifts of so many poor parents to their children. This son took from them as little as he could in material things: at the age of fourteen he went on a bursary to Aberdeen Grammar School, with its fame for sound learning, where the great Latinist, Dr. Melvin, was still a living memory. Latin Prose – 'the version' – was still the basis of study. There he worked hard, read widely, sometimes rising at three o'clock to study before breakfast, then catch the eight o'clock train to Aberdeen. He had the double gift of concentration and of quickness, and could move from Latin Prose to English novels, from a school debate to games, without effort. Already he had the faculty for going to the heart of the matter which would be invaluable to him as a Bishop.

The mystique of games had not yet spread to Scotland where the boys played for fun and to work off their energy. Anthony was good at games and played with zest. He enjoyed, also, the game of writing, producing quantities of stories and poems, the former inclining to horror – one was called 'The Bloody Buccaneer' – the latter ranging between sweet sorrow and deft lightness, as his poem to his cat:

> Little cat, pussy cat,
> How I love to see you thinking,
> At the cosy fireside winking,
> Gently purring, slyly blinking,
> Sitting just like that.
>
> Are you deeply meditating
> On your misdeeds, or regretting
> That you lately have been getting
> Really rather fat?
>
> But 'tis more than I can bear,
> When the evening stars are shining,
> Mortals on their beds reclining,
> Earth and heaven both inclining
> To give rest from care;
>
> When you howl with your appalling
> Voice, and rend the air with squalling,
> Till, to stop your caterwauling –
> I blow you through the air.

He absorbed more than book learning. He used to visit old Dr. Walker of Monymusk, a living source of Scottish Episcopal tradition, and saw through his eyes the priests and Bishops of the years of penalties and poverty, saw the emergence of the Church into daylight, her growth in strength.

In 1886, with the School Gold Medal and a bursary, he went up to King's College, Aberdeen, to wear the red gown as a bejan and proceed through the succeeding years as semi, tertian and magistrand; the old terms were still in use. His energy of mind and body did not flag: he read Classics for Honours as well as the usual subjects for the ordinary degree of M.A., played in the College Fifteen and Eleven, joined the Literary and Debating Societies, and contributed to the University Magazine *Alma Mater*.

His chief intellectual inspiration came from the Professor of Humanity, Sir William Ramsay, the great Pauline scholar. Besides his formal lectures Ramsay used to give talks on the social life of ancient Rome, always with a practical and contemporary application. Religion was not mentioned, but religion informed those talks. He was something of a hero to this student who came to him for counsel at a spiritual crisis. Already Anthony had become aware of his vocation to the priesthood and had begun pastoral work in an East End Mission, teaching a Sunday School class of small, tough boys. But doubts were beginning to trouble him. The atmosphere of the university was more than tinged with scepticism and materialism. The remark of one of the medical faculty was much quoted:

'I have dissected many a body, but such a thing as a soul has never yet come under my notice.'

The theological students were few and lightly esteemed. Ramsay helped Anthony, though indirectly. He gave no spiritual counsel but he was wholesomely astringent, telling the anxious boy that 'he did not know enough to feed his own mind'. Anthony accepted the criticism. Ramsay advised him to go to Cambridge and consider an academic career. Accordingly he went up to Gonville and Caius for the summer term of 1889 (the Scottish University year then ended in the spring), went up with a fine cluster of academic honours, prizes in Greek, in logic, in classical philology. Cambridge taught him something, including the fact that the enclosed, academic life was not for him. In the autumn he returned to Aberdeen for his final year as magistrand, which ended triumphantly in First Class Honours in Classics.

There were still moods of bewilderment, even of foreboding.

'I always feel that I shall not live long, and so, what I do I'll have to do quickly.' It was a sadly true presentiment and it was reflected in a poem:

> I would not pray for length of years,
>   To feel my eye grow dim,
> And drink the last dregs of the cup
>   Now trembling at the brim;
> Nor high renown – a little while
>   In men's report to be;
> Then leave my name to reap the fame
>   That death denied to me.

He never lost faith or hope, his doubts vanished; well grounded in the faith by Dean Harper, his mind was fortified by the tradition and discipline of the Church, and he was always a practising Christian.

So, having paid his way through College with bursaries and prizes, he was capped M.A. with Honours and won the Seafield Gold Medal in Latin: besides that scholastic glory he had a book of verses to his name: *Tatters From a Student's Gown* published in 1890 and dedicated to his fellow classmen. It is a pleasant collection of lyrics, parodies and echoes of balladry, a medley of the wistful and the daft. One poem celebrates 'The Minister's Gweed Black Coat': a garment so fine as to win veneration for its wearer:

> For mony a day
> The principle topic o' a' conversation
> Was the Meenister's new black coat.

The coat covered the minister's rotundity and its cause – 'He drank something stronger than water or yill' – and covered that and other failings in every way until 'ae day he was laid in the mool'. Then tongues wagged freely:

> But whaure'er he was gane
> There is ae thing I ken-
> Nae cheenge was made in his destination
> Because o' the gweed black coat!

A variant of *Hey Diddle-Diddle* runs:

> Hey tiddle-tum, the pig played the drum,
>     And the elephant walked up the tree;
> The tall kangaroo put his head in his pouch,
>     And the haddock was drowned in the sea.

One poem deftly takes off the current vogue for melancholy:

Soft the shades of eve are falling, and from out my lattice door
I can hear the billows breaking all along the misty shore;
And my soul is filled with sadness, and I feel I'm all at sea,
For I'm sewing on a button, and I'm thinking, love, of thee!

Lone I sit, and sadly wonder, what you do when in your thumb

Half an inch you push the needle – where you thought it
    couldn't come.
Do you sit and suck it calmly? or get mad as mad can be?
I've just done it, and I'm thinking, sadly thinking, love, of thee.

Another bursary, the Walker, commemorating the Bishop who
was the first Pantonian Professor of Theology, took him to the
Theological College now occupying two houses in Rosebery
Crescent; Coates Hall was in process of building. This was for
him a complete change of atmosphere, discipline and way of life.
Intellectual discipline he had known from his school-days; it was
now instinctive. The discipline of poverty had always been
accepted. This new discipline was of the soul; it was partly
exercised in College rules, in the mild, semi-monastic regimen.
At King's, he had known little community life, although much
good comradeship; the former was no part of Scottish university
life. Now he was one of a community, living by rule.

The day began with the butler's call, 'Seven o'clock, sir', the
chapel bell ringing half an hour later for Matins and the Eucharist:
breakfast followed, with a brief space afterwards for glancing at
the newspapers, smoking a pipe, walking quickly round the
Crescent. At half-past nine the men were in chapel again for
silence and meditation: perhaps the most difficult discipline of all.
Lectures took them to one o'clock and dinner; the afternoon was
free except for those who (twice a week) had a lesson in Hebrew,
and was the time for exercise, for browsing in book-shops, for
discovering Edinburgh. Between tea and supper was study time;
after supper came recreation in the Common Room, and at ten
o'clock Compline and silence. Chapel was quite as important as
the lecture room, prayer mattered even more than study, and
prayer must be learned and practised. At first, Anthony was ill at
ease.

'To be a scholar was a natural ambition. . . . To be a saint had
hardly entered his head.'

The sacramental life was more intense than he had known.
His practice had been to receive Holy Communion once a month;
here it was given every Sunday and once during the week as well.
The old instinct which had little indifference in it and much awe,
much sense of unworthiness, was still strong in him; after much

prayer and counsel he came thankfully to accept this frequent Communion.

The College was still barely furnished but it held riches of learning. The profoundest influence upon Anthony was that of the Vice-Principal, Charles Davey-Biggs, newly come from Oxford and Cuddesdon, a disciple of Bishop Gore, a scholar and a true priest. Between these two a strong and lasting affection developed; there became evident in the student 'a new refinement and seriousness, a firmer hold upon Divine truth, a growing sense of the Divine Presence . . . Christian truth had become something to do and live, as well as to study'. The making of a priest had begun.

The scholar also grew in strength. Bishop Dowden lectured on Church History with immense stimulus:

'A fact of history is worth a bushel of speculation' was one of his sayings, never forgotten by one hearer. Dowden was then writing his *History of the Celtic Church*. Having discovered Anthony's poetic talent, he suggested a verse translation of St. Columba's *Altus Prosator* and this was accomplished, although not until after College days were over. The Principal, Canon Keating, thought Anthony the best all-round student he had known. All three men, the Bishop, the Principal, the Vice-Principal gave him friendship, encouragement, counsel – gifts he had not been given so richly since his boyhood at Inverurie with Dean Harper. Some years later he wrote:

'The most precious and enduring gift which one who aspires to enter the priesthood of the Church can ask or obtain, is a realization of and a beginning of growth in the priestly character.'

Looking back he saw how all things had been ordered to that end:

'We found ourselves bathed in an atmosphere of gentle, albeit powerful spiritual influence, and when we left the protecting walls of the College and faced our new duties in the world, we found our possession to be no delusive or stinted one. We had not to learn, but to go on learning.'

Ordained deacon by Bishop Dowden on Trinity Sunday 1892, he was appointed to a curacy in the cathedral, with charge of the new Church of the Good Shepherd, Murrayfield, then a dependent Mission. His friend Suther Presslie was curate at All Saints, and

Anthony, not over-burdened by the care of his own small congregation, went there often, learning, according to his biographer, 'more about parish work than he ever gained from the stereotyped ways which prevailed at the cathedral'. Arriving for Evensong on the Vigil of All Saints, he was asked by Canon Murdoch to preach.

'Well, Canon, if you give me *poynts.*'

The Canon gave the necessary points in about five minutes, and Anthony preached a very good sermon.

'Well, Anthony, ye're gey quick in the uptak',' was Canon Murdoch's tribute.

He was indeed quick in the uptake as regards both preaching and pastoral work. He knew how to deal with people. In 1893 he was offered the curacy of St. John's, Dumfries; he had been priested that year and now he married and took his wife to this new setting. It was a change of atmosphere as well as of region. In Edinburgh, Episcopacy had long been approved as a gentleman's religion. In the south-west it was tolerated, known as The English Church, regarded as alien but harmless. This had a subduing effect upon Episcopalians who tended to stay in the background, keeping their beliefs and practices to themselves. It was an ethos different from that in which he had grown up. The church in Dumfries was, for all that, in a flourishing condition, the congregation built up by the Rector, J. R. Denham. Socially it was well mixed, ranging from county families to working people.

The new curate made many friends. He found the county people easy and sympathetic, and they liked him; and he worked ardently among the poor. There was a Mission at Maxwelltown, there were Sunday School and day school classes, and there was the chapel at the Crichton Asylum where St. John's clergy served every other Sunday. It was varied and valuable experience for a young priest and he matured in every way. His gift for storytelling endeared him to the children; he had a talent for teaching.

For a year all went well: then some misunderstanding or antagonism arose between rector and curate. This was in later years to be overcome, but at the time it appeared to be making their work together impossible. At this crisis the Bishop of Glasgow, Dr. Harrison, offered Anthony the charge of St. Andrews-by-the-Green, Glasgow – 'a call . . . to the most forlorn hope in

Scotland', to the oldest Episcopal Church in the south-west, and to evangelistic work which was to complete the making of this already devoted priest.

St. Andrew's stood in the centre of Glasgow, in what, a hundred years before, had been a prosperous and genteel quarter but was now on the borders of the slums. The prosperous and genteel citizens had long since moved west, to dignified terrace houses, or south, over the river, to large villas. The church, having been an English or 'qualified' chapel, had never known penalties and in the late eighteenth and early nineteenth centuries had not known poverty. Its congregation had been chiefly of 'carriage folk'; ladies and gentlemen arrived, followed by a footman carrying their Prayer Books, and were shown into their pews by a verger or pew-opener. The service was accompanied by the organ which had come from the Presbyterian Cathedral, the 'kist o' whistles' which gave St. Andrew's its name of 'The Kirk o' Whistles'. But that was a long time ago; poverty had replaced gentility, indifference had reduced what was left of the congregation to some fifty members. There was an oddly large baptismal register, but this was due less to parental piety than to the easy attitude of the previous incumbent. He asked no questions, made no conditions; he had accepted any child for baptism whose parents would pay half a crown into congregational funds.

The new Rector stopped all this. He was at once more strict and more pastoral: those who came from other districts were directed to their own church; the churchless poor were gently treated, visited, most of them drawn into the congregation.

St. Andrew's was poor to the verge of bankruptcy and was kept going financially only by help from the Bishop of Glasgow's Fund. There was no Rectory; the Mitchells, three of them now, a daughter having been born to them, lived in a flat in a poor street. Besides the shadow of poverty on the church there was one almost of disrepute; previous incumbents had been negligent, even eccentric. The difficulties were heart-breaking, but this young priest had a brave as well as a compassionate heart. He visited his people faithfully and with kindness.

'He seems to bring peace into the house,' one parishioner declared.

Realizing that social work must be related to teaching and to worship, he gradually worked out a synthesis. The worship at St. Andrew's-by-the-Green was devout and reverent, the preaching was instructive and truly attractive. This scholar never talked down to his people, he drew them to the Gospel. On the secular side he arranged Saturday night parties in the hall, presiding himself and contributing to a programme of songs, stories and comic turns; a dance followed. More and more people came, and more and more of them appeared next morning at the altar.

A penny-a-week fund was started to pay off the congregational debt, and in one year this raised £200. In 1897 a Parish Mission was conducted, not by the Rector alone or by an inner group of the devout but by the whole congregation, including the children. One of the Missioners was Dr. Davey-Biggs, the former Vice-Principal of the Theological College. The results were solid and lasting. In the following Lent there was a notable increase of members; fifty-six confirmands were presented to the Bishop, two hundred and forty communicants made their Easter Communion.

The whole diocese was growing under the pastoral and missionary care of Bishop Harrison. New churches were being built, the Home Mission Board was very active. The Bishop from south of the border, whose coming had been, by some, resented, and the priest from the very cradle and home of Scottish Episcopacy, were alike in their zeal.

At the end of the century Anthony served for a time as Chaplain to the Forces in the Boer War. To this new venture he adapted himself well; his forthright manner set him on good terms with the men. He was amused by the report of a medical officer in reply to his query about the wounded:

'Only two bad enough for you. You see, when they are beyond me, I hand them over to you.' Again he did not water down doctrine. Once, in the mess, an officer declared that if he found his wife going to confession he would divorce her and horse-whip the priest. Some of the others agreed that this would be right and proper conduct. The new padre listened, waited, then spoke; he pointed out that there was spiritual as well as physical illness and that it was reasonable to discuss this in strict confidence with someone qualified to diagnose the cause and prescribe a remedy. The priest was a spiritual physician. The officers listened, impressed by his argument; they had not thought of it like that, but they were fair-minded; they began to see a glimmering of the sacramental life.

His ministry at St. Andrew's-by-the-Green ended in 1904 when he went to St. Mark's, Portobello; there he stayed only a year, being made principal of the Theological College in 1905. The College had come a long way since Miss Panton left her legacy of endowment, a long way from Bishop Walker's classes in his own house and from the meagre days at Glenalmond. Now this place of north-eastern foundation had a son of the north-east to rule it. His rule was wise, strict in essential discipline, relaxed in small matters. The men found him patient, sympathetic, firm without fuss, always accessible; the more discerning were aware of a tolerant amusement behind some of his rebukes.

It was a brief rule. In 1912 he was consecrated Bishop of Aberdeen and Orkney, and so returned to his own country, to gather up, continue and strengthen the tradition he had received in boyhood from those good priests William Walker and Dean Harper.

As Principal and as Bishop he belongs to the present century, but the making of him began in the 1870's, a decade which remembered, through living witnesses, the old days of poverty and austerity. The poor boy of rich mind who had inherited those memories, who had won scholastic glories, who had, as a priest, accepted new discipline, fulfilled his vocation among the poor – these younger Anthonies were part of Anthony the Bishop. With his consecration he received new grace, a deepening of spiritual wisdom and compassion which made him one of the great Bishops of our Church and our century.

He is still a living and beloved memory, his episcopate recalled with pride and thankfulness, and sorrow that it ended so soon. Physically he had little reserve of health and strength. Was he, like so many of the poor scholar-lads of Scottish history, paying for the intense work and frugal living of college days?

It was a full episcopate and he was the ideal Bishop: pastor and teacher, Father-in-God, experienced in the care of souls, a scholar well learned in the faith. His *History of the Church in Scotland* was written during his Principalship. A volume of *Biographical Studies in Scottish Church History*, including a brief Life of Bishop Dowden, grew out of the Hale Lectures he delivered in Chicago, a strengthening of the old bond between the Church in Scotland and the Church in America. The excellence of both books makes the lack, through his death, of other, ampler studies the more grievous.

In his time St. Andrew's Church, Aberdeen, became the cathedral of the diocese. He died in 1917 in the thick darkness of war, when the lights of Europe had one by one gone out; but the lamp of faith, tended through penal days, poverty and every hardship, by the faithful Scottish Church, still burned clear.

# Epilogue

When the writing of this book was nearly finished, something happened very quietly, in a small company and a small place, which the future historian may find as exciting and important as the consecration of Bishop Seabury. It happened in the old and lovely chapel at Roslin, on the Feast of the Transfiguration, 1965. There, the Bishop of Edinburgh received the vows – to celibacy, poverty and communal life, for one year of postulancy – of three priests, one of them the chaplain of Roslin, admitting them to a brotherhood of service. Then he celebrated the Eucharist by the Scottish Rite; the new Brothers, the other clergy present, and the people received the Sacrament. The atmosphere was that of the mountain of vision and Transfiguration. The descent to the plain and the crowd must follow; of that, and of all that may be done by the Brotherhood in prayer, worship, daily life and work it is too soon to write. But something began that bright evening in the little chapel, planned five hundred years ago as a great collegiate church to perform the Work of God, which may prove greater than that plan; something was born in the Scottish Church which may bring renewal to the Church and to Scotland.

We are happy in many Retreats and Missions conducted by visiting Religious of the Anglican Communion: Benedictines from Nashdom, The Society of St. John from Cowley, the Community of the Resurrection from Mirfield, the Franciscans from Dorset and from Alnmouth. We have our own Retreat House at Walkerburn under the care of the Sisters of St. Peter. The Community of St. Mary and St. John, and that of St. Margaret of Scotland, still live their devoted lives of prayer and work in Aberdeen, and the former Community is of Scottish foundation. But this Brotherhood of three is the first Community of men to be founded in our Scottish Church. The chapel that festal evening was full of prayers.

The Religious life – in the monastic or conventual sense of the word – returned to the Anglican Church more than a hundred years ago in the renewal of the Oxford Movement. Today again there is a new sense of vocation and of *aggiornamento* as good Pope John called it, which may bring a revival of this particularly dedicated Christian life and communal living within the great Christian family, whether chiefly in the active service of God to meet the desperate needs of our time or in the hidden way of prayer.

The Church has been awakened by painful thrusts of conscience about two scandals: that of social evil which includes unemployment, bad housing, corruption of morals, ignorance of religion; and that of disunity. We cannot be complacent, we dare not be somnolent. We need not be self-defensive or apologetic in a feeble way. We must be generous, self-critical, self-giving and out-going.

Awareness of social evils has led to an enlargement of social service. The Church is following the people as they move to new districts; the clergy are making new encounters, new approaches in their pastoral work. One good new thing has been the forming of The Scottish Episcopal Church Housing Society to help to provide decent homes at a decent price.

As for unity, the way is long and hard and we have far to go, if we trust only our own eyesight; but there can be an illumination of sight by the Holy Spirit. And we have already come a long way, in the past ten years or so, from the old antagonisms. There may not, even now, be many Presbyterians who would go as far as Professor Cooper in that approach we saw him make; but it is generally admitted in Scotland that Bishops are Christian, even that they may have some notion of theology and can preach a good sermon. During one week of Prayer for Unity, when there was an interchange of preachers in the various churches of one city, a Presbyterian lady was heard to say:

'You'll never guess who was preaching in our church yesterday. The Bishop! He was quite good.'

It was a generous admission; but acceptance of Bishops as successors of the Apostles, transmitting Order, holding an inherited spiritual authority, is still difficult. Other prejudices have become light, almost to evanescence. There is now very little objection to 'read prayers' and to liturgic worship. The Prayer Book has conquered by its own beauty and devotion; the desire is growing in non-Episcopal Churches for a pattern of prayer, a worshipful service. Along with this has come increasing observance of the Church Year, notably of Holy Week.

But for many Presbyterians the Bishop remains a menace. In himself he may be good, in his office he is seen as an intruder, an autocrat, a dictator, a door-keeper more alert to shut out arrivals than to welcome them in. There is still a great deal of bad history, confused thinking with vague literary associations to strengthen the prejudice. Many Scots, otherwise intelligent, tolerant and amicable, appear to see the Bishop in general as a mixture of Archbishop Sharp, any proud English prelate of the eighteenth century, and Bishop Proudie. No one has met this prodigy, but there is a strong fear that he does exist and, in a united Church, would appear and take action.

The Scots thistle is strong; so is the Anglican spike, and sometimes the spike is intertwined with the thistle. We Scots Episcopalians may well be proud of our heritage and loyalty, and our poverty is no disgrace although very harassing, but we can be unbearably complacent, sentimental about the past and damnably arrogant. We all, as Christians, need to purge our consciences of dead works, but we in Scotland have a particular need to purge our historical memories of passions which, far from being dead, thrive and breed and multiply. Is it altogether the fault of other kirks that they fail to see the Bishop as we do, or is it we who have failed to present the true picture of him as pastor, teacher, guardian of the faith, inheritor and transmitter of sacramental Order, bearing an office and authority greater than his own personal gifts and quality, of him as, above all, the Father-in-God of his people?

This picture has indeed been seen by many Presbyterian ministers who have found their need of a spiritual father to whom they may go, in confidence and privacy, for help and counsel at once paternal and authoritative. Committees, Courts and Presbyteries have their place and function, but a man cannot open his heart and conscience to a committee. He may go to a fellow minister, to one older and wiser than himself, and receive true comfort and counsel; but if the problem or trouble be congregational or parochial, that other minister cannot interfere. The Bishop can take action, with full knowledge and balanced judgement; he can listen, speak and act.

There is still an idea that Episcopacy is undemocratic, and it is

hoped that this history may have removed something of that idea.
Presbyterians and Episcopalians often appear to look at the Bishop
under different aspects. To the Presbyterians he is the G.O.C.,
the principal, the head of the firm; he has been promoted, he is
probably more distinguished in scholarship, administrative
capacity or other talents than other clergy, but he is not essentially
different from them. To the Episcopalian he is the source, origin
and centre of the priesthood: he is a maker of priests: himself
once priested by a Bishop he has had his priesthood carried up
into full authority by his consecration at the hands of other
Bishops, who hold and transmit that authority, that fullness of
Order. We see him at the centre; Presbyterians see him at the top
of the line. The true concept of the Bishop will have to be realized
before much progress can be made.

Dialogue and discussion have helped, and can help more and
more; thinking with clarity and in charity should surround all
discussion. We must see the essentials rather than the accidents
of our faith and of the faith of others. And we must realize that
there is a difference of thought deeper than that between Presbyterian and Episcopalian, Protestant and Catholic: the difference
between secular and Christian thinking. If we think only with our
own minds, no matter how well instructed, balanced and tolerant,
we see all the difficulties and differences, solid as walls and rocks,
deep as chasms between us and unity. We must go on seeing them
for it is useless to pretend that they do not exist. But we need not
sit down and stare hopelessly ahead. Thinking with the Mind of
Christ we see one thing only – His desire that all be made one.
What He desires He must have, and He will show us the way. We
must not ignore the rocks and chasms, but if we look with Him
we shall see here and there a gap, a bridge; and having somehow
or other dodged round the rock or over the gulf we meet our
separated brethren, pause, gasp rather breathlessly, and laugh:
'So you're here too. Let's go on together.'

Talking of bridges, most Anglicans, Scottish and others, are
bored by the title of The Bridge Church. No one wants to live
on a bridge or even linger there; and if we claim to own the
bridge and impose tolls on those who would cross it, we may find
them doing without it altogether, pushing off in a boat from the
Roman or the Presbyterian side, meeting mid-stream, landing on

some island for a friendly, ecclesiastical picnic. There have been many happy encounters between Roman priests and Presbyterian ministers without intervention or interpretation by Episcopalians. Scottish Episcopacy is having to revise its idea of itself as interpreter or reconciler. Yet we can and should play that part, and must think, with the Christian mind, how far we can go towards either side without sacrifice of principles and essentials. What can we offer that the others lack? Can we help to explain one to the other, make, for example, Episcopacy more acceptable than Papacy, our Eucharistic doctrine and worship more easily understood than that of the Roman mass?

It is indeed at the altar that separated Christians long to meet. At one gathering of Presbyterians, Roman Catholics and Episcopalians, all three representative speakers laid great stress on the Sacrament of Baptism, our re-birth into the family of God. There we are together with Christ in the household of the Father, renewed by the Holy Spirit. But at the altar there is still separation.

L. S. Thornton has written in his great book on *The Common Life in the Body of Christ*:

'The common life here treated of is something more mysterious than the visible fellowship of Christians . . . The life shared is embodied. The Church is related to Christ in His mystical complement in the organism of the new creation. . . . The Church is thus defined Christologically in terms of the creed and the two greater Sacraments. In the beginning the Church entered a baptismal life corresponding to her confession of faith. The essence of this life consists in Eucharistic worship, prayer, and fraternal love, grounded upon, sustained by and manifesting union with the Divine-Human Priest Victim in His eternal sacrifice and His regnant glory.'

That conception of the Eucharist has been held continuously by the Scottish Episcopal Church, even when it appeared to be half forgotten or ill expressed in worship. It is the teaching of a long line of priests and Bishops – Scougal, Rattray, Jolly, Robert Forbes and Alexander Forbes. We receive the Sacrament, we offer and plead the Sacrifice, we adore the Presence of the Victim-Priest, the Crucified, the Glorified. It is so unspeakable a joy that we must share it.

In the groups who debate this problem of access to the altar some see intercommunion as the end of the quest, to be reached after all the difficulties have been resolved, all the barriers passed; but only then. Others see it as the immediate need, the centre from which all acts, all efforts must radiate. One party says:

'Let us settle this matter of the Apostolic Succession, Order and so on, then come happily together at the altar.'

The other:

'Let us worship and receive Our Lord together, and then we shall know what more we can do.'

Discipline and authority erect some barriers or defences, but prejudice heightens them. Belief may bring us closer together than we imagine. The Anglican Articles repudiate the doctrine or theory of transubstantiation, but the Anglican Liturgy and Catechism hold and convey belief in the Real Presence, the Sacrifice, the reception of Christ's Body and Blood. The formularies of the Presbyterian Church of Scotland present Holy Communion as much more than a mere commemoration of the dying Saviour, much more than an act of Christian fellowship, even although these two aspects may be most often stressed. Many devout Presbyterians would declare:

> Christ was the Word that spake it,
> He took the Bread and brake it,
> And what His Word doth make it
> That I believe and take it.

Here again discussion may help, although sometimes there may seem to be another barrier of thought; a barrier of words. We seem on each side to be using a language foreign to the other, or else the same words with a different meaning. It is as if one were to use 'prevent' in its old sense of 'go before' or 'lead', the other in its modern meaning of 'hinder'. In such a case 'The Lord prevent you in all your ways' would have a very different significance for two different hearers.

Many Anglicans dislike the mode of celebration followed in many Presbyterian churches, the giving of the Wine in individual cups; they may be shocked by the disposal of the unused Elements. It is easy to be shocked and to condemn; our own history, as we have seen, administers a sharp reminder that at one period we were far from seemly in our celebration and reception of Holy

Communion. Our Eucharistic worship has reached a height of beauty and reverence hardly imagined by our spiritual forebears in the seventeenth century. There are many signs of a similar development in Presbyterian worship.

Validity of Orders, intention to consecrate, form and rite all appear to present difficulties. A way may have been opened at Pentecost, 1963, the fourteenth centenary of the landing of St. Columba on Iona. Then, on his island, there was a Celebration of the Eucharist which was a true Sacrament of Unity. The Rite was that of the Church of South India which was acceptable by both Presbyterians and Episcopalians. The celebrant was Bishop Newbigin; with him were the Bishops of Durham and Edinburgh, the Moderator of the Church of Scotland and his predecessor in office. These four, having received the Sacrament, gave it to thirty other men, including a Bishop of the Church in Wales, and ministers and elders of the Church of Scotland. These thirty in turn served the congregation of men and women from many Churches.

Celtic legends are full of magic adventures, a passing from this world into fairyland through a door in the hill-side or a cave. A greater adventure than that, a holy magic may begin at one single encounter; a door may suddenly be opened into a world larger and brighter than we have imagined.

The past few years, the 1960's, have left many pictures, shown many open doors. This, on Iona, is the loveliest, but there are others. There have been meetings during the Week of Prayer for Unity: one with an Episcopalian layman in the chair, a Cistercian Abbot, a Presbyterian minister, an Episcopal Provost as speakers: another under the presidency of a Bishop, with three laymen, again Roman, Presbyterian, Anglican, expressing their faith. Then there was a memorable celebration in Edinburgh Cathedral, by Archbishop Bloom of the Eastern Orthodox Liturgy, followed later in the day by a talk by him about the condition of our suffering brothers in the Church of the Silence. The old bond between Eastern Orthodoxy and Scottish Episcopacy was strengthened, and many were made aware of a great heritage of spirituality hitherto hardly guessed. For some, the Archbishop's stories of the Church in Russia recalled the history of our own penal period.

There are many meeting points, many talking points where frank discussion clears the air like a wind driving away the mist. It may not always be comfortable, for the wind can be chill, but it is bracing. There is the meeting-point of social service; best of all is the meeting-point of prayer.

Discipline and organization can raise barriers, which may God forbid, or demolish them, which may God grant. And in our highly variegated Anglican Communion there are two parties on the ecumenical march: one looking hopefully towards Rome – for recognition and reconciliation, not submission or conversion; the other towards the non-Episcopal Churches. The former hold that the Apostolic Succession of Bishops from the Apostles appointed by Our Lord Himself cannot be changed, that the threefold Order of Bishop, Priest and Deacon is of primitive establishment; they doubt, if they do not deny, the validity of non-Episcopal Orders. The others are ready to discuss terms, to review their own conceptions. Rome has pronounced – though not by an infallible decree – that Anglican Orders are invalid; this judgement may be revised. May the Anglican view of Presbyterian Orders also change?

The Scottish Episcopal Church, free, as she is, to order her affairs, democratic and representative in her government, may yet become the interpreter, the reconciler.

Within this Church, as in most others, there is at present a renewal of the liturgic life, which may show itself in revision of the Liturgy itself. There is already a more faithful obedience to the Divine bidding: *Do This*; words used as the title by the Bishop of Edinburgh for his pamphlet on Eucharistic Worship and the meaning of the Sacrifice. 'He took, He blessed, He gave it away' – the food of the Last Supper, of the Eucharist, His Own Body and Blood which the Bread and Wine represent and convey.

The most notable renewal of form has been the increased share of the people in the Liturgy; there is more and more a participation by act and dialogue as well as by private and silent prayer. More and more of the prayers are being said with the priest by the people. The use varies from one church to another, but it is not uncommon to find the Prayer of Humble Access made by all together, and the response 'We beseech Thee' uttered during the Prayer for the Church; and that Prayer offered after the Creed, instead of after the Consecration, making a better balance than the old way. The Oblation is, in many churches, made obvious by a small procession of lay folk carrying up to the sanctuary the alms, the bread, the wine.

With so many changes the pattern of Scottish Episcopacy may appear more intricate than formerly, but the intricacy becomes a richer harmony if the threads and colours are interwoven with prayer. Worship and service, the traditional and the modern, the hidden life and the outward going are all to be traced in the glorious tapestry of our faith. The hidden life of the Faithful through past generations and centuries is more powerful for good than we, most of us, realize; it endures to the end of time. History tells of events, and our Church history should be cherished with pride. Actions have expressed ideals and loyalties. Even the disputes and antagonisms, of which this history may seem to be disconcertingly full, can express loyalty, a passion for what is held to be right. What cannot be told but only thankfully guessed and accepted is that hidden life of prayer in Bishops, priests and people, in the humblest no less than the greatest: the life of those who loved and followed one way of faith, who worshipped the Presence, offered the Sacrifice, and maintained, by sheer devotion, the Church of their allegiance.

We have come a long way in a short space of time towards unity, in charity fostered by mutual courtesy. In the way of truth we are coming more slowly, for none must concede or discard what is essential, and to judge what is essential is not easy. Truly the way ahead may seem long. To the secular mind the barriers appear, at times, impregnable. To the Christian mind they are dwarfed and outspanned by the crucifix. *There* is our Unity, made for us by Christ.

'For He is our peace Who hath made both one, and hath broken down the middle wall of partition between us; having abolished in Himself the enmity . . . to make in Himself of twain one new man, so making our peace, and that He might reconcile both unto God in one body by the Cross.'

# Bibliography

*Discourses on Important Subjects.* Henry Scougal (Foulis Press).

*The Works of the Right Reverend Thomas Rattray.* (Pitsligo Press).

*A Catechism Dealing Chiefly With the Holy Eucharist.* Robert Forbes. Edited by John Dowden (R. Grant).

*The History of the Church in Orkney.* J. B. Craven. (Pearce, Kirkwall).

*The Records of the Diocese and the Isles.* J. B. Craven. (Pearce, Kirkwall).

*Ecclesiastical History of Perth.* George Farquhar. (Jackson, Perth).

*An Ecclesiastical History of Scotland.* George Grub. (Edmonstoune & Douglas).

*Mystics of the North-East.* G. D. Henderson. (Third Spalding Club).

*Memoir of the Right Reverend Alexander Jolly.* William Walker (R. Grant).

*The Life of the Right Reverend George Gleig.* William Walker. (Douglas).

*The Life and Times of John Skinner, Bishop of Aberdeen.* William Walker (Edmond & Spark, Aberdeen).

*Three Churchmen: Bishop Terrot; Bishop Russell; George Grub.* William Walker. (R. Grant)

*Reminiscences Academical, Ecclesiastical and Scholastic.* William Walker. (Wyllie, Aberdeen).

*Biographical Sketch of the Right Reverend David Low.* Matthew Forster Conolly. (R. Grant).

*Daniel Sandford, Bishop of Edinburgh: Remains. With a Memoir by John Sandford.* (Waugh & Innes, Edinburgh).

*The Life and Times of Patrick Torry, Bishop of St. Andrews.* J. M. Neale. (Joseph Masters.)

*Bishop Forbes. A Memoir.* Donald Mackey. (Kegan, Paul & French).

*My Years in Dundee with Bishop Forbes of Brechin.* George Grub. (R. Grant).

*Alexander Penrose Forbes, Bishop of Brechin.* William Perry (S.P.C.K.)

*George Hay Forbes.* William Perry, (S.P.C.K.).

*The Episcopate of Charles Wordsworth.* John Wordsworth. (Longmans Green.)

# Bibliography

*Annals of My Early Life* and *Annals of My Life*. Charles Wordsworth. (Longmans Green).

*Memoir of Alexander Ewing, Bishop of Argyll and the Isles*. Alexander Ross. (Dalby Isbister).

*Memoir of George Howard Wilkinson*. A. J. Mason. (Longmans Green).

*A Pastoral Bishop: Memoir of Alexander Chinnery-Haldane*. Thomas Ball. (Longmans Green).

*A Victorian Diarist:* Lady Monkswell. (John Murray).

*Anthony Mitchell, Bishop of Aberdeen and Orkney*. William Perry. (Hodder & Stoughton).

*Biographical Studies in Scottish Church History*. Anthony Mitchell. (Mowbray).

*The Story of the Church in Scotland*. Anthony Mitchell. (Winter, Dundee).

*The Oxford Movement in Scotland*. William Perry. (Cambridge).

*The Scottish Liturgy*. William Perry. (Mowbray).

*The Call of the Cloister*. Peter Anson. (S.P.C.K.).

*The Annotated Scottish Prayer Book*. John Dowden. (R. Grant).

*The History of Glenalmond*. G. St. Quintin. (T & A. Constable, Edinburgh).

*Hely Hutchinson Almond*. Robert Mackenzie. (Constable).

'The Scottish Guardian'. *The Dictionary of National Biography*.
   *The Year Book of The Episcopal Church in Scotland.*
   *The Annual Report of the Representative Church Council.*

The following books are also recommended:

*John Keble*, by Georgina Battiscombe (Constable) for a picture of the Church of England in the nineteenth century;

*The Making of the Scottish Prayer Book* by Gordon Donaldson (Edinburgh University Press) for a detailed and scholarly account of the liturgical process in the seventeenth century;

*A Short History of the Scottish Episcopal Church*, by Frederick Goldie (S.P.C.K.) as an excellent summary and introduction;

*Rival Establishments in Scotland* 1560–1690 by Agnes Mure Mackenzie (S.P.C.K.). as a summary of Church History until 1688;

*Some Scottish Links With the American Episcopal Church*, 1685–1785, by Reginald Foskett. (privately printed, Edinburgh); and two Scottish Episcopal Church Booklets: *The Apostolic Succession*. by John W. A. Howe; *Scottish and Anglican*. by Duncan Macgregor

# Index